The Second Austrian Republic

Marc Landry and Eva Pfanzelter, eds.
Christian Stenico, Associate Editor

CONTEMPORARY AUSTRIAN STUDIES | VOLUME 31

UNO PRESS

innsbruck university press

University of New Orleans Press
2000 Lakeshore Drive, Earl K. Long Library, Room 221
New Orleans, LA, 70148, USA
www.unopress.org

Printed in the United States of America on acid-free paper

Published in the United States by
University of New Orleans Press
ISBN: 9781608012435

Published and distributed in Europe
by *Innsbruck* University Press
ISBN: 9783991060796

UNIVERSITY OF NEW ORLEANS PRESS

iup

Library of Congress Cataloging-in-Publication Data

Names: Landry, Marc, editor. | Pfanzelter, Eva, 1969- editor. | Stenico, Christian, editor.
Title: The Second Austrian Republic / Marc Landry and Eva Pfanzelter, eds. ; Christian Stenico, associate editor.
Description: New Orleans : University of New Orleans Press ; Innsbruck University Press, 2022. | Series: Contemporary Austrian studies ; volume 31 | Includes bibliographical references.
Identifiers: LCCN 2022036149 (print) | LCCN 2022036150 (ebook) | ISBN 9781608012435 (paperback) | ISBN 9781608012442 (ebook)
Subjects: LCSH: Austria--History--1955- | Austria--Politics and government--1945- | National characteristics, Austrian. | Holocaust, Jewish (1939-1945)--Austria--Influence. | Collective memory--Austria.
Classification: LCC DB99.2 .S43 2022 (print) | LCC DB99.2 (ebook) | DDC 943.605/3--dc23/eng/20220727
LC record available at https://lccn.loc.gov/2022036149
LC ebook record available at https://lccn.loc.gov/2022036150

Publication of this volume has been made possible through a generous grant by the Austrian Federal Ministry of Education, Science and Research through Austria's Agency for Education and Internationalization (OeAD). The Austrian Marshall Plan Anniversary Foundation in Vienna has been very generous in supporting Center Austria: The Austrian Marshall Plan Center for European Studies at the University of New Orleans and its publications series. The College of Liberal Arts at the University of New Orleans, as well as the Vice Rectorate for Research and the International Relations Office of the University of Innsbruck provided additional financial support.

THE UNIVERSITY of NEW ORLEANS
CENTER AUSTRIA

universität innsbruck

The Dietrich W. Botstiber FOUNDATION

Federal Ministry
Republic of Austria
Education, Science
and Research

Marshallplan-Jubiläumsstiftung
Austrian Marshall Plan Foundation

Contemporary Austrian Studies

Sponsored by the University of New Orleans and University of Innsbruck

Table of Contents

The Second Austrian Republic

Introduction

Marc Landry and Eva Pfanzelter

The Second Austrian Republic emerged from the destruction and misery of the Second World War and is now in its seventy-seventh year of existence. On April 27, 1945, mere weeks after the Red Army had captured Vienna, the Soviets declared Austria independent and installed a provisory government led by Karl Renner. The former representative in the legislature of the Habsburg Monarchy and state chancellor of the First Austrian Republic stood at the head of a broad coalition of socialists, the People's Party, and communists. His government, however, would not be recognized by the western Allies until months later, at the end of October that year. It would take still another ten years for Austria to achieve sovereignty with the signing of the State Treaty and the departure of occupying forces. In this sense, from the very beginning, observers have held differing interpretations about the nature of the new state. To some extent this variance has been carried over into the historiography on the Austrian state.

The "Proclamation on the Independence of Austria" from April 27, 1945, together with the "Constitutional Transition Act" of May 1, 1945, clearly proclaimed the intention of Austria's Provisional Government to reinstall the Constitution of the First Austrian Republic in its latest iteration of 1929. The two laws swept away both the Constitution of the Austrian Corporate State (the so called *Maiverfassung* or May Constitution of 1934) as well as the "Law on the Reunification of Austria with the German Reich" (*Anschlussgesetz* or Law of Annexation) of March 13, 1938, which together with the "Law on the Administration in the Ostmark" (*Ostmarkgesetz* or *Ostmark*-Law) from April 14, 1939, had got rid of the never-actually- functioning May Constitution. With the reversion to the Constitution of 1929, the Proclamation declared both the Anschluss and the Corporate State as null and void, the governments of the past twelve years as something imposed on the Austrian people. At the same time, the annexation of 1938 was classified as having been "initiated by military threat from the outside and treasonous terror of a Nazi-fascist minority" and as "forced upon the helpless people of Austria by military, warlike occupation of the country." Austria was then declared independent and the reinstalment of the "democratic republic of Austria in the spirit of 1920" was announced.[1] In its first issue on April 23, 1945 – several days before the official end of the war in Austria – the daily newspaper *Neues Österreich* jubilantly declared: "Austrians! For the first time in seven years, you may once again be addressed by this name so dear to us all."[2] Sentiments oscillated between euphoria about the end of the war and fear of reprisals by the Allies.

But who were those Austrians the newspaper addressed? As with the status of the political entity, national identity was far from certain. Being Austrian in 1945 did not per se mean belonging to the re-installed republic. Ever since the end of the Habsburg Empire and World War I, the constitution of a national identity remained in flux. Despite these obvious uncertainties research has been slow to address both the elimination of the Austrian Corporate State and the period of Nazi collaboration from collective memory as well as the formation and consolidation of national identity in the years after World War II. It would not be until the early 1970s that Austrian historians set out to try to capture the Republic in scholarly form. By that point the Alpine republic had already established many of the hallmarks that would come to define it. From its pretensions as a *Kulturgroßmacht* (cultural great power), to its comparatively high concentration of state-owned industries (*Verstaatlichte*), to the welfare state and *Sozialpartnerschaft* (Austro-Corporatism) that buttressed social peace and general prosperity. This all took place in an era of unprecedented economic growth, part of a broader postwar trend that in retrospect appears to be nothing less than a golden era. In the realm of party politics, the consociational democracy (*Konkordanzdemokratie*) practiced by the ÖVP and SPÖ defused earlier hostilities. This newfound willingness to give-and-take saw its greatest expression in the grand coalition governments that reigned uninterrupted until the mid-1960s.

The first major effort to take stock of the Second Republic was the two-volume history edited by Erika Weinzierl and Kurt Skalnik in 1972.[3] It set the tone in many ways by characterizing the new state in broad strokes as a success. Ernst Hanisch is surely correct in arguing that viewing the Second Republic as a comparative "*Erfolgsgeschichte*" ("success story") has been in fact a central pillar of the *Koalitionsgeschichtsschreibung* (coalition historiography) that dominated the Austrian guild until the end of the Cold War.[4] This does not mean that the historiography has been lacking in critical appraisals. Still this basically positive disposition toward the Second Republic, particularly when compared to its predecessor polities, is widespread. To take only one prominent example, Oliver Rathkolb's 2005 study of the Second Republic suggested the state was best understood as a "paradox".[5] His cross-section of Austrian society revealed significant contradictions in the development of Austrian identity and democracy. Among other things it emphasized the persistent latent authoritarian leanings of many Austrians. But a paradox can also be a success, and Rathkolb finds numerous sources for optimism as well. Of course, the ultimate success or failure of the Second Republic is only one of many consequential yardsticks that historians have employed. As the historical discipline has witnessed a proliferation of new methodologies in recent decades, we will increasingly see new approaches to and even conceptions of the nature of the Second Austrian Republic.[6]

The papers assembled here started their lives as part of a GSA seminar on the theme of "The Second Austrian Republic: Building the Nation, Shaping the State." As conceived, the organizers sought not to aim for comprehensive coverage of broad aspects of Second Republic history, but specifically to solicit research on efforts to construct the new Austrian nation. Here we meant not only efforts to construct a national identity, but also the material basis for a functioning state. This focus on nation and state-building is thus reflected in the contours of this volume. A primary goal of the seminar was to bring together scholars at all stages working in all areas of Austrian Studies, and this too is reflected in the final product. When Günter Bischof and Anton Pelinka began editing Contemporary Austrian Studies in 1992, they sought to center the history of the Second Republic in the annual volumes. This is the first time that the Second Republic has been the explicit theme.

When the idea behind this volume first emerged in 2019, there were many reasons to seek new scholarship on the Austrian Second Republic, and in particular efforts to rebuild an Austrian state and identity after the ravages of the Second World War. For one thing, the year 2020 would mark the seventy-fifth anniversary of the Second Republic. This seemed an opportune time to reflect on nation-building measures, particularly when their continuing influence on many aspects of present-day Austria society is still clear. Moreover, events such as the migrant crisis of 2015 seemed to call into question major facets of both Austrian state institutions and identity.

There are reasons why the history of the Second Republic should perhaps find broader resonance as well. In an important sense, its experience seems to represent something quite unique. As Oliver Rathkolb notes: "Looking back historically, there are few examples that show such rapid identity formation in a small-state society, a society that had to cope with the trauma of two world wars and the loss of Great Power status."[7] Austria does indeed seem to have been particularly successful in this regard. The accomplishment raises the question of the peculiarity of the Austrian situation. What role has the former Great Power status played? Is the territory somehow able to draw upon a greater reservoir of potential identity-creating symbols? How much of the accomplishment is domestic, so to speak, and how much must be attributed to international circumstances and contingency? Answers to these questions, and many more similar ones, promise insights into the history of the nation-state, a topic of enduring importance in our current globalized world.

The seminar that inspired this volume was supposed to meet in the fall of 2020 in Washington, DC. However, the coronavirus pandemic forced the GSA to hold its first ever online conference, and our seminar opted to convene in the digital world rather than postpone for a year.

Eva Pfanzelter's opening article examines a facet of postwar Austrian identity formation that has not yet received attention: the role of the so-called "Option". This international agreement, forged between Hitler and Mussolini in 1939, gave German-speaking South Tyroleans the option of "voluntarily" relocating to the German Reich to become citizens there. Thousands ended up migrating to and remaining in Austria, permanently changing the country in numerous ways. Perhaps most visible were the "South Tyrolean settlements" that were constructed to house the newcomers. Additionally, streets across Austria were also renamed to commemorate the arrival of the South Tyroleans, and in the postwar period those South Tyroleans that remained in Austria created "*Südtiroler Vereine*" that tried to uphold the traditions of their homeland. Taken together, Pfanzelter argues, these constitute a "landscape of remembrance" which in contrast to memorialization in South Tyrol, has not yet been the focus of historians. For Austrians, the presence of this landscape further underlined the feeling of victimization at the hands of the great powers, even though the "Option" itself has faded from public memory.

In his piece, Christian Karner explores how, since the turn of the millennium, core symbols of the Second Republic have once again become the focus of debate and political anxiety. Surveying a range of media from across the ideological spectrum and of varying reach, Karner uses "snapshots" to show that once uncontroversial elements of Austria's national identity are being called into question. Karner builds upon theories of Pierre Bourdieu and Michael Bilig to explore the crisis conditions under which the habitus and "cultural commonsense" (or *doxa*) can be transformed from "banal" into "hot" aspects of national self-understanding. The central symbols analyzed here include the social welfare state, political stability, and the country's rural landscapes. Karner joins other scholars in locating critical antecedents for these changes in perceptions already in the 1970s. Viewing these changes through the prism of key national symbols purportedly in crisis has only heightened the politics of national identity.

Sarah Oberbichler's contribution emphasizes another way in which South Tyrol played a role in early Austrian nation-building efforts. As Austria emerged from the Second World War, its relationship to the former Habsburg land once again became a point of intense discussion. Would it once again be reunited with an Austrian state? Oberbichler's piece uses a large corpus of publicly available digitized Austrian newspapers to trace which discourses accompanied the South Tyrol Question after 1945, and how the process of creating an Austrian nation framed these discourses. With both qualitative research methods and digital history tools—largely of the text mining repertoire—the essay shows how Austrian elites began to refer to South Tyroleans as an "Austrian" minority. This was in stark contrast to the period prior to 1945, when they were overwhelmingly referred to as German. The digital analysis provides data on when the South Tyrol discourse was most intense and suggests that the economic aspects of the South Tyrol Question loomed largest. Ultimately nation-building extended into the linguistic realm, and South Tyrol became an essential pillar in Austria's national reorientation.

An important component of postwar Austrian identity was the self-perception of Austria as a welcoming place for refugees. Not only did this align Austria with western values and lifestyles, it served to mark a departure from the barbarity of the National Socialist period. In her essay, Judith Welz looks at the shift to more restrictive migration policies of the early 1990s and asks whether this also entailed a change in the nation-building project. Applying a Foucauldian biopolitical approach, Welz argues that the discursive construction of the "economic refugee" redefined what it meant to belong to Austrian society. On the one hand, it determined which migrants were no longer desired and thus worthy of expulsion. On the other, it increased the value of legal residence and compelled legal residents to comply with desired ways of conduct, particularly at the workplace.

Alexandra Sterling-Hellenbrand shifts the attention to contemporary Austria's memory landscape, mining the rich field of memory and place in the Second Republic. The focus here is on recently constructed or modified monuments to Siegfried—a fixture of German-speaking culture since the medieval *Nibelungenlied*. Siegfried's historical entanglements with German nationalism make the figure an example of difficult heritage. But Sterling-Hellenbrand shows that since the 1980s, high-profile monuments to Siegfried have been motivated by a desire to move beyond this troubled legacy. In Pöchlarn, Tulln, and at the University of Vienna, we can see a process in which Austrians have worked to reimagine Siegfried in a framework of "peace-making and hoped-for tolerance." As the twenty-first century progresses, major efforts to engage with the medieval past even seek to go beyond Siegfried to recover more local inheritance.

In his piece, Christoph Leschanz focuses on another crucial aspect of cultural life in the Second Republic, namely Austrian literature. He engages with the thorny question of whether something like an "Austrian literature"—separate from its German neighbors to the north—actually exists. Leschanz shifts the question somewhat by employing sociological concepts–particularly the idea of a "literary field"—from Bourdieu among others. The essay shows that the peculiar social, political, and economic circumstances at work in postwar Austria did indeed lead to the forming of a distinct Austrian literary field. In particular, because of official efforts to use Austrian high culture as the basis of a new (but historically anchored) Austrian identity, the Austrian literary field both contributed to the formation of new Austrian people while benefitting from the accompanying state support.

Like all states, the Second Republic has depended on a certain mythmaking to legitimize its existence and to provide a basis for collective identity. To the well-known victim thesis and "Habsburg myth" Vanessa Maria Carlone and Bernhard Alexander Achhorner add the myth of "Musikland" Austria. Their piece poses the question how the political functionalization of Austrian musical heritage has acted as a mediating instrument to enforce idealized notions of a collective "Austrian" identity. They note that cultural memory is also part of the construction of identity and show how the canonization, heroization, and invention of musical traditions were important tools in distancing the Second Republic from the failures of the First Republic and the National Socialist period.

Marc Landry's contribution rounds out the topical essays by addressing an important aspect of postwar Austria's physical infrastructure. Given the outsized role that they have played both in the postwar imaginary and the country's electricity supply, the *Tauernwerke Glockner-Kaprun* have captured the attention of journalists and historians since the 1990s. Exploring the intense debates over the ultimate design of the Kaprun dams that began during the First Republic and proceeded through the National Socialist and Allied occupation periods, the article shows that from the very beginning Austrian engineers succeeded in advancing a scheme that primarily conformed to perceived Austrian interests. The finding suggests the presence of a self-confident Austrian identity already in the interwar years—at least among engineers. It also raises the question whether additional aspects of Austria's material and immaterial infrastructure possess such continuities with the past.

This volume is also fortunate to contain a Forum representing the papers delivered at the German Studies Association panel on Pioneering Austrian Holocaust Scholars held online after being postponed in 2020. Gerald Steinacher's essay is devoted to Simon Wiesenthal, Joseph W. Moser's addresses his father, Jonny Moser. Finally, Winfried Garscha writes about the communist Hermann Langbein. As Günter Bischof notes in his introduction to the forum, in addition to providing important contributions to Holocaust scholarship, it is noteworthy that these Austrian scholars were all active at a time when the Second Republic leadership was proffering the theory that the state had actually been a victim of Hitlerite aggression.

Finally, in addition to our annual book reviews we present here two review essays. In the first one, Jason Dawsey contextualizes and analyzes the *The Red Vienna Sourcebook* in a moment of increased interest in the legacy of Karl Marx and Marxism. It has been about twenty years since CAS last published a review of literature on the Second Republic. Very fitting then, that Günter Bischof has picked up where he left off in providing one in a volume dedicated to the Second Republic.

A number of people have been instrumental in making the completion of this volume possible. Series editor Günter Bischof facilitated the book reviews and forum and was always available to draw upon his three decades of experience publishing CAS. Thanks are also due to our co-convenor, Michael Burri, for his part in making the seminar a great virtual success. We are sincerely thankful to all the contributing authors for submitting their essays in a timely fashion and for responding favorably to all editing suggestions from our production team. Associate Editor Christian Stenico, the 2021/22 Nick Mueller Fellow and first ever UNO Press & Center Austria Publishing Fellow, has done a fine job tracking every manuscript through both the copyediting and proofreading processes and toward final publication. Christian introduced a superior management system for handling manuscripts using Microsoft OneDrive. He also has been relentless in correcting and aligning footnotes with our style sheet and humoring authors toward completion of their manuscripts. Finally, Christian was also instrumental in designing the cover. This year represents the end of an unprecedented three-year run of fellowships for

Christian at Center Austria. He will be missed, and we wish him the best in his future endeavors.

We would also like to thank our anonymous outside peer reviewers for their thorough and timely assessments.

Center Austria is fortunate to work with two dedicated university presses on both sides of the Atlantic. Caroline Moore at UNO Press copyedited some of the individual manuscripts, and Alex Dimeff skillfully typeset the final text of the volume and designed the cover. G.K. Darby and Abram Himelstein, the leadership team at UNO Press, have as always been hugely supportive to spirit this volume through to final publication. At Center Austria: The Austrian Marshall Plan Center for European Studies, Gertraud Griessner conducted the center's daily business with superb efficiency (and cheer) to allow the coeditors to work on managing the completion of this volume. Without the dedicated teams at Center Austria and UNO Press, there would be no CAS series. At *innsbruck* university press, Birgit Holzner was helpful with the final round of proofreading and then producing the volume for the European market. Cooperating with her has become a big bonus in the production of these volumes. We would also like to thank all institutions on behalf of our contributors for being helpful with photo material for this volume and thereby making the volume more attractive.

As always, we are happy to acknowledge our sponsors and supporters for making the publication of the *Contemporary Austrian Studies* series possible at all—not a small matter in the age of diminishing budgets for higher education in general and the social sciences and humanities in particular. At the Universities of Innsbruck and New Orleans, our thanks go to Vice *Rektor* for Research Ulrike Tanzer for a grant toward the printing of this volume. Matthias Schennach at the International Relations Office, and Barbara Tasser, head of International Services, have always been supportive. At Center New Orleans in Innsbruck thanks to our counterparts Gerhard Rampl and Hannah Rofner. At UNO, Kim Long, the dean of the College of Liberal Arts, Education, and Human Development has given us green lights and much support whenever needed. We are also grateful to President John Nicklow and *Rektor* Tilmann Märk for their support of the entire UNO-University of Innsbruck partnership agenda, including its publication series. In the Federal Ministry of Education, Science, and Research and the OeAD, we are grateful to Barbara Weitgruber, Christoph Ramoser, Felix Wilcek, Josef Leidenfrost, Lydia Skarits, and Florian Gerhardus. Markus Schweiger, the executive secretary, and Ambassador Wolfgang Petritsch, the chairman of the board, as well as the board members of the

Austrian Marshall Plan Foundation, have been our strongest supporters for more than a decade now. It is a great pleasure and privilege to work with them all and acknowledge their unwavering support of Center Austria: The Austrian Marshall Plan Center of European Studies at UNO and its activities and publications.

St. Leonhard in Passeier/Kufstein, June 2022

Endnotes

1 See the first issue of the *Staatsgesetzblatt für die Republik Österreich*, May 1, 1945.

2 *Neues Österreich*, April 23, 1945.

3 Erika Weinzierl and Kurt Skalnik, eds., *Die Zweite Republik*, 2 vols. (Graz: Styria Verlag, 1972). Later published as a new one volume edition: Erika Weinzierl and Kurt Skalnik, eds., *Das neue Österreich. Geschichte der Zweiten Republik* (Graz: Styria, 1975).

4 Ernst Hanisch, "Der forschende Blick. Österreich im 20. Jahrhundert: Interpretationen und Kontroversen," *Carinthia* 189 (1999): 567-583. A recent overview of the historiography of the Second Republic can be found in: Günter Bischof, "Zweite Republik," in *Österreichische Zeitgeschichte – Zeitgeschichte in Österreich*, ed. Marcus Gräser and Dirk Rupnow (Vienna: Böhlau, 2021): 160-177.

5 Oliver Rathkolb, *Die paradoxe Republik: Österreich 1945 bis 2005* (Vienna: Paul Zsolnay Verlag, 2005).

6 For example, from an environmental history perspective, states are understood as components in the broader terrestrial ecosystem. See Martin Schmid and Ortrun Veichtlbauer, *Vom Naturschutz zur Ökologiebewegung: Umweltgeschichte Österreichs in der Zweiten Republik* (Innsbruck: Studienverlag, 2006).

7 Rathkolb, *Die paradoxe Republik*, 415.

Memorializing the South Tyrolean "Option" of 1939 North and South of the Brenner Pass. Building Blocks of Differentiating Identities.

Eva Pfanzelter

Introduction

Whoever walks from the center of Kufstein, a little town in the Tyrolean Alps near the border to Germany, toward the touristically popular Kaisertal, inevitably passes spacious housing estates built along streets carrying names like "Meraner Straße," "Sterzinger Straße," "Brixner Straße," "Brunecker Straße," and even "Terlaner Straße," and "Toblacher Straße"—names that bring South Tyrolean towns and villages to mind. This is because the settlements were built between 1939 and 1943 to offer a new home to people emigrating from the then Italian South Tyrol. The South Tyrolean settlements are thus also symbolic of the border at the Brenner Pass, which was drawn up in the 1919 peace treaty of Saint Germain between Austria and Italy, and the subsequent fascist decades. For it was Italian Fascism and German National Socialism that in 1939 laid the political, economic, and legal foundations for a large-scale emigration of South Tyroleans from their ancestral homeland between Eisack and Etsch and brought them to Austria and Germany.

With the agreements of German and Italian signatories from the two fascist sates on June 23, 1939 and the signing of the "Richtlinien für die Rückwanderung von Reichsdeutschen und Abwanderung der Volksdeutschen aus dem Alto Adige in das Deutsche Reich" ("Guidelines for the return of Reich Germans and the emigration of ethnic Germans from the Alto Adige to the German Reich") on October 21, 1939, the German-speaking population south of the Brenner Pass was given the opportunity to "voluntarily" opt for resettlement to the German Reich and thus apply for Reich German citizenship. Since the people were given the option to choose, it was called the "Option Agreement" or simply "Option," those deciding to leave became the "Optants," those who remained the "*Dableiber*" (Remainers). For thousands of people in the country, this marked the beginning of the road to a future that had been painted in the most dazzling colors by propaganda: jobs and housing for all, farms for all, not just the first-born sons, but above all membership in the "German National

Community," and an enclosed settlement area, where the South Tyroleans would find themselves once again among families and friends.[1]

The reality of emigration, however, was different. The enclosed settlement area never came into being. Men of military age were drafted into the German Wehrmacht upon arrival at the train station in Innsbruck, the first stop for all resettled persons. Jobs were allocated to the arriving men—and (unmarried) women—according to their qualifications. This had consequences for the largely unskilled and uneducated South Tyrolean workforce, which depending on professional aptitude, was distributed mainly to western Austria and southern Germany.[2] Furthermore, living space for the immigrating people had to be created during the war. Settlement projects like the above-mentioned *Südtiroler Siedlung* (South Tyrolean settlement) in Kufstein were initiated all over Austria (e.g., Image 1 and Image 2). They are thus stone monuments to a unique migration history that call the historical events of the war and of people immigrating, integrating, or emigrating again, as well as the commemoration of these events, to mind. Gradually, however, not only are these stone witnesses disappearing from the towns—which replace them with modern homes and apartments—but also the people who had been part of the "Option" of the South Tyrolean population between 1939 and 1942 and their direct descendants are becoming fewer and fewer.

This article takes as its starting point the question of how the landscapes of remembrance concerning the "Option" resettlements influence the collective memory of German-speaking South Tyroleans. It also seeks to find out just how pronounced and profound the memory of the "Option" is. Ultimately, the thesis of this article is that the victim theory —meaning that the "Option" was a collectively-experienced stroke of fate brought about by foreign powers or fate itself—still lives on in the collective memories of German- and Ladin-speaking South Tyroleans and is endorsed by both those who stayed in South Tyrol and those who emigrated. At the same time, the "Option" eventually also became part of Austrian identity, since those who remained in Austria stood as a symbol of the manipulation that international politics had inflicted upon the German-speaking minority after World War I and again after World War II. The culture of remembrance among the "Optants" and their descendants in Austria, however, became disassociated from the "motherland" South Tyrol through time and place and resulted in an almost mythical memorialization of the past, the South Tyrol, and the alleged sufferings of their ancestors. The "Option" became part of Austrian identity through the "Optants" integrating into their new homes, through the street and place names in Austrian towns, villages, and South Tyrolean settlements, and through the work of many so-called *Südtiroler Vereine* (South Tyrolean Associations) that tried to keep the traditions of the former "motherland" and connections to it alive.

Figure 1: Resettling people and property: Annotated photo album of the Egebrecht family. The wooden bay was made in 1941 in Egebrecht's own carpentry in Meran, a small town in South Tyrol, and then erected in the family's home in Meran (© Inge Egebrecht, Kufstein).

Figure 2: Annotated photo album of Egebrecht family. The wooden bay was transferred to the new home in Kufstein in 1942 and became the center of many family celebrations, like here during Easter 1943 (© Inge Egebrecht, Kufstein)

Memorializing the "Option" in South Tyrol[3]

Academics in South Tyrol are increasingly discussing the conceptual twins *History* and *Commemoration*, stimulated not least because of the effective media wars of the last two decades. These have been triggered by the monuments left as legacies of Fascism, such as the Monument to Victory in the provincial capital Bolzano or the ossuaries near the border to Austria with imported remains of Italian soldiers who had never fought on that soil. These stone relics of the Fascist dictatorship of the 1920s and 1930s stand alongside "monuments" to the statutes of autonomy, e.g., incorporated by the nine South Tyrolean state museums. They are considered an expression of South Tyrolean identity—in accordance with the law, exhibits are in all three official South Tyrolean languages—and they fulfill an important cultural-political, almost *nation-building* function by documenting regional diversities and specific features, as well as by displaying the vitality and independence of the region.[4]

Awareness of the constructiveness of history, the efficacy of monuments and symbols, changing historical-political instrumentalization, and especially of the identity-generating effects of historical remembrance thrives superbly in this regional-historical context. However, it was the primacy of memory that really brought to the fore to what degree the collective memory of the German and Ladin-speaking[5] South Tyroleans differs from that of the Italian-speaking populace.[6] To adequately understand the German-language remembrance, it is necessary to ascertain the emergence of a distinct historiography. Historian Georg Grote calls this—in lieu of a more suitable term—the "National Historiography of South Tyrol."[7] Within this historiography, the discourse on victimization plays a central role. It reinforces the formation of a separate identity, in the sense of a "dissociative identity" or an "identity of differentiation," and it defines itself by the German speakers' own suffering—for which Italy as a nation and Fascism as a regime is seen to be responsible.[8] Even today, the "Option" of 1939 is presented as evidence for the correctness of this theory of victimhood.

In academic literature, the "Option" of 1939 is consistently portrayed as a "trauma of South Tyrolean society," a "profound rift," the greatest social "breakdown of solidarity," a "deep wound" and "long-lasting weakening" of the minority, and even "the most sorrowful chapter in history, which was written by the people in their own country."[9] However, the facets of German-language remembrance of the "Option" have changed significantly during recent decades.

A first phase can be identified between 1945 and the 1960s when a politicization and standardization of the "Option"-remembrance took place.

Immediately after the end of World War II, at the beginning of May 1945, the German-speaking minority in South Tyrol was deeply divided on questions relating to the "Option" and its complexities during the wartime, or at the least since September 8, 1943. Due to the liabilities of the Optants, those who had remained behind in South Tyrol, the "*Dableiber*" ("remainers"), took over the political responsibilities and almost overnight filled in the deep gaps of the past years.[10]

Italian politics, in turn, exploited the statelessness of all "Optants" for the German Reich in 1939 as a bargaining chip at the peace negotiations and thereby helped to promote the formation of a South Tyrolean theory of victimization.[11] This victimization thesis ultimately served not only the interests of the political elite of South Tyrol: The German-speaking minority was stylized as a victim of two dictatorships, and the "Option" was seen as the result of two decades of Fascist oppression. It was "seen in undifferentiated contexts, as an endured collective stroke of fate, which the South Tyroleans suffered in their passive role."[12] Debates about exoneration served to obscure or mask the endemic brown (i.e., Fascist) past, even though collaborators and delinquents could often be found among their own political ranks.

In the beginning, discussions about victimization served to promote the united demand for self-determination, then later to support the legitimation of autonomy. Nevertheless, the debate always included an urgent statement directed against Italy—against the Italian-speaking state and the Italian-speaking minority in South Tyrol, which represented this state.[13] The actual strategic necessity of this case for victimization was, however, only feasible immediately after the end of the war—from 1945 to 1948—with the Gruber-De Gasperi Agreement, the revision of the "Option" agreement, and the Italian State Treaty in mind. Thus the "Option" had a historical-political function after 1945 and has enduringly influenced South Tyrol's political culture, with some lasting effects up to today. The "ideology of national heritage" was superimposed by a "fetishism of unity." Dissension was considered treason against one's own ethnic group.[14]

The phase between the 1970s and the early 1990s can then be viewed as a period of controversy and scientification. The changes of the 1960s and 1970s, subsumed under the catchword "1968," deeply shocked all social and political sectors and, with some delay, also reached the peripheries, such as South Tyrol.[15] Also, in South Tyrol, a critical generation began questioning the Wehrmacht generation. Despite sealing the division of language groups by proportional representation in the official administration, the foundations for a cautious pluralism were laid by the Second Autonomy

Statute of 1972, since this brought about political and social peace. The traditional historical picture of South Tyrol began to totter for the first time, at the end of the 1960s, under the criticisms of journalists, literary figures, and contemporary historians. The most prominent of these figures were Claus Gatterer and Joseph Zoderer.[16] Numerous debates were also fought and printed in the magazine *Skolast*, published in the name of the South Tyrolean Students' Union by Rainer Seberich and Franz von Walther.[17] However, conservative social groups which supported the victim theory maintained a particularly persistent inertia up into the first half of the 1990s. This was quite evident in the polemics of Alfons Gruber's volume "South Tyrol under Fascism" in 1974. Gruber's central thesis was based on a denial of any solidarity and ideological proximity of South Tyroleans with National Socialism and reduced the "Option" to a form of homeland confiscation by the fascists.[18] Among the authors' followers were advocates who wanted to deny South Tyrol's own National Socialism and instead portray it as having been brought in, since 1933, from Germany. They denied South Tyroleans' active participation in and perpetration of Nazi activities. Some of the groups supporting the thesis of "imported" National Socialism were from opinion-forming elitist groups and could also be found in the South Tyrolean People's Party, the main representation of the German-speaking minority. The media foundations of this conservative bulwark were to be found primarily in the daily newspaper *Dolomiten*. Its "letters to the editor" section was used as a forum for the tempestuous and polemic discussions about South Tyrol's history during the 1980s. This forum was primed and stocked by several media confrontations which offered opportunities for staging intense avowals of National Socialist ideology, as can be found, for example, in the support of the radically National Socialist book by Willy Acherer, . . . *Mit seinem schweren Leid* . . . (. . . *With his Enormous Suffering* . . .).[19]

In contrast, contemporary South Tyrolean history—and particularly the "Option"—became a public political issue from 1975 onwards. The critical contemporary historiography of the 1970s and 1980s can now be understood as a sort of delimiting and emancipatory process with respect to a conservative "official memory," which based itself on "stereotyped and undifferentiated assertions" about the suffering of the South Tyrolean *Volk*, and about the dictatorship of Fascism. Many names can be quoted as protagonists of this phase of thinking; perhaps exemplary for all of them are the historian and teacher Rainer Seberich, the young historian and student of Claus Gatterer, Leopold Steurer, the Munich Jesuit priest Reinhold Iblacker, the exponent of the New Left/Neue Linke/Nuova Sinistra,

Alexander Langer, with the "Initiativkommitee gegen die Option 1981" (Initiative Committee against the Option 1981),[20] the historians Martha Verdorfer, Walther Pichler, Alessandra Zendron, Piero Agostini, and many others. The "Option"-era became a fashionable topic in the historiography, fiction, and biographic literature of the 1980s. The literary productions took the form of a veritable "coming out" of many of those involved. In numerous (auto-)biographies, plays, and novels, first the *Dableiber*, then the Optants, and finally—with Franz Thaler—even the deserters had their say.[21]

A time of intense historical debate, in which broad strata of the population were involved, was initiated through an assertion by Reinhold Messner, the world-famous extreme mountain climber, in an Italian RAI-Uno television interview in 1981. Alluding to the "Option," Messner stated that "Penso che nessun popolo ha tradito tanto la 'Heimat' come gli altoatesini" (no people have ever so betrayed their homeland as have the South Tyroleans).[22] The regional RAI branch subsequently began to deal with South Tyrolean contemporary history in several documentary films. Among the most viewed and commented on broadcasts is the television interview from January 1982 between Reinhold Messner, Josef Rampold, and Friedl Volgger. While both Rampold, the editor-in-chief of the local newspaper, and Friedl Volgger were members of the Wehrmacht generation, Volgger showed understanding and support for a new way of examining the interwar and war periods.[23]

Encouraged by support from the South Tyrolean Students' Union and its backers, on the one hand, and fueled by the media-supported, conservative establishment on the other, verbal blows were exchanged for almost ten years in the print media, on the radio, and on the newly-founded television station, RAI-Bozen.[24] The 1980s were thus a time of upheaval, in which the mass media and, above all, the pluralization of the media landscape were to play a decisive role.

The climax of this decade of reappraisal was the year 1989, commemorating the "Option's" 50th anniversary. Although the proposal by the Green-Alternative List to make this a commemorative year was rejected, the South Tyrolean State Government financed the exhibition "Option – Heimat – Opzioni" (Option – Homeland – Opzioni), which the Tyrolean Historical Association organized in Bolzano, and which was attended by around 30,000 visitors. With this highly successful exhibit and with Felix Mitterer's film *Verkaufte Heimat: Eine Südtiroler Familiensaga* (*Homeland Sold: A South Tyrolean Family Saga*)—directed by Karin Brandauer as a co-production of Austrian, German and Italian broadcasters, produced and broadcast for the first time in 1989—[25] the "Option" definitively expanded beyond its academic framework and became part of a general social discourse. This, however, is not meant to detract from the numerous additional lecture series, academic publications, and instructional curricula for secondary schools that were published during this period of change.[26]

If 1989 represented the climax of public debates about the "Option" and the era of the two fascisms, this had primarily to do with it being a commemorative year. Anniversaries attract the public's attention at regular intervals, but they are forgotten soon thereafter. In fact, 1989 was not only a special year for South Tyrol, but also a memorable year throughout Europe and the world. It represented a caesura for cultural remembrance. In 1992, Tony Judt wrote that Europe's identity had been formed—up to the fall of the Berlin Wall and the end of Communism—above all by issues of separation, both by the Iron Curtain at the end of World War II, and by forgetting the immediate past preceding this separation. The manner in which Europe "distorted, sublimated, and appropriated" the experiences of war, left behind a basically false European identity, which constructed a feeble, unstable boundary between the past and the present in collective memories. The remembrance problems consequently left unsolved, formed the hub of a deep European identity crisis in the 1990s.[27]

Although the upheavals of 1989 removed the decade-old taboos about war remembrances, new myths and misinterpretations arose at the same time, especially about the time after 1945:[28] The many social and political continuities, the incomplete democratizations, the Resistance myths, accompanied by an insufficient de-Nazification and the rivalry for remembrance of Communist oppression (in historiographic circles known as victim rivalry) forced their ways into the collective memory of Western European societies over the following decades. In Germany, there were fierce debates about economic continuities, the political continuance of the National Socialist ideology, and the uninterrupted careers of Nazis. In Italy and France, the socially germane controversies of the 1990s did away with the myths of "resistance" and "resistenza."[29] Paradoxically, this breaking of taboos also led to the fact that those who told a different version of history were and are now acceptable again: Holocaust denial, antisemitism, radical nationalism, and a new right-wing radicalism are phenomena that have been cropping up increasingly throughout Europe since the middle of the 1980s, and in the 1990s began to become once more socially acceptable, due, in part, to globalization and the media revolution—a world-wide crisis of modernization.[30]

Can these European and international remembrance phenomena also be discovered in South Tyrol's handling of the "Option"? In fact, academic and popular scientific interest in the "Option" has remained unabated since 1989: There is a deluge of literature about coming to terms with this subject. Consequently, 1989 can more properly be seen as a turning-point year than a climax year. In the subsequent decades, numerous regional-historical issues of the Fascist and National Socialist era were tackled, yet interest in the subject more and more shifted to the academic arena. It is indisputable that in this last phase, the "Option" has experienced a historicization: even if the distortions of the past—depending on personal concerns—are still present, most contemporary witnesses look back on the events of those times *sine ira et studio*. At the same time, the victim theory also has survived strongly in collective memory. Not only that: The public handling of the Fascist and National Socialist past is in no way critical or without reservations these days. The traditional practices of covering up, re-interpreting, denying, and belittling are on the daily order of affairs in society, as recently exhibited with the historical review of the Homeland Cultural Clubs (from music bands to societies for traditional costumes to the companies of traditional militia, the *Schützen*). On the one hand, these inadequate methods of dealing with history enable the propagation of erstwhile right-wing thinking (also in the powerful political parties)—in South Tyrolean jargon affectionately called "ultrapatriotic." On the other hand, they foster trivialization and denial, as can be seen above all on television and the internet in recent years.[31]

Memorializing the "Option" in Austria

Analyzing the history of the memorialization of the resettlement of 1939 in Italy's northern neighbor, a totally different picture is revealed, and it becomes clear that the history of the culture of remembrance concerning the "Option" in Austria still has to be written. In Austria, which became the new home of many thousands of those who had left South Tyrol during World War II, beyond the propaganda celebrating their arrival "back home," the "Optants" were first and foremost an additional burden for the strained economy. Housing, food, and jobs were scarce in the years after 1940, and the immigrants from the south seemed to be given privileged access to all of these. During the war, however, resentments were voiced only quietly since NS propaganda celebrated the "Option" as a success story and with the *Sondermaßnahme Südtirol* or *Sondermaßnahme "S"* (Special Measures South Tyrol) the largest wartime civil construction project of the Third Reich was initiated. Construction companies like the *Neue Heimat Tyrol* (New Homeland Tyrol) and the "Vogewosi" (*Vorarlberger gemeinnützige Wohnungsbau- und*

Siedlungsgesellschaft, Vorarlberg non-profit Housing, Construction, and Settlement Society) were commissioned with building residences for the expected migrants from the south (e.g., Image 3). The construction of the settlements began during wartime—also by using prisoners of war and forced laborers and despite the displeasure of the local population, who was struggling with sometimes extremely difficult housing situations itself.[32]

Figure 3: The "South Tyrolean settlement" in Kufstein around 1960 (© Heimatverein Kufstein and Gerhard Lehmann, Kufstein)

After the end of World War II in 1945, the Province of Bolzano remained part of Italy, although Austria brought forth a strong plea to the Allies to reincorporate the southern part of the Tyrol. The situation for the inhabitants of South Tyrol at this point was almost dramatic: all those who had opted for the German Reich were stateless persons—whether they had left or not. The Italian government treated them as foreigners without civil rights and political representation. Only the *Dableiber*, those who had not opted at all or opted to remain in Italy, possessed Italian citizenship. It took arduous and lengthy negotiations until this issue was solved. The "Gruber-De Gasperi-Agreement" of September 5, 1946, which was included in the Italian Peace Treaty in 1947, and the *Optantendekret* (Decree on the Optants), the law for the "Revision of the Options of the South Tyroleans" of February 2, 1948, reversed the "Option Agreement" and finally created the legal basis for the reacquisition of the Italian citizenship and a return to South Tyrol.[33]

The situation was even more complex for those who had moved abroad: Already during World War II, some South Tyroleans returned occasionally to their homeland, but their number was limited. Immediately after the end of the war, South Tyrolean emigrants faced an uncertain future: Should they, who had now become stateless, go back to their homeland, or should they try to strengthen their foothold in their country of immigration? In the first few days after the end of the war in May 1945, those who made up their minds quickly illegally crossed the newly emerging borders between the occupying powers and found their way back to South Tyrol via the Brenner or Reschen Pass. After a couple of days, this illegal transition was only possible via the mountains, e.g., via the old smuggler and cattle trails in the Ziller Valley, or together with Italian returnees on resettlement trains.[34]

Only after 1948 could those who had moved abroad officially apply for the reacquisition or retention of Italian citizenship. The reacquisition of citizenship or the return, however, was denied if the applicant had been a member of the SS, the Gestapo, the SD, or the SOD (the *Südtiroler Ordnungsdienst* was the South Tyrolean military police installed after 1943). The same applied if they had held a major position at the offices organizing the "Option" resettlement program, the ADERSt (*Amtliche deutsche Ein- und Rückwanderungsstelle*, Official German Immigration and Repatriation Office), the AdO (*Arbeitsgemeinschaft der Optanten für Deutschland*, Association of Optants for Germany), or if they had been convicted of war crimes. Also excluded were those who had demonstrated explicit "Nazi partiality" when making propaganda for the "Option." This, of course, was a very vague phrasing that allowed for subjective decisions and personal judgments.[35]

The number of those who were finally allowed and still wished to return is still unknown. Historian Stefan Lechner estimated that about one-third of the 75,000 emigres returned to the Province of Bolzano after 1948,[36] but it could have been many more or many less. This means that many of those who had left South Tyrol per the 1939 agreements remained in Austria.[37] After the end of World War II, their situation changed rapidly, especially concerning the attitude of locals towards the immigrants. Prejudices and accusations were voiced in the press and during political meetings. The newly immigrated were seen as a burden to the social and economic system. Also, in Austria, the South Tyroleans were now stateless people without entitlement to welfare and social benefits. Also, for them, gaining Austrian citizenship was only possible after the "Decree on the Optants" of 1948, and even then, they had to pay for citizenship, as many witnesses keep stressing resentfully when talking about their past. Even if they did, sometimes it took years for them to be granted full citizenship. Eventually, however, the situation of the former "Optants" normalized, they integrated well, and especially the children quickly became part of Austrian society.[38]

Many of the immigrants from South Tyrol lived in the *Südtiroler Siedlungen*, where they were among themselves, often had their own restaurants or butchers, and sometimes, as in Innsbruck, even their own cinema. In collective memory, the settlements, therefore, became synonymous with the South Tyroleans living abroad, although not only "Optants" and their descendants inhabited them. The "South Tyrolean settlements," therefore, seem an ideal starting point when trying to map the memorial landscape of the "Optants" in Austria and the legacies of the "Option" in collective memory. Since many of the settlements in recent years were targeted for reconstruction programs aiming at renewing the outdated houses and arguing for compact construction in cities and villages,[39] some public and academic effort has been put into the history of the residential areas of the "Optants." Some projects aimed at interviews with the former inhabitants, others at the history of architecture and urban planning. Others again had a more artistic approach, and some thought about memorials to commemorate the remigration movement of the late 1930s.[40]

The history of the "South Tyrolean Settlements" and the memories of the many generations of South Tyrolean descent living there can therefore be seen not only as a concrete building block of Austrian identity but also as a migration history that became part of this identity unawares (e.g., Image 4 and Image 5). Due to the origins of these migrants, ever since the 1940s, South Tyrol became both a mythical homeland of origin and, since the 1960s, a popular vacation destination for the families living in the settlements and for the cities where they exist.

Figure 4: A little girl and an older woman in the “South Tyrolean Settlement“ in Kufstein in the Stuttgarterstraße, Kufstein in 1964 (© Heimatverein Kufstein and Gerhard Lehmann, Kufstein)

Figure 5: Renovated “South Tyrolean Settlement” in the Langstrasse in Pradl in Innsbruck in 2014 (© Eva Pfanzelter)

Another building block worth investigating in connection with the "Option" in Austria are the *Südtiroler Vereine* (South Tyrolean Associations) that came into being soon after World War II in every federal state of Austria and in many localities, where "South Tyrolean Settlements" were built. Over the years, the "South Tyrolean Associations" and especially its central organizing body, the *Gesamtverband der Südtiroler in Österreich* (General Association of South Tyroleans in Austria), had many functions: First, they served as meeting points and places of exchange among like-minded people. Also, they were needed for organizational matters and when it came to communication with the local and state authorities in both Austria and Italy. Their role as a "migrant organization" included the printing of a migrant newspaper, the *Südtiroler Heimat* (*South Tyrolean Homeland*), which was published as part of the *Volksboten* in Innsbruck from 1946 and, starting in 1952, became the "General Association's" own newspaper.[41] Later on (and in fact until today), questions of pension settlements and payment transfers became the central concern of the associations.[42]

Over the years, many local organizations lost their members, were dissolved, or combined with others, their legacies scattered, and the memories of their members recorded only infrequently. However, even today, they seem to fulfill an important community-building function when they gather the descendants of the "Optants" for monthly meetings and for major festivities where traditional costumes and customs are being held up and displayed. At the same time, they still are a place for lived community.[43]

Finally, concerning memorialization, it is interesting to note that monuments to the "voluntary" resettlement of South Tyroleans have so far not been built in South Tyrol itself, but some have been installed in Austria. In northern Tyrol, for example, a stone with a corresponding inscription to commemorate the "Option" was installed at the center of the former "South Tyrolean Settlement" in Pradl, Innsbruck, in 1984 (Image 6), and another one meant to imitate the South Tyrolean Dolomites mountain range, was installed in the city of Jenbach in 1981.[44] Also, in the context of the reconstruction of the outdated "South Tyrolean settlements," several art monuments have been erected to commemorate the former settlement buildings as part of the "*Kunst am Bau*" (art at construction sites) initiative of the housing company Neue Heimat Tirol.[45]

Figure 6: Stone memorial commemorating the "Option" of 1939 in the "South Tyrolean Settlement" in Innsbruck, Pradl, installed in 1984 (© Eva Pfanzelter 2014)

Conclusion: "Option" and Identity

Despite the arguments above, this paper is not a plea for a monumentalization of the South Tyrolean "Option." On the one hand, in South Tyrol itself, several museums and exhibitions are dealing with South Tyrolean history, where the "Option" plays a central role (e.g., The Tower of Memory to South Tyrol in the 20th century in the Castle Tyrol by Meran[46] and the exhibition "BZ '18–'45 one monument, one city, two dictatorships: A Permanent Exhibition within the Monument to Victory"[47]). On the other hand, the relationship between the people living in South Tyrol today and their past is still complicated, and monumentalization, therefore, remains difficult: The "Option" up until today stands as a symbol of victimhood, complicity, and perpetration with two dictatorships. At the same time, monuments, like the Monument to Victory in Bolzano, are closely intertwined with discourses of oppression, national supremacy, and neglect of minority rights.

Despite a good academic analysis of the South Tyrolean resettlement of 1939, however, the issue still seems to be an interesting starting point for further investigating questions of identity—not only in South Tyrol but also in Austria. While the "Optants" have reached an almost myth-like status south of the Brenner Pass and seem to stand for all the reasons why dictatorships and minorities can never coexist, in Austria, they seem to have disappeared from public awareness. But is this truly so? Are not their legacies, their thousands of descendants scattered all over the nation, the work of the Südtiroler Vereine, the many street names, the remaining South Tyrolean settlements, and memorials proof of a subtle influence on Austrian identity? It would be worth pursuing the history of the "Optants" in Austria further, to analyze their heritage, organizations, and migrant newspaper *Südtiroler Heima*t as well as their memories and careers before it is too late and the traces of this particular migration history disappear in the folds of history.

Finally, it is also time to reanalyze South Tyrolean history with postcolonial approaches, where the Italianization efforts of Mussolini's Fascism are seen as a process of internal colonization. If this is so, then the "Option" was one instrument of this colonization that enforced a tense interrelationship between all parties involved, that was to determine the coexistence in the region for many decades into the post-war period. In postcolonial theory, this relationship is called "othering" (after Edward Said, Johannes Fabian, and here especially Gayatri Chakravorty Spivak). The "othering" of the German/Ladino-speaking minority could be described as the self-image of a group that always felt apart from the national group in Italy, whereby this apartness, the "being foreign," always seemed threatened by everything Italian. The "othering" of the Italians, however, is equally evident: After the Italianization during the fascist regime, Italy has never unreservedly welcomed its new minority on the northern border as a new child into the national community. The new members of the state always seemed to be culturally and linguistically too "different," too "foreign" – and they always had the threat of their big brothers Germany and Austria on their backs, where they instantly became part of a very powerful, economically thriving community of Germanness, thus turning the "othering" around again. To reanalyze the "Option" as an instrument of colonial oppression and the Second Statute of Autonomy of 1972 as an instrument of decolonization would therefore provide ample room for discussions on identity.

Endnotes

1 For a very short introduction to the history of the Option see Eva Pfanzelter, "The South Tyrol Question and the Option Agreement: Fascism and National Socialism in the Nineteen-Twenties and Nineteen-Thirties," in *Dialogue Against Violence: The Question of Trentino-South Tyrol in the International Context*, Annali dell'Istituto Storico Italo-Germanico in Trento Contributi 32, ed. Giovanni Bernardini and Günther Pallaver (Bologna: Società editrice il Mulino; Berlin: Duncker & Humbolt, 2017), 33–56.

2 The strong economic impetus was already hinted at by Helmut Alexander, Stefan Lechner, and Adolf Leidlmair, *Heimatlos: Die Umsiedlung der Südtiroler* (Vienna: Franz Deuticke, 1993). Some more recent case studies stress this even more, e.g., Eva Pfanzelter and Sarah Oberbichler, "Über steinerne Zeugen einer traumatischen Vergangenheit: Die Südtirolersiedlungen in Tirol am Beispiel Kufsteins," in *Einmal Option und zurück: Die Folgen der Aus- und Rückwanderung für Südtirols Nachkriegsentwicklung*, ed. Günther Pallaver, Leopold Steurer, and Martha Verdorfer (Bolzano: Raetia, 2019), 313–31.

3 This chapter is a very shortened version of the essay: Eva Pfanzelter, "The (Un) Digested Memory of the South Tyrolean Resettlement in 1939," in *A Land on the Threshold: South Tyrolean Transformations, 1915–2015*, ed. Georg Grote and Hannes Obermair (Bern et al: Peter Lang, 2017), 119–43.

4 Thomas Ohnewein, "Die Südtiroler Landesmuseen: Ausdruck einer neuen Landesidentität," in *Südtirolismen: Erinnerungskulturen—Gegenwartsreflexionen—Zukunftsvisionen*, ed. Georg Grote and Barbara Siller (Innsbruck: Wagner, 2011), 113–21 (here 121).

5 In order to facilitate reading the terms German-speaking versus Italian-speaking shall be used, esp. since in this context the Ladino-speaking memory developed alongside the German-speaking one.

6 Hans Heiss and Hannes Obermair, "Erinnerungskulturen im Widerstreit: Das Beispiel der Stadt Bozen/Bolzano 2000–2010," in *Der Grenzraum als Erinnerungsort: Über den Wandel zu einer postnationalen Erinnerungskultur in Europa*, Histoire 34, ed. Patrick Ostermann, Claudia Müller, and Karl-Siegbert Rehberg (Bielefeld: Transcript, 2012), 63–80 (here 77–80).

7 Georg Grote, *I bin a Südtiroler: Kollektive Identität zwischen Nation und Region im 20. Jahrhundert* (Bolzano: Athesia, 2009), 255–57.

8 Heiss, Obermair, "Erinnerungskulturen," 77–80.

9 See also Günther Pallaver, "Die Option im Jahr 1939: Rahmenbedingungen, Ablauf und Folgen," in *Deutsche! Hitler verkauft euch! Das Erbe von Option und Weltkrieg in Südtirol*, ed. Günther Pallaver and Leopold Steurer (Bolzano: Ræetia, 2011), 13–34 (here 24–29); Grote, *I bin a Südtiroler*, 138; Rolf Steininger, *Südtirol im 20. Jahrhundert: Vom Leben und Überleben einer Minderheit* (Innsbruck: Studienverlag, 1997), 155.

10 A detailed account of the phases of memorialization of the Option, e.g., Brigitte Foppa, "Vom 'Reich im Herzen' bis zum 'Boden unter den Füßen': Zur Option in der Südtiroler Literatur," in *Deutsche! Hitler verkauft euch! Das Erbe von Option und Weltkrieg in Südtirol*, ed. Günther Pallaver und Leopold Steurer, (Bolzano: Raetia, 2011), 26–30. Also to be considered: Günther Pallaver and Gerald Steinacher, "Leopold Steurer: Historiker zwischen Forschung und Einmischung," in *Demokratie und Erinnerung: Südtirol, Österreich, Italien. Festschrift für Leopold Steurer zum 60. Geburtstag*, ed. Christoph von Hartungen, et al. (Innsbruck: Studien-Verlag, 2006), 51–91; Eva Pfanzelter, "Die (un)verdaute Erinnerung an die Option 1939," *Geschichte und Region/Storia e regione* 22, no. 2 (2013), 13–40.

11 Eva Pfanzelter, *Südtirol unterm Sternenbanner: Die amerikanische Besatzung Mai–Juni 1945. Mit Fotodokumentation und DVD* (Bolzano: Rætia, 2005), 230–32.

12 Pallaver, "Die Option im Jahr 1939," 26.

13 Martha Verdorfer, "Geschichte und Gedächtnis: Die Erinnerung an die Option von 1939," in *Deutsche!*, ed. Pallaver and Steurer, 365–83 (here 368–70).

14 Pallaver, "Die Option," 25–30; Verdorfer, "Geschichte und Gedächtnis," 367–68.

15 See also Pfanzelter, "Die (un)verdaute Erinnerung."

16 Claus Gatterer, *Im Kampf gegen Rom: Bürger, Minderheiten und Autonomien in Italien* (Vienna: Europa Verlag, 1968); Joseph Zoderer, *Das Glück beim Händewaschen* (Munich: Relief, 1976).

17 Brigitte Foppa, "Nur net rogeln! Zum Umgang mit Option und Widerstand in Südtirol," in *Skolast: Zeitschrift der Südtiroler HochschülerInnenschaft* 54, no. 2 (2009): 74–87 (here 74).

18 Günther Pallaver and Gerald Steinacher, "Leopold Steurer: Historiker zwischen Forschung und Einmischung," in *Demokratie und Erinnerung: Südtirol – Österreich – Italien. Festschrift für Leopold Steurer zum 60. Geburtstag*, ed. Christoph von Hartungen et al. (Innsbruck: Studienverlag, 2006), 51–91 (here 60–61).

19 Foppa, "Nur net rogeln," 74–80.

20 Verdorfer, "Geschichte und Gedächtnis," 376–78; Pallaver, "Option," 31–33.

21 An extensive bibliography of the historiographic and literary productions can be found in: Eva Pfanzelter, Elisa Heinrich, and Sabine Merler, "Literaturliste Option und Erinnerung," in *Die Erinnerung an die Südtiroler Option*, 2013–2017, accessed February 15, 2022, http://www.optionunderinnerung.org/wp-content/uploads/2014/11/Literaturliste-Option-und-Erinnerung.pdf.

22 Cited in Foppa, "Nur net rogeln!" 78.

23 Pfanzelter, "Die (un)verdaute Erinnerung."

24 Pallaver and Steinacher, "Leopold Steurer," 58–60.

25 Parts one and two, directed by Karin Brandauer, deal with the time-period of the "Option" itself, that is 1938–1945, parts three and four, directed by Gernot Friedel, take place in the post-war years.

26 E.g., Klaus Eisterer and Rolf Steininger, eds., *Die Option: Südtirol Zwischen Faschismus Und Nationalsozialismus*, Innsbrucker Forschungen zur Zeitgeschichte 5 (Innsbruck: Haymon, 1989); and, of course, the companion volume to the exhibition: Benedikt Erhard, ed., *Option–Heimat–Opzioni: Eine Geschichte Südtirols/Una storia dell'Alto Adige*, Katalog zur Ausstellung des Tiroler Geschichtsvereins (Bolzano: Tiroler Geschichtsverein, 1989).

27 Tony Judt, "The Past Is Another Country: Myth and Memory in Postwar Europe," *Daedalus* 121, no. 4 (1992): 83–118 (here 84), accessed February 15, 2022, https://doi.org/https://www.jstor.org/stable/20027138.

28 More on this topic: Pfanzelter, "Die (un)verdaute Erinnerung."

29 Robert A. Ventresca, "Mussolini's Ghost: Italy's Duce in History and Memory," in *History and Memory* 18, no. 1 (2006): 86–119 (here 89–91).

30 Frank Decker and Marcel Lewandowsky, "Was ist Rechtspopulismus?," Dossier Rechtsextremismus, Populismus (Bundeszentrale für Politische Bildung, June 3, 2009), accessed February 15, 2022, http://www.bpb.de/politik/extremismus/rechtsextremismus/41192/was-ist-rechtspopulismus.

31 Pfanzelter, "Die (un)verdaute Erinnerung."

32 Eva Pfanzelter, Marcel Amoser, and Sarah Oberbichler, *Von Zugewanderten, Weggegangenen und Dagebliebenen: Beiträge zur Migrationsgeschichte Kufsteins im 20. Jahrhundert*, Kufstein Edition 5 (Kufstein: Stadtgemeinde Kufstein, 2022).

33 Stefan Lechner and Helmut Alexander, "Die Rücksiedlung," in Alexander, Lechner, and Leidlmair, *Heimatlos*, 181–273.

34 For the situation at the end of the war: Pfanzelter, *Südtirol unterm Sternenbanner*.

35 "Decreto Legislativo 2 Febbraio 1948, n. 23—Revisione Delle Opzioni Degli Alto Atesini," in *Gazzetta Ufficiale Della Repubblica Italiana, Serie Generale* 29 (February 5, 1948), accessed September 19, 2019, http://www.gazzettaufficiale.it/eli/id/1948/02/05/048U0023/sg.

36 Stefan Lechner, "Alles Retour: Rückoption und Rücksiedlung nach 1945," in *1940–1959: Totaler Krieg und schwerer Neubeginn*, Das 20. Jahrhundert in Südtirol, vol. 3, ed. Gottfried Solderer (Bolzano: Raetia, 2001), 76–87.

37 Currently two digitization projects at the University of Innsbruck in conjunction with the Tiroler Landesarchiv, the Tyrolean Regional Archive in Innsbruck, and the Staatsarchiv, the State Archive in Bolzano, are being carried out. It is hoped that some of these questions will be answered after the end of the projects, see: Eva Pfanzelter, Dirk Rupnow, and Andrea Di Michele, "Option museal – Option digital," 2022, accessed February 15, 2022, https://www.uibk.ac.at/zeitgeschichte/optionmudi/; Eva Pfanzelter, Andrea Di Michele, Sarah Oberbichler, and Valerio Larcher, "ReMIGRA: Return Migration as an Interdisciplinary Research Area Using the Example of the South Tyrolean 'Return Option,'" 2021, accessed February 15, 2022, https://www.uibk.ac.at/zeitgeschichte/remigra/.

38 Pfanzelter, Amoser, and Oberbichler, *Von Zugewanderten*.

39 E.g., in February 2022 the "Neue Heimat Tirol" has ten "re-construction" projects in former "Südtiroler Siedlungen" all over the region: search Neue Heimat Tirol website for "Südtiroler Siedlung," accessed February 15, 2022, https://www.neueheimat.tirol/.

40 To name only a few: Helmut Alexander, Stefan Lechner, and Adolf Leidlmair, *Heimatlos: Die Umsiedlung der Südtiroler* (Vienna: Deuticke, 1993); Elisa Heinrich, and Sabine Merler, "Südtiroler-Siedlung," in *Die Erinnerung an die Südtiroler Option*, 2013–2017, accessed September, 14, 2020 http://optionunderinnerung.org/index.html@p=162.html; Michael Astenwald, "Genese, Transformation und Persistenz der Südtiroler Siedlungen in Innsbruck – Neu-Pradl: Politische, ideologische und städtebauliche Hintergründe einer Siedlungserweiterung der NS-Zeit, sowie deren Verflechtung mit Österreichs Sozialem Wohnbau von 1918–1945" (Diploma-thesis, University of Innsbruck, Austria, 2011); Sabine Schweitzer, "Wanderndes Gedächtnis – Wandelnde Erinnerungen. Migration und Akkulturation von Südtiroler Umsiedlerinnen und Umsiedlern" (PhD diss., University of Fiesoly, Italy, 2002); red./tirol.ORF.at, "'Verkaufte Heimat' in Südtiroler Siedlung," tirol.orf.at, July 25, 2019, accessed February 15, 2022, https://tirol.orf.at/stories/3005952/.

41 Gesamtverband der Südtiroler in Österreich, ed., *Südtiroler Heimat.* A collection of paper-editions can be found at the Tiroler Landesmuseum Ferdinandeum/Bibliothek. The collection's search catalogue turns up the following results: Tiroler Landesmuseen Bibliothekskatalog, ed. "Südtiroler Heimat," 1946–ongoing, accessed February 15, 2022 http://opac.tiroler-landesmuseen.at/webopac/index.asp?MedienNr=0066703.

42 Sabine Merler and Elisa Heinrich, "Südtiroler Vereine," in *Die Erinnerung an die Südtiroler Option*, 2013–2017, accessed September 14, 2020, http://optionunderinnerung.org/index.html@p=183.html.

43 See the website of the Gesamtverband der Südtiroler in Österreich, accessed February 15, 2022, https://verband-der-suedtiroler.at/.

44 Heinrich and Merler, "Südtiroler-Siedlung."

45 E.g., Eva Schlegel, "In den Palästen der Erinnerung, Südtiroler Siedlung Innsbruck," Neue Heimat Tirol, ed., "Kunst am Bau," accessed February 17, 2022, https://www.neueheimat.tirol/projekte/kunst-am-bau/innsbruck-eva-schlegel; Jürgen Bauer, "House Repetition 5. FE Jenbach," ibid., https://www.neueheimat.tirol/projekte/kunst-am-bau/jenbach-juergen-bauer; Michael Fliri, "Maske 'Topo Antro' in Innsbruck Pradl," ibid., https://www.neueheimat.tirol/projekte/kunst-am-bau/innsbruck-topo-antro; Gabriela Oberkofler, "Eine Geranienblüte in Kufstein," ibid., https://www.neueheimat.tirol/projekte/kunst-am-bau/kufstein-gabriela-oberkofler; Peter Niedertscheider, "Flachrelief in St. Johann in Tirol," ibid., https://www.neueheimat.tirol/projekte/kunst-am-bau/st-johann-in-tirol-peter-niedertscheider; Franz Wassermann, "Die Vertriebenen Telfs," ibid. https://www.neueheimat.tirol/projekte/kunst-am-bau/telfs-franz-wassermann; Claudia Barcheri, "Ich trag' meistens ein Poloshirt: Wörgl Südtiroler Siedlung," ibid. https://www.neueheimat.tirol/projekte/kunst-am-bau/woergl-claudia-barcheri; Christine S. Prantauer and Manfred Moser, "YinYang-Uhr: Zams Südtiroler Siedlung," ibid., https://www.neueheimat.tirol/projekte/kunst-am-bau/zams-christine-s-prantauer.

46 Due to the COVID-19-pandemic the exhibition has also been turned into a virtual tour: Schloss Tyrol, “Der Turm der Erinnerung: Südtirol und das 20. Jahrhundert (Virtual Tour),” accessed February 17, 2020, https://www.schlosstirol.it/virtualtour/de/main_tour/.

47 Culture Department of the City of Bolzano et al., “BZ ‘18–’45 One Monument, One City, Two Dictatorships: A Permanent Exhibition within the Monument to Victory,” accessed February 17, 2022, https://www.monumenttovictory.com/en/menu/privacy.html.

The Second Republic's National Symbols in Crisis? When *Doxa* Becomes Discourse (Again)

Christian Karner

Introduction

On 26 November 2003, Austria's most popular newspaper, the tabloid *Kronen Zeitung*, took stock of what it portrayed as a "dark week for us Austrians." What had started with an Austrian skier's allegedly unjustified disqualification was followed by the passing of new legislation that the paper predicted would negatively impact pensioners and job-seekers. Even more disconcerting—for an (increasingly) EU-skeptical medium against the backdrop of the then still recent fallout from the formation of the first "black-blue" (Austrian People's Party, ÖVP-Freedom Party of Austria, FPÖ) coalition government and the temporary "sanctions" by Austria's fourteen European partners three years previously—were developments on the EU-level during this purportedly *schwarze Woche für uns Österreicher* in November 2003. The *Kronen Zeitung* suggested that the decision not to penalize French and German financial deficits had revealed stark discrepancies favoring the big and powerful within the European Union and prophesized that the European parliament's recent regulations regarding truck traffic would exacerbate Austria's problems with the much-discussed *Transitverkehr* and lead to trucks "thundering across" the country unrestrictedly.[1]

Sport, social change, criticisms of European politics, and environmental concerns intermingled in a thematic mix typical of Austria's most widely-read newspaper and tabloid journalism across much of Europe. However, there was more to this. Implicit in the *Kronen Zeitung*'s headlines on the day in question was an assessment that some of the core symbols of Austria's Second Republic—and hence sources of well-documented "national pride" for many of her citizens[2]—were in a state of acute crisis. In what follows, I argue that these claims and perceptions back in 2003 were anything but isolated. On the contrary, they encapsulate much of the politics of national identity in Austria since the turn of the millennium. To illustrate this, I begin with outlines of a pertinent theoretical trajectory and well-known studies of the Second Republic's symbolic repertoires of national self-identification, which will lead to a brief methodological note for the ensuing discussion. This is followed by four analytical sections demonstrating how some of those core symbols—namely social protection and other institutional pillars of the Second Republic, political stability, Austria's landscape, water, and the environment—have been at the heart of key developments and core episodes reflecting Austria's shifting political field since the *Kronen Zeitung*'s headline in November 2003 mentioned above.

Contexts: Theoretical, Historical, and Methodological

It has long been recognized that Pierre Bourdieu's account[3] of social reproduction accomplished through the emotional, cognitive and dispositional "structuring structures" of the *habitus* and its practices is also more narrowly relevant to the study of national identities in Austria and elsewhere.[4] This tradition of research focused on people's socialization into, and symbolic reproduction of, national cultures extends to more recent work on "everyday" nationalism and "nationhood" that work in the "realm of the unself-consciousness."[5] Concerning the latter, namely in the taken-for-granted linguistic and semiotic domains of *Banal Nationalism*, Michael Billig's seminal study[6] continues to provide significant points of reference. Much less widely noticed, however, is the fact that in both paradigmatic conceptual strands, Bourdieu's and Billig's, there are explicit acknowledgments that not all social reproduction occurs in a non-reflexive fashion and that many forms of nationalism are anything but banal. For Bourdieu,[7] habitus and its associated domain of "cultural commonsense" (or *doxa*) are transformed into a contested discursive field of competing political positions in moments of *crisis*. For Billig, meanwhile,[8] the distinction between *banal* (i.e., ubiquitous but generally unnoticed) and *hot* nationalism (i.e., emotionally charged and politically mobilizing) is crucial. Building on recent work,[9] the following discussion demonstrates that our understanding of Austria's politics of national identity today benefits from an analytical synthesis and application of these sub-strands in Bourdieu's and Billig's respective oeuvres: the crisis-induced transformation of previously taken-for-granted cultural meanings (*doxa*) into competing discourses also manifests in formerly banal, though widely cherished, symbols of national identity "turning hot" (i.e., becoming the objects of debate and the focus of politicized anxieties).

In a further preliminary step to such a discussion, important scholarship on the *symbolic* and identificatory dimensions of Austria's post-war "reconstruction" or nation-building[10] needs to be mentioned. Research periodically conducted since the mid-1950s revealed the widening availability and taken-for-grantedness of a distinctly Austrian habitus and hence a growing distancing from previously dominant pan-Germanic self-understandings.[11] The proportion of Austrians considering themselves "a separate people" (*ein eigenes Volk*), rather than part of a larger, *deutsch-nationale* and hence ethno-linguistically defined ingroup, increased from 49 percent in 1956 to 66 percent in 1970, and 75 percent in 1987.[12] Similarly noteworthy was the *symbolic content* of this newly emerging, distinctly Austrian banal nationalism. Valorized in popular Austrian cinema of the first postwar decade,[13] rural space was beginning to play an important role. By the mid-1980s, in a study on "objects of national pride," 80 percent of the participants ranked the country's "scenic beauty" first, while 67 percent also emphasized its "historical treasures," and 64 percent further included Austria's skiing achievements.[14] In a comparable survey in 1980, 97 percent of participants expressed "great pride" in Austria's "scenic beauty," 96 percent celebrated the country's political stability and social peace, 93 percent stressed their attachment to "their common language,"[15] 87 percent mentioned political neutrality, 79 percent the country's artistic history, and 74 percent Austrian food as their sources of positive national self-identification.[16] Data from interviews and focus groups from more recent research on Austrian national identities[17] has added to this frequently corroborated list of symbols of purported Austrianness (see below) by revealing pronounced pride in or gratitude for the country's social welfare system.

By the 1990s, Austria reported some of the most pronounced forms of national pride measured in comparative international surveys.[18] Against this background, it is worth noting that previous research has traced growing anxieties surrounding each of the symbols of national self-identification reported above—from landscape and natural resources to historical treasures, sporting performances, and the particularities of Austrian German, to political stability and social welfare—during the early years of the new millennium and the neo-nationalist turn in evidence by then.[19] Building on this, I here ask how and in which contexts some of the Second Republic's core symbols have featured in more recent public discussions. The analytical "snapshots" to follow reflect recent perceived crises,[20] their purported effects on some of Austria's most widely-cherished symbols, and the political contests to which some such crises have given rise.

As a final preliminary step, a methodological note is needed. What follows is the result of a qualitative, thematic analysis of how the symbolic pillars in the literature on Austrian national identities summarized above have been discussed in national media—and other relevant sources—at key moments in recent years. This article thereby draws on an extensive corpus of data—an archive of media materials personally collected since

2002—which span much of Austria's diverse mediascape (i.e., materials from the ORF, the country's public broadcasting network; the tabloid as well as the broadsheet press; quality dailies and weeklies with different ideological leanings). More specifically, my focus and selection below, from this very extensive corpus of data, are directed by three considerations: first, *ideological breadth*, which this discussion ensures by considering materials from media located at very different points along the political spectrum (e.g., the strongly right-leaning, EU-skeptical tabloid *Kronen Zeitung*, and Vienna's weekly, left-liberal *Falter* respectively). The second consideration is one of the relative reach or discursive prominence of the positions being examined: particular emphasis thus lies on the *Kronen Zeitung*, Austria's most widely-read paper that for some time reached some 43 percent of Austria's population and thus enjoyed the reputation of being the "world-champion in circulation relative to population size" (*Reichweitenweltmeister*);[21] discursive prominence also underpins my brief mention of a relevant recent installation on Vienna's *Heldenplatz* in the conclusion of this article. The third consideration has directed me towards including media with a proven *agenda-setting* ability, such as the weekly *Profil*, that have demonstrably shaped the broader public debate in Austria.[22] The data thus selected and discussed includes voices from very different political positions and diverging degrees of discursive power and reach (e.g., politicians, journalists, and newspaper readers expressing their views through letters to editors).

With the conceptual, contextual, and methodological foundations thus in place, I turn to my first thematic focus. This illustrates how Austria's welfare state and other core institutions have recently been declared to be under threat. Notably, some such perceptions implicate, or are articulated from, otherwise very different ideological positions.

Social Protectionism and Institutions under Threat

The first collection of discursive "snapshots" pertains to how the protections afforded by the Austrian welfare state—some of the earlier-quoted studies showed that these have come to feature among the Second Republic's most widely-valued accomplishments—have recently been constructed as being in jeopardy or, unsustainable by certain parts of the ideological spectrum. Such claims have been particularly prominent in, but not exclusive to, the *Freiheitliche Partei Österreichs*. What is more, the FPÖ offers an unambiguous scapegoat for the purported crisis affecting the welfare state: migration and "foreigners" allegedly depleting resources and structures that the party defines as quintessentially national.

Such claims already implicitly resonate in the party's self-stylization as a *soziale Heimatpartei* that the FPÖ has cultivated since 2005; its preferences for neo-liberal economic policies notwithstanding.[23] As I have argued elsewhere,[24] the term performs some of its rhetorical and ideological work subtly through insinuations about political competitors: the subtext to this self-designation are implicit claims that the FPÖ outperforms the ÖVP in terms of patriotism and is more supportive of the socially marginalized than the Social Democratic Party of Austria, SPÖ. However, the party's full assessment of the current state of Austria's welfare systems emerges from a closer look at the 2013 FPÖ *Handbuch freiheitlicher Politik*. Premised on the party's insistence that the "social state was not invented for foreigners,"[25] regardless of their tax contributions, the FPÖ's handbook includes the following statements and demands: opposing EU-citizens' unconditional freedom of movement; opposing social support payments for non-EU-citizens; for the unemployment services (AMS) to only support Austrian citizens; for the creation of a separate social security system for "guest-workers," and for non-EU-workers' work-permits to be withdrawn in case of prolonged or repeated periods of unemployment; "ultimately," the FPÖ claims, "Austria's social state becomes unaffordable if citizens and foreigners retain rights to the same welfare provisions."[26]

The (FPÖ's) claim that one of the Second Republic's core features, its social welfare system, was under acute strain due to migratory flows became yet more prominent in the context of the much-discussed "refugee crisis" of 2015/16. In a video address concerning Austria's purported "asylum-emergency" published on the FPÖ's YouTube channel in September 2015, the party's then *Bundesparteiobmann* Heinz-Christian Strache posed the following ideologically loaded questions:

> What consequences are awaiting our health- and social systems? … We already have FAR too few affordable flats for our own population. What does accepting so many people mean for our schools? Who can guarantee that terrorists and fundamentalists are not also being smuggled into our country? … How much does all this cost? … At a time when there is not enough money for the fight against poverty and unemployment in our country and when people suffer from cuts.[27]

Taken together, these (and many similar) pronouncements on perceived present crises affecting the Austrian welfare state, one of the Second Republic's institutional pillars and core symbols, reveal what Nancy Fraser[28] describes as an ethnically exclusionary (and "unsavory") form of *social protectionism*. Typical of our neo-nationalist era, such nationalist "closure"[29] constitutes a prominent, always contestable, and indeed frequently contested response to contemporary social changes and perceived crises.

More recently, other core institutions of the Second Republic have been declared to be under threat. What is more, some such pronouncements have been articulated from the other end of the ideological spectrum, opposite the nationalist Right. For the present discussion, such critical assessments are particularly telling considering the earlier-mentioned contrasting findings from 1980, when 96 percent of survey respondents professed their pride in Austria's "political stability,"[30]—which would surely presuppose well-functioning democratic institutions. In August 2021, against the backdrop of the parliamentary inquiry into the "Ibiza-affair" (see below) and a succession of scandals revealed in its aftermath involving the FPÖ, ÖVP, and Sebastian Kurz, philosopher and journalist Isolde Charim detected an "illiberalism" corrosive of democracy: its symptoms, Charim argued, included a government that undermined the separation of powers, that "delegitimized" the judiciary and sought control over the media.[31] As had been reflected by an "external voice" two months earlier, this was not an isolated assessment: in an interview published in *Profil*, German SPD-politician Martin Schulz likened Sebastian Kurz—who had portrayed the judiciary's inquiries into his statements concerning the "Ibiza-affair" parliamentary inquiry as "a politically motivated campaign"—to "Orbán, Kaczyński, Berlusconi, and Trump" and their democratically damaging strategies.[32] Particularly criticisms of (now former) Chancellor Kurz's alleged attempts to instrumentalize parts of the press and the ORF were already voiced prior to the next scandal in early October 2021, which led to Kurz's resignation as Chancellor. Two months before this particular scandal (revolving around accusations that Kurz and the ÖVP may have used public money to ensure favorable opinion poll data in the tabloid *Österreich*)—the full fallout of which cannot yet be assessed at the time of writing—the editors of the ideologically differently positioned *Profil* and *Falter* had both and independently argued that Kurz's government's influence on the public broadcasting network ORF threatened to destabilize Austrian democracy.[33]

These first illustrations thus suggest that institutions (e.g., the welfare system or the public broadcasting network) that in the earlier decades of the Second Republic were seen as guarantors or signs of social and political stability—and hence as some purported core symbols of "Austrianness" and national pride—are now commonly seen as being under threat. Significantly, some such diagnoses emanate from very different positions along the political spectrum and partly cut across the otherwise profound ideological contrasts between them. The following section illustrates that assessments of systemic crises extend even further.

(In-)Stability—Political/Financial, National/European

As we saw in the surveys from the 1980s quoted earlier, political stability and "social peace"[34] ranked highly in Austrians' appreciation of what they had come to value in the course of the history of the Second Republic and its consensual democracy. Since Austria's EU accession in 1995, forms of EU skepticism and, in some formulations, outright EU phobia have made frequent, romanticizing references to the pre-EU-accession period and the 1960s and 1970s, in particular. The well-known trope of Austria as an "island of the blessed" (*Insel der Seligen*), first formulated by Pope Paul VI during a visit by Austrian president Franz Jonas in 1971,[35] has been widely re-appropriated to negatively contrast a present found wanting compared to the post-war, pre-EU-accession era. A discursive realm in which such positions are routinely encountered are the "letters-to-the-editor" pages of Austria's most popular newspaper, the tabloid *Kronen Zeitung* mentioned earlier. The latter primarily represents an EU-skepticism[36]—occasional counter-discourses notwithstanding—that is paradigmatically encapsulated in the following readers' letters,[37] which are representative of argumentative positions one encounters on a near-daily basis in the paper's *Leserbriefe zum EU-Theater* section:[38]

> Austria has changed radically over recent decades: arrogant politicians are merely led by the EU ... [T]he finance minister wastes millions on European projects while 400,000 Austrians live in poverty ... The health system is misused ... most media only report what the government and the EU want them to.[39]
>
> People in our country were considerably better off in the 1960s than today... [N]ews about our politicians were largely positive, whereas today they just make up the numbers at EU-summits. There were no concerns about UV-light, HIV ... genetically modified food, nuclear accidents, or rising crime.[40]

With regard to political stability and "social peace" as some of yesteryear's purported symbols of "Austrianness"—nowadays nostalgically projected back upon a bygone era of the country's alleged former status as an island of the blessed that has since, so the claim continues, been overtaken by social transformations and political changes—the *Kronen Zeitung* and many of her readers have found great fault with the Eurozone's responses to the Greek (and other) sovereign debt crises since 2009. The juxtaposition of a positively evaluated (post-war) past to a negatively judged present is here discursively overlaid by another binary; Austria and other net-contributors (*Nettozahler*) are constructed as being at the mercy of a "bottomless pit" (*Fass ohne Boden*) in a Eurozone portrayed as a union of debt (*Schuldenunion*). The following two readers' letters, published at the height of the Eurozone crisis, are paradigmatic of discursive positions that have recurred with some regularity on the pages of the *Kronen Zeitung*:

> Greece's bankruptcy has shown that the EU is a pack of lies ... other Mediterranean countries will also receive Austrian tax money... We should either get out of the EU immediately, or Greece should be removed from it.[41]
>
> The Greek and Irish bailouts are causing the EU to hemorrhage ... Blood donors only give as much as they comfortably can. The European donor countries, by contrast, are now incurring unmanageable debts themselves.[42]

The wider and enduring political traction of such positions is reflected in the current Austrian government's place within the European Union's so-called "frugal" states and their position concerning the EU's attempted budgetary response to the COVID-19 pandemic.

A proposition emerging from the discussion thus far is that analysis of some prominent—though certainly also widely contested—political positions in Austria requires a deeper historical lens and an understanding of the country's politics and symbolisms of national identity in periods of crisis. The positions briefly summarized in this section amount to an EU-skeptical[43] politics of nostalgia,[44] which evaluates the present negatively and in direct contrast to a highly romanticized narrative of the Second Republic's earlier decades up until the discursively constructed "turning-point" of Austria's EU-accession. As the next analytical step illustrates, perceptions of crises are not confined to the domain of political institutions. Other such perceptions manifest in relation to what the studies of Austrian "national pride" mentioned earlier revealed to be the most widely-cherished symbolic domain: the country's (rural) landscape(s).

"Landscape"—The National Scenery in Crisis?

As we saw earlier, emotional attachments to Austria's scenic beauty came to rank highly among respondents' reported sources of national pride during the post-war decades. Recent literature has done much to critically illuminate Austria's complex environmental histories[45] in general and the symbolic significance of various natural environments to the "nation-building process"[46] in particular. Building on this, it bears analytical dividends to pay attention to how recent years and decades have seen growing concerns about the future of Austria's landscapes and central identity-bestowing symbols in the face of environmental changes.[47]

A recent public debate on how rural landscapes—and hence some of Austria's central symbolic domains—are impacted by construction-work and infrastructural developments was triggered by the lawyer, author, and *Kronen Zeitung* columnist Tassilo Wallentin. Having written about the scale of construction in Austria's (formerly) rural spaces, Wallentin followed this up by reporting some of his readers' reactions. Those included statements to the effect that the ubiquitous "construction madness," with leading participation of the tourist industry (i.e., through cable cars, mountain-bike tracks, and viewing platforms), "has to stop." They also expressed gratitude for Wallentin's interest in the issue, which another reader described as "one of our era's most pressing problems, rapid environmental destruction through the exploitative appropriation of nature by neoliberal consumers." Wallentin himself responded by predicting that the currently "parasitic" appropriation of rural space would lead to all of Austria being "paved over" (*zugepflastert*) by 2050:

> One has to picture this: in Austria, every year, an area the size of the city of Salzburg disappears underneath concrete. Every day, forests, meadows, and fields amounting to twenty football pitches are turned into streets, parking spaces, shopping areas, and apartment blocks. Seventy percent of animals and plants have disappeared since 1986. The most fertile soil is transformed into artificial towns, although the space taken up by unused buildings already matches the size of Vienna. We can no longer produce all our food ourselves ... Spatial planning cannot be left to local politicians anymore ... We need a national plan prioritizing agricultural land ... Our survival is at stake.[48]

For the present discussion, it is crucial to emphasize that these are anything but isolated concerns. In a regional, Styrian context, the *Kronen Zeitung* already reported a decade earlier that every year Graz and its hinterlands were losing "green space" the size of "90 football pitches."[49] Elsewhere, and more recently, Austrian author Barbara Frischmuth has reported an unparalleled "construction mania" (*Bauwut*) in her native Altaussee,[50] one of Austria's most photographed and most (stereotypically) Alpine sceneries. Similarly, environmentalists have warned against the consequences of seemingly unhindered construction along the shores of Burgenland's *Neusiedler See*.[51] Related discussions have shown that the issue of "soil sealing" (*Bodenversiegelung*)—the construction of buildings or infrastructural developments on formerly agricultural or natural/unused land—is increasingly recognized as a major environmental problem across ideological camps and boundaries. In February 2021, *Profil* reported that thirteen hectares of land were turned into construction sites across Austria every day.[52] This figure was adjusted to a daily loss of eleven and a half hectares in natural habitat in a European Union "state of nature" report, which still means that "soil sealing" is progressing at a faster rate in Austria than in any other EU member-state; critical commentators have attributed this, in part, to widespread, cultural aspirations for living in single-family detached houses.[53] Meanwhile, other experts have called attention to a wider set of historical, legal, and economic conditions threatening the destruction of more and more of Austria's (formerly) rural spaces; these conditions include the growing power of Austria's publicly owned corporation in charge of motorway expansion and maintenance (Asfinag).[54]

Discussions of the symbolic importance of particular landscapes to Austrian self-understandings do well to remember that the country's darkest historical period between 1938 and 1945 saw many of the same environments constructed as quintessentially "Germanic," as "living-space" and a protective "bulwark" for all Germans.[55] The speed with which the Second Republic's natural environments were subsequently refashioned into quintessential sources of *Austrian* pride and particularism can be taken as an indicator of the success and efficacy of the country's post-war nation-(re)building in the symbolic domain. What the present discussion adds to this is a recognition that recent years have seen a new awareness: of the precarity of environments and, with them, of a central symbol of national identity. As the next and final thematic section illustrates, environmental concerns extend considerably beyond changes affecting specific landscapes as widely-endorsed markers of national identity.

Ibiza, Water, and Climate Change

Building on the issue of environmental concerns, the background to our set of final snapshots includes long-established cultural anxieties—traceable at least to the 2006 Austrian parliamentary elections when those anxieties manifested, albeit to differing degrees, in each of the main parties' electoral programs,[56] with a specter of widening commodification: i.e., with the impact of global market forces on areas like higher education, agricultural production, or the environment more broadly. Arguably foremost among such concerns with the growing "marketization" of formerly non-commodified realms[57] has been opposition across the political spectrum to any prospect of Austrian water being privatized and turned into a commodity for the international market. Put more simply, there has been a widespread political consensus that water is, and should remain, a national, public good not for sale.

It is in this context that core aspects of Austria's biggest political scandal in decades need to be read: the undercover recordings of Heinz-Christian Strache and Johann Gudenus in highly compromising discussions with a pretend-Russian oligarch's niece revealed by the *Süddeutsche Zeitung* and *Der Spiegel* in May 2019, now known as "Ibizagate" and until very recently subject to a parliamentary inquiry. Parts of the subsequent account by the two investigative journalists at the heart of the initial revelations (though not the recordings) showed how Strache was—his subsequent and repeated protests to the contrary notwithstanding—prepared to circumvent Austria's cultural and political consensus concerning water:

> At this point, the Russian's chaperon takes over. He sketches several possible quid-pro-quos for the Russian: one could reciprocate by awarding her state contracts at artificially inflated prices or by privatizing the art collections … Perhaps, he suggests, she could get a share of Austria's water through potential legislative changes … Strache replies: "A privatization of water is unthinkable," for when it comes to "the white gold" Austrians are "allergic." However, what is possible, he says, is a structure whereby "we sell water, granting the state an income, and the buyer (or trader) also certainly makes a profit." One would have to "discuss percentages." … It is a remarkable statement since, at least publicly, the FPÖ's head had consistently argued, for instance, in a party video in 2013, that water was not "a source of profit for corporations, nor to be speculated with."[58]

The Ibiza-affair has been multi-dimensional, protracted, and complex. It has led to a series of subsequent revelations and continues to involve much of Austria's political- and media establishment in attempts at explaining, fact-finding, and variously attributing or deflecting responsibility for the many disconcerting statements and connections captured in the undercover recordings.[59] What is crucial for the present discussion, however, is that part of the outrage caused by the scandal derived from the apparent contradiction that had emerged: between Strache's public statements, made consistently since 2007, against any form of privatization of Austrian water supplies on the one hand;[60] and, on the other, his suddenly revealed preparedness—on a supposed backstage—to bargain with one of the country's most widely cherished symbols of national self-identification in his pursuit of power.

Water has been only one issue among several (including media ownership and political corruption) that have been highlighted by the Ibiza affair and the succession of still unfolding scandals it has triggered. What matters for present analytical purposes is that the "water issue" also interfaces with wider concerns about environmental degradation and climate change. Notably, some debates about these core issues of our current historical era are being discursively framed in distinctly national terms. Put differently, global challenges and threats are viewed through the symbolic lenses of the national narratives of self-identification that were established in the post-war period and recorded in the studies mentioned earlier. Writing in *Profil*, Eva Linsinger has shown how far current realities now diverge from Austria's carefully-styled image as a model of environmentalism: Austrian per-capita meat consumption and CO_2 emissions, for example, are among the highest in the world, contradicting widespread, myth-like self-understandings[61] of Austria as a model country of environmentalism (*Umweltmusterland*).[62] Concerning the earlier-mentioned issue of soil-sealing, meanwhile, it has been pointed out that the Austrian rate of nearly twelve hectares of green space being turned daily into shopping centers, residential areas, or infrastructural developments compares very unfavorably in international terms and is far above the EU target of two and a half hectares.[63] Quite how complex contemporary environmental politics can be has also become apparent in the context of current controversies surrounding some major infrastructural developments in Austria (e.g., a planned ring road and tunnel east of Vienna and their impact on the Danube Woodlands National Park in the area[64]): as argued by the *Falter* columnist Peter Michael Lingens, environmental conservationism here runs into infrastructural disadvantages endured in many a rural area; put differently, without major investments in public transport rural dwellers often have little choice but to rely on their environmentally and economically costly cars.[65] Projected back onto the conceptual screen that formed my starting point for this discussion, this shows how—against the backdrop of climate change and our urgent need for environmentally responsibly changes—Austrian rurality and "scenic beauty," as long-established and often reified symbols of national identification, have themselves become contested political terrain. In the context of growing concerns about the scarcity of natural resources (e.g., water) and the (un)sustainability of late modern lifestyles, some of Austria's natural and symbolic capital is, as this section has begun to show, now widely seen to be facing profound crises.

Concluding reflections

Parts of a recent public installation on Vienna's Heldenplatz (see figure 1) reflected the continuing cultural salience of many of the symbols of national self-understanding recorded in the studies from the 1980s mentioned earlier. According to a 2019 follow-up study conducted by Diem and Bruckmüller and cited by the installation, the following "symbols of Austrianness" still rank prominently and in descending order: *der Bundesadler*, *Berge*, *die Nationalflagge*, *der Stephansdom*, *Seen*, *das Riesenrad*, *Wiener Schnitzel*, *Mozart*, *Landschaft*, *Wien*, *Großglockner*, *Donau* (see figure 2). This provides important corroboration of the continuing importance of some of the core symbols of national pride recorded in the 1980s, including those of scenery and particular landscapes widely associated with Austria, some of the country's historical (i.e., artistic and architectural) treasures, food, and the kind of symbolic reservoir typically associated with banal nationalism.[66] However, there are also limitations to such rather decontextualized, potentially static recordings of what citizens profess pride in and associate with national belonging.

Therefore, the present discussion offers a necessary complement to the quantitative recording of different symbols' relative, perceived importance at specific points in time. Several features have characterized this complementary, more carefully contextualized and qualitatively oriented approach applied here: first, the materials drawn upon for the present discussion have included a range of contributions to public discussions in Austria; each of the discussions in question has revealed perceptions of crisis-scenarios affecting a widely-cherished symbol of Austrian self-identification.[67] Second, the debates reviewed here, although each of them was presented as a set of discursive "snapshots" in its own right, have covered core episodes since the start of the new millennium and, jointly, capture discursive developments over this period of time. Third, on a theoretical level, the present analysis has made reference to two mutually complementary strands that, combined, provide a dynamic conceptualization of how symbols of national belonging have been re-debated and re-thought in light of changing circumstances.

The two conceptual strands in question have been Michael Billig's distinction between "banal" and "hot nationalism";[68] and Bourdieu's account of the crisis-induced transformation of the habitus and the domain of *doxa*, or taken-for-granted cultural commonsense, into a domain of heightened consciousness and competing political positions. When synthesized—and therein lies the specific, conceptual contribution of the analysis offered here[69]—Bourdieu's framework can help illuminate the conditions (i.e., structural, perceived, or discursively-politically exploited crises) conducive to the transformation of formerly *banal* into now positively—though invariably contestable and indeed frequently contested[70]—*hot* nationalisms. As this discussion has begun to show, such an analytical switch captures anxieties and changing forms of Austrian national consciousness and identity politics in the twenty-first century. As such, the argument developed here subsumes but also pushes beyond Peter Ulram's summary of the political and civil society changes discernible in Austria since the 1970s: those have included a "loosening" of older political bonds; growing "civic competence,"; newly emerging political concerns with issues like environmentalism or immigration; but also widening disillusionment with, if not outright anger at, the political system among significant proportions of the population.[71] The discussion developed here has shown how issues, both local/national and global, are commonly interpreted through the prism of long-established, widely-endorsed symbols of national identification. The common denominator of the public concerns and debates examined above is that diverse contemporary issues are thereby perceived as affecting, or sometimes threatening, some of Austria's institutional and symbolic pillars. Heightened crisis-consciousness thus becomes a driver of the politics of national identity.

Put differently, the synthesis of parts of Pierre Bourdieu's and Michael Billig's conceptual apparatuses enables a *processual* understanding of national identifications: survey and other data on the relative prominence of symbols of national pride are thereby read in their respective contexts and moments of production; concurrently, changes over time in how such symbols are either silently celebrated or explicitly talked about, and the (often contrasting) political positions which debates surrounding a previously *banal* and now *hot* nationalism give rise to, can then be recognized. The crux of the argument developed here is that an understanding of Austria's national identity politics today benefits from an acknowledgment of how widely-shared, previously taken-for-granted symbols of national identification have, over recent decades, entered what Bourdieu[72] described as a "universe" of crisis-induced reflexivity and competing discursive positions. What is more, the processual approach sketched and applied here is also potentially highly relevant for our critical understanding of, and possible responses to, neo-nationalist politics more generally, including the various crises the current and wider renationalization of European societies purports to address.

Image 1, taken by the author: Installation (summer 2020) on Vienna's *Heldenplatz*—"2020 – Ein Jahr der Jubiläen (25 Jahre Österreich in der Europäischen Union, 75 Jahre Zweite Republik, 100 Jahre Bundesverfassung)"—against the backdrop of a police car and the renovation of Austria's parliamentary building.

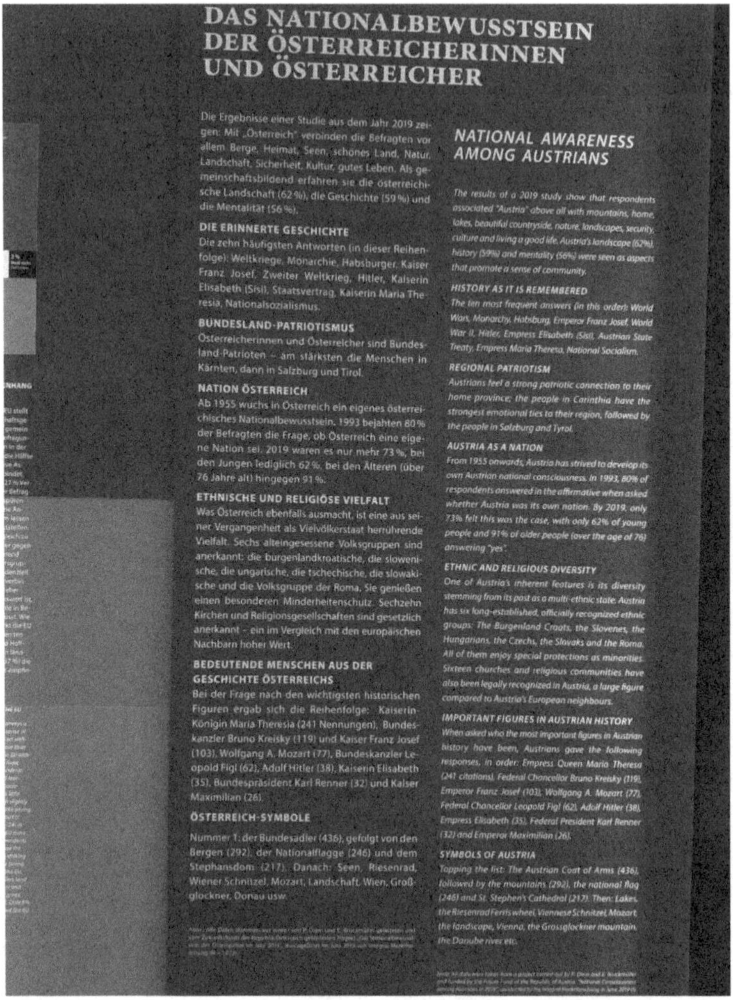

Image 2, taken by the author: contribution to the Heldenplatz installation in figure 1, focus: national consciousness and symbols of "Austrianness."

Endnotes

1 See Christian Karner, "National Doxa, Crises and Ideological Contestation in Contemporary Austria," *Nationalism and Ethnic Politics* 11, no. 2 (2005), 232.

2 See, for example, Oliver Rathkolb, *Die paradoxe Republik: Österreich 1945 bis 2005* (Vienna: Zsolnay, 2005), 25–26.

3 Pierre Bourdieu, *Outline of a Theory of Practice* (Cambridge: Cambridge University Press, 1977).

4 For example, see Rudolf De Cillia, Martin Reisigl, and Ruth Wodak, "The Discursive Construction of National Identities," *Discourse & Society* 10, no. 1 (1999), 149–73; Ruth Wodak, Rudolf de Cillia, Martin Reisigl, and Karin Liebhart, *The Discursive Construction of National Identity* (Edinburgh: Edinburgh University Press, 1999).

5 Jon Fox, "The Edges of the Nation: A Research Agenda for Uncovering the Taken-for-Granted Foundations of Everyday Nationhood," *Nations and Nationalism* 23, no. 1 (2017), 26; Jon Fox and Maarten van Ginderachter, "Introduction: Everyday Nationalism's Evidence Problem," *Nations and Nationalism* 24, no. 3 (2018), 546–52.

6 Michael Billig, *Banal Nationalism* (London: Sage, 1995).

7 Bourdieu, *Outline*, 167ff.

8 Billig, *Banal Nationalism*, 43ff.; also see Michael Skey, "The National in Everyday Life: A Critical Engagement with Michael Billig's Thesis of Banal Nationalism," *Sociological Review* 57, no. 2 (2009), 331–46.

9 Christian Karner, *Nationalism Revisited: Austrian Social Closure from Romanticism to the Digital Age* (New York: Berghahn, 2020).

10 See, for example, Peter Thaler, *The Ambivalence of Identity: The Austrian Experience of Nation-Building in a Modern Society* (West Lafayette: Purdue University Press, 2001).

11 Karner, *Nationalism Revisited*, 128.

12 Ernst Bruckmüller, "Das Österreichbewußtsein," in *Politik in Österreich,* ed. Wolfgang Mantl (Vienna: Böhlau, 1992), 262.

13 Maria Fritsche, *Homemade Men in Postwar Austrian Cinema* (New York: Berghahn, 2013).

14 Albert Reiterer, ed., *Nation und Nationalbewußtsein in Österreich* (Vienna: Verband der wissenschaftlichen Gesellschaften Österreichs, 1988), 118–19.

15 Given the phonetic and semantic particularities of Austrian German, very considerable regional variations between different dialects notwithstanding, and an often wide linguistic "gulf" experienced by many Austrians vis-à-vis Germans, it seems more plausible to interpret such linguistic pride as a sign of Austrian particularism rather than as a neo-romantic return to pan-Germanism. This is also

corroborated by recent data collected by De Cillia, Wodak, Rheindorf, and Lehner, whose research participants also emphasized the importance of Austrian variants of German to them: see Rudolf De Cillia, Ruth Wodak, Markus Rheindorf, and Sabine Lehner, *Österreichische Identitäten im Wandel: Empirische Untersuchungen zu ihrer diskursiven Konstruktion, 1995–2015* (Wiesbaden: Springer, 2020), 81–107.

16 Ernst Bruckmüller, *Nation Österreich: Kulturelles Bewußtsein und gesellschaftlich-politische Prozesse*, 2nd ed. (Vienna: Böhlau, 1996), 70.

17 De Cillia et al., *Österreichische Identitäten im Wandel*, 49.

18 Rathkolb, *Die paradoxe Republik*, 26.

19 Karner, "National doxa."

20 De Cillia et al. *Österreichische Identitäten im Wandel*, 206–7, rightly emphasize the "discursive construction" and concurrent political instrumentalization of various crises. For the purposes of the present discussion, I opt for the term "perceived" crises: in line with W. I. Thomas' "first law of social constructivism," this acknowledges that socially shared and enabled beliefs and perceptions are real in their consequences to those holding or experiencing them. Such perceived crises, so my claim, yield themselves to the Bourdieu-ian analysis sketched here, although they arguably meet a lower condition than Bourdieu's original emphasis on "objective crisis" (*Outline*, 168–69).

21 Rathkolb, *Die paradoxe Republik*, 241; also Karner, *Nationalism Revisited*, 168.

22 For a recent summary of the *Profil*'s journalistic self-understanding, see Robert Treichler, "Suchen Sie Streit?" *Profil*, September 12, 2021, 7.

23 See, for example, Heribert Schiedel, "Die FPÖ und der freiheitliche Antisemitismus," *Der Standard*, September 13, 2017, accessed October 25, 2021, http://derstandard.at/2000063919322.

24 Christian Karner, "National Mythologies: Theoretical Reflections, Empirical Applications," in *Myths in Austrian History*, ed. Günter Bischof, Marc Landry, and Christian Karner, Contemporary Austrian Studies 29 (New Orleans: UNO Press, 2020), 21–42.

25 See Herbert Auinger, *Die FPÖ – Blaupause der Neuen Rechten in Europa* (Vienna: Promedia, 2017), 56.

26 All quoted in Auinger, *Die FPÖ*, 52–56, all translations are mine.

27 Quoted in De Cillia et al., *Österreichische Identitäten im Wandel*, 203, original emphasis, my translation.

28 Nancy Fraser, "Can Society Be Commodities All the Way Down? Post-Polanyian Reflections on Capitalist Crisis," *Economy and Society* 43, no. 4 (2014), 541–59.

29 Karner, *Nationalism Revisited.*

30 Bruckmüller, "Das Österreichbewußtsein," 70.

31 Isolde Charim, "Demokratische Helden braucht das Land," *Falter*, August 4, 2021, 9.

32 Siobhán Geets, "Martin Schulz: 'Kurz ist noch gefährlicher,'" *Profil*, June 6, 2021, 38–41.

33 Christian Rainer, "Die Vergewaltigung der Pressefreiheit," *Profil*, August 8, 2021, 7; Armin Thurnher, "Wozu braucht Österreich einen öffentlich-rechtlichen Rundfunk?" *Falter* 31, August 4, 2021, 5. For a discussion of the longer continuities and, arguably, the recent intensification of the entanglements between politicians and the tabloid press, also see Florian Klenk, "'Ein Sumpf aus systemischer Korruption,'" *Falter*, June 16, 2021, 21–23. Also see Hubert Patterer, "Regierungskrise in Österreich: Wenn Kurz die Kanzlerschaft für die ÖVP retten will, muss er ein Opfer bringen: sich," *Kleine Zeitung*, October 7, 2021, accessed October 22, 2021, https://www.kleinezeitung.at/meinung/meinungktnhp/6044474/Regierungskrise-in-Oesterreich_Wenn-Kurz-die-Kanzlerschaft.

34 Also see, for example, John Fitzmaurice, *Austrian Politics and Society Today* (London: Macmillan, 1991).

35 See Konrad Paul Liessmann, *Insel der Seligen* (Innsbruck: Studienverlag, 2005); Konrad Paul Liessmann, "Austria, Insel der Seligen: Fortunate Isle?" in: *Myths in Austrian History*, ed. Günter Bischof, Marc Landry, and Christian Karner, Contemporary Austrian Studies 29 (New Orleans: UNO Press, 2020), 211–24.

36 Christian Karner, "The Uses of the Past and European Integration: Austria Between Lisbon, Ireland and EURO 08," *Identities: Global Studies in Culture and Power* 17, no. 4 (2010), 387–410; Christian Karner, "'Der Balkan' in der *Krone*: Austria between 'Frontier Orientalism' and Amnesiac Nationalism," *Interventions: International Journal of Postcolonial Studies* 22, no. 6 (2020), 783–801.

37 Also see Karner, *Nationalism Revisited*, 185.

38 Constraints of space allow for no more than the presentation of illustrative examples: the following readers' letters are typical of frequently recurring positions and arguments encountered on the readers' letters pages of the *Kronen Zeitung*. All translations from German are mine.

39 *Kronen Zeitung* reader, June 6, 2008, 25.

40 *Kronen Zeitung* reader, May 31, 2008, 31.

41 *Kronen Zeitung* reader, May 3, 2010, 23.

42 *Kronen Zeitung* reader, December 2, 2010, 28.

43 In some of its most forceful articulations, such EU-skepticism can certainly turn into outright EU-phobia. See Christian Karner, "(Kon-)texte kontrastierender Europapolitik in Österreich," in "(Kon-)Texte des Politischen," ed. Lukasz Kumiega, Christian Karner, 3. Beiheft, *Zeitschrift für Diskursforschung* (2018): 54–79.

44 See, for example, Christian Karner and Bernhard Weicht, eds. *The Commonalities of Global Crises: Markets, Communities and Nostalgia* (London: Palgrave Macmillan, 2016).

45 Marc Landry, Patrick Kupper, and Verena Winiwarter, eds., *Austrian Environmental History*, Contemporary Austrian Studies 27 (New Orleans: UNO Press, 2018). Georg Rigele, "'Land of Mountains…': Austria's Exceptional

Environment and Its Myths," in *Myths in Austrian History*, ed. Günter Bischof, Marc Landry, and Christian Karner, Contemporary Austrian Studies 29 (New Orleans: UNO Press, 2020), 225–41.

46 Marc Landry, Patrick Kupper, "Introduction," in *Austrian Environmental History*, ed. Marc Landry, Patrick Kupper, and Verena Winiwarter, Contemporary Austrian Studies 27 (New Orleans: UNO Press, 2018), 16.

47 See Karner, "National Doxa."

48 Tassilo Wallentin, "Bauwahnsinn Teil 2," *Krone Bunt*, July 26, 2020, 22, my translation.

49 *Kronen Zeitung*, "Graz wird zubetoniert," August 31, 2012, 30–31.

50 Sebastian Fasthuber, "'Mich hat niemand aufgehalten,'" *Falter* 26, June 30, 2021, 28–30.

51 *Der Standard*, "Der Neusiedler See wird verbaut auf Teufel komm raus," August 14, 2021, accessed October 22, 2021, https://www.derstandard.at/story/2000128897691/der-verbaute-seeamneusiedlersee-wird-gebaut-auf-teufel-komm?ref=nl.

52 Robert Prazak, "Bodenlos," *Profil Spezial*, February 28, 2021, 44–46.

53 Benedikt Narodoslawsky, "Heile Welt," *Falter*, October 6, 2021, 48–50; Maik Novotny, "Traumhaus oder Traum aus?" *Falter* 14, April 6, 2021, 34–37.

54 Hermann Knoflacher, "Autos, Autos über alles," *Falter*, August 18, 2021, 36–37.

55 Laura Morowitz, "Hitler as Liberator, Ostmark as Bulwark, and Other Myths of the Anschluss," in: *Myths in Austrian History*, ed. Günter Bischof, Marc Landry, and Christian Karner, Contemporary Austrian Studies 29 (New Orleans: UNO Press, 2020), 131–49.

56 See Christian Karner, "The Market and the Nation: Austrian (Dis)agreements," *Social Identities* 14, no. 2 (2008), 161–87.

57 Fraser, "Can Society Be Commodities All the Way Down?"

58 Frederik Obermaier and Bastian Obermayer, *Die Ibiza-Affäre* (Cologne: Kiepenheuer & Witsch, 2019), 62–63, my translation.

59 Christian Karner, "Ibizagate: Capturing a Political Field in Flux," *Austrian History Yearbook* 52 (2021), 253–69.

60 See *Der Standard*, "'Kein Spekulationsobjekt': Strache wollte Trinkwasser 2013 noch schützen," May 20, 2019, accessed May 21, 2019, https://derstandard.at/2000103489586/Kein-Spekulationsobjekt-Strache-wollte-Trink.

61 See Georg Rigele, "'Land of mountains.'"

62 Eva Linsinger, "Bitte aufwachen, Herr Bundeskanzler!" *Profil*, August 1, 2021, 7.

63 Joseph Gepp, Christina Hiptmayr, Clemens Neuhold, and Franziska Tschinderle, "Kein Sommer wie damals," *Profil*, August 8, 2021, 8–18.

64 Gerlinde Pölsler, "Stau & Lobau: wir brauchen eine modernere Verkehrspolitik," *Falter*, July 7, 2021, 7; also see Christa Zöchling, "Die neue Gretchenfrage," *Profil*, August 15, 2021, 25–27.

65 Peter Michael Lingens, "Die tückischen (ersten) letzten Kilometer," *Falter*, August 3, 2021, 8.

66 Billig, *Banal Nationalism*.

67 A further example that cannot be discussed in detail here relates to the significance of skiing to Austrian discourses of national identity, which was also captured in one of the aforementioned studies (Reiterer, *Nation*, 119). It is worth remembering how prominently skiing featured in political discussions surrounding COVID-19-related restrictions during the winter of 2020/2021: during the pandemic as a quintessential moment of crisis, and when Italy, France and Germany insisted on keeping ski-slopes closed, the Austrian government chose a different approach and allowed (socially distanced) skiing, a decision ÖVP club chairman August Wöginger explained, in part, by reasserting that "wir sind eine Skifahrernation" (Eva Linsinger, "ÖVP-Klubobmann Wöginger: 'Impfplan gilt auch für alle Politiker,'" *Profil*, January 24, 2021, 25–27. For a critical commentary, see Robert Treichler, "Ski Unheil!" *Profil*, November 29, 2020.)

68 Also see Skey, "The National in Everyday Life"; De Cillia et al., *Österreichische Identitäten im Wandel*.

69 Also see Christian Karner, *Negotiating National Identities: Between Globalization, the Past and "the Other"* (Farnham: Ashgate, 2011), 55–88; Karner, *Nationalism Revisited*.

70 To state the obvious, each of the discursive positions and claims considered here has certainly been widely discussed and contested from other vantage points along Austria's/ Europe's ideological spectrum. Limitations of space have made a focus on merely one set of contributions to a considerably larger, internally contested discursive-political field (à la Bourdieu's predictions) necessary.

71 Peter Ulram, "Political Culture in Austria," in *Austrian Studies Today*, ed. Günter Bischof and Ferdinand Karlhofer, Contemporary Austrian Studies 25 (New Orleans: UNO Press, 2016), 269–78.

72 Bourdieu, *Outline*, 164–71. As I have previously argued (Karner, "National Doxa," 227–29), the (crisis-induced) transformation of widely taken-for-granted national narratives into discursive contests and political polarization also describes the "Waldheim-affair" of 1986, as a result of which the long-cultivated myth of Austrian World War II "victimhood" was, at long last, turned into an object of political debate and critical, cultural introspection. (See Richard Mitten, *The Politics of Antisemitic Prejudice* [Boulder: Westview Press, 1992]; for pertinent, recent reflections in Austrian media see, for instance, Eva Lisinger, "Wolfgang Schüssel: 'Ich habe mit 30 haarsträubende Positionen vertreten,'" May 29, 2020, 12–17.) Such recurrent patterns of the transformation of "cultural common-sense" into political debate are captured by the last word in the title of the present article.

From "German Minority" to "Austrian Minority" – South Tyrol in Austrian Newspapers Post 1945

Sarah Oberbichler

While Austria sought to reshape its identity after the 1938-1945 period,[1] the relationship of the German-speaking minority in South Tyrol – the northernmost province of Italy and former (until 1919) part of Austria-Hungary – to Austria and its continued existence also became an important discussion. Identity creation and the discourse about the German-speaking minority seem interwoven with how political parties in Austria spoke about the "lost" minority in the south of Tyrol. E.g., some politicians, parties, interest groups, authorities and the media began to use the term "Austrian minority" when referring to German-speaking South Tyroleans, thus replacing the previously common "German minority" after 1945. The same applies to the rejection and critique of Germany's interference in the so-called South Tyrol Question. This question had its beginning when South Tyrol was ceded to Italy in 1919, making its German-speaking population a minority in Italy. Italy's attempts to Italianize the German-speaking population during the fascist era from 1922 to 1943 failed, and after World War II the question of how to resolve the divergent interests between South Tyrol/Austria and Italy became an international issue.[2] Austria's desire and attempts to unite South Tyrol with Austria shaped the political discourse after 1945. The failure of these attempts, however, led to the Gruber-De Gasperi Agreement in 1946, which had to be incorporated into a Statute of Autonomy for South Tyrol. The question and the importance of a possible or desired autonomy as well as the question of the return of those South Tyroleans who had emigrated to the German Reich between 1939 and 1943 in the framework of the so called "Option Agreement" [3] between Adolf Hitler and Benito Mussolini in 1939 accompanied the political and public debates in Austria.[4]

This paper discusses the question of which discourses accompanied the South Tyrol Question in Austrian newspapers after 1945 and how the process of nation building framed these discourses. It is assumed that the media in Austria reflected the highly political and ambivalent discourses about South Tyrol, which were led predominantly by a few political leaders. Newspapers as a source of indirect experience give a rich insight into those discourses and its disseminator.[5] It is also indisputable that mass media such as daily newspapers influence the perception of realty, the shaping of opinions and consequent changes in thinking and argumentation of a society, since information conveyed through the media offers recipients patterns of ideas and concepts[6]

The goal of this paper is to reveal such arguments and linguistic patterns and to shed light on South Tyrol's role in the quest for a new national self-perception of Austria. A combination of qualitative and quantitative methods, i.e., a combination of human and computational analyses, is used for the analysis. In concrete terms, this means that analysis methods from the text mining repertoire – methods that help to extract implicit knowledge from large amounts of textual data – are combined with the necessity of reading, interpreting and contextualizing individual texts of a bigger text corpus.[7] The combination of these methods makes it possible to identify recurring patterns as a whole without losing sight of the sensitive specifics of individual texts. For the Austrian postwar discourse on South Tyrol, this approach does not only help to confirm or support existing hypotheses, but also to raise new questions. For instance, the analysis of linguistic patterns in thousands of media reports proves Austria's demarcation from Germany in the South Tyrol discourse but it also reveals a strong focus on economic issues in the South Tyrol negotiations and thus uncovers previously unexplored aspects of this topic. This makes it possible to raise new questions: While language undoubtedly seemed to play a role in the "realignment" of Austrian nationality, and Austrian politicians did not fail to openly use this language in their announcements and speeches (which then found space in the newspapers), the role of South Tyrol for postwar Austria seemed to be much more than symbolic or political. Indeed, South Tyrol was seen as essential to a severely economically weakened post-World War II Austria – as will be shown in this article. Reunification could have strengthened Austria economically, whereby the discourse on South Tyrol could easily be integrated into Austria's new national self-image and victim theses. All this would have been beneficial for Austria in a very difficult time.

The primary source for this contribution are digitized Austrian newspapers of the online newspaper platform ANNO[8]. This interface provides free access to selected historical Austrian newspapers and journals, which are continuously being digitized (24 million pages in 2022). The corpus extracted from the ANNO platform for the qualitative and quantitative analysis consisted of the following digitized newspapers[9]: *Österreichische Volksstimme*, *Das kleine Volksblatt*, *Neues Österreich*, *Österreichische Zeitung*, and *Wiener Kurier*.[10] In order to create a specialized subcorpus on South Tyrol, 4,035 text blocks[11] that contain the keyword *Südtirol** (South Tyrol*) have been extracted from the mentioned newspaper issues. This topic-specific corpus was manually "cleaned" after the automated extraction of text blocks. For example, newspaper clippings that did not refer specifically to South Tyrol, such as mention of a street or square in Austria named after South Tyrol (*Südtirolerstraße* or *Südtirolerplatz*), were excluded from the corpus.

The programming code and results of the computational analysis have been made publicly available on GitHub[12] in the form of a Jupyter Notebook[13]. The interactive and narrative nature of computational notebooks provide a good opportunity for sharing computational results, allowing reproducibility and publishing scientific research.[14]

The South Tyrol Question in the Context of Austrians' National Reorientation

Austrians' national reorientation also affected the relationship to German-speaking minorities of the former Habsburg Monarchy. Today, it is known that Austria no longer saw itself as the protector of these minorities. German-speaking refugees from Habsburg successor states who came to Austria in the post-Cold War period, for example, were viewed with skepticism. This rejection, though, did not concern South Tyrol, which, unlike other minority areas such as Gottschee, became part of the Austrian reorientation.[15] In 1945, there was a strong desire of Tyroleans to be reunited. The governor (*Landeshauptmann*) of North Tyrol and later Austria's Foreign Minister, Karl Gruber, appealed to the Allies and called for reunification. The same applied to the newly founded South Tyrolean People's Party (*Südtiroler Volkspartei*).[16] The hopes, which were also strongly supported by the Austrian Chancellor Leopold Figl, however, proved to be an illusion.[17] While Leopold Figl spoke at one of the largest demonstrations in Innsbruck in April 1946, calling the return of South Tyrol a prayer of every Austrian, followed by the exclamation: "*Jawohl, Mannder, es isch Zeit, wir wollen unser Südtirol wieder*,"[18] the Council of Foreign Ministers (CFM) had already accepted an American proposal that Italy's frontier with Austria would be unchanged. This decision, according to the historian Rolf Steininger, was of historical importance and remained unchanged notwithstanding the pleas of Austrian politics and people.[19]

But how does all this relate to Austria's new self-definition? After 1945/46, Austria began to push to change the German-national image of South Tyrol. South Tyrol from now on was described as a specifically Austrian concern, classified as part of the Austrian people, thus establishing a changed memory and enabling Austria to perceive itself as a nation. South Tyroleans were now increasingly referred to as "Austrians," "Austrian minority," or "Austrian people." Although the return of South Tyrol to Austria was not possible, Austria institutionalized the memory of the lost territory with the Gruber-De Gasperi Agreement, which was concluded between Austria and Italy in Paris in the fall of 1946.[20]

The historian and lawyer, Peter Thaler, concluded that Austria took responsibility for South Tyrol primarily for pragmatic reasons. The South Tyrol question unified Austrian society and supported national self-perception, and it was less risky to support a minority in Italy than in the Eastern Bloc.[21]

South Tyrol itself accepted the perception as an Austrian minority, and South Tyrolean politicians regularly used and still use the term (it clearly contained a more political component than the neutral term "German-speaking minority"), while on the other hand Italian politicians rejected the concept of an Austrian minority.[22] From the Italian perspective, even in 1960, the expression included thoughts of a border revision, which is why the term "German-speaking Italian citizens" seemed more appropriate.[23]

The South Tyrol Question in Austrians News between 1945 and 1948

After the Second World War, the South Tyrol Question was regularly discussed in Austrian daily newspapers. However, South Tyrol did not have the same importance for each publication.

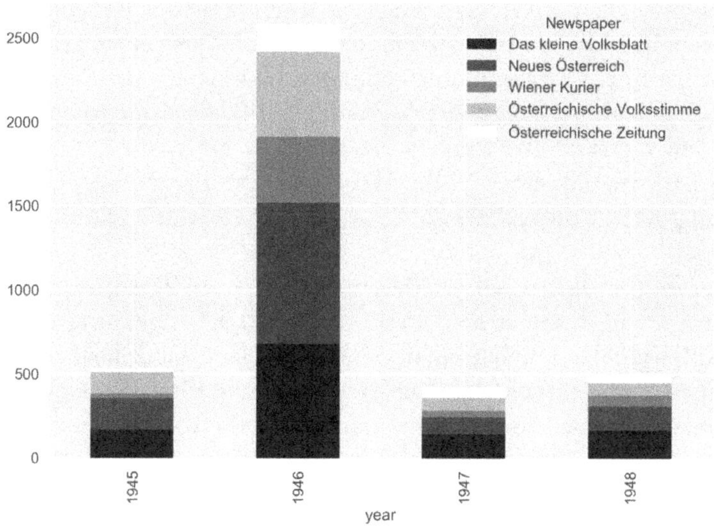

Figure 1: Distribution of the South Tyrol corpus between 1945 and 1948

As Figure 1 shows, South Tyrol was a particularly prominent topic in the ÖVP-newspaper *Das kleine Volksblatt* and in the *Neues Österreich*, which has been the organ of democratic unification. Also the newspaper *Österreichische Volksstimme*, the organ of the Communist Party of Austria (KPÖ), regularly reported about South Tyrol. Both parties, the ÖVP and the KPÖ, referred to a separate and independent Austrian nation and both verifiably shaped the discourse about the Austrian identity.[24] The fact that the ÖVP and KPÖ newspapers strongly took up the subject of South Tyrol indicates the importance of South Tyrol in Austrian identity formation. Media often serve as a political platform for influencing public discourse, whereby, as Teun A. van Dijk noted, leading politicians are usually asked for their opinion or allowed to speak, especially in conflicts.[25] This is also true in the media reporting on the South Tyrol Question in Austria.

Looking at the most frequently used nouns within this South Tyrol corpus,[26] the words *Frage* (question), *Lösung* (solution), as well as *Abkommen* (agreement), *Anspruch* (claim), *Rückkehr/Rückgliederung/Rückgabe* (return), *Unrecht* (injustice) and *Recht* (justice) belong among others to the top words in the Austrian discourse on South Tyrol. Besides the South Tyrol Question in general, solutions were sought for the question of power (*Machtfrage*[27]), the question of dispute (*Streitfrage*[28]), the border question (*Grenzfrage*[29]), the question of traffic (*Verkehrsfrage*[30]), and, very importantly, the Option Question (*Optionsfrage*[31]), i.e. the question of the return of South Tyroleans who migrated to the German Reich as a result of the Hitler-Mussolini Agreement in 1939. However, the return of South Tyrol to Austria was a far more important issue communicated in the newspapers in 1945 and 1946, next to the Gruber-De Gasperi Agreement. When it came to questions of justice and injustice, the language in the daily newspapers was emotional with patriotic undertones. The *Wiener Kurier*, for example, quoted the Tyrolean government in 1946:

> Despite the united will of the entire people of Tyrol north and south of the Brenner Pass, despite the 150,000 signatures of the South Tyrolean population, despite the declaration of former men that with the tearing apart of Tyrol after the First World War a grave injustice was done to the country and the seeds of permanent discord were sown, despite the fact that the whole world knows exactly that justice is on our side, South Tyrol is to be awarded Italy, without even listening to us.[32]

And the *Österreichische Volksstimme* quoted from a rally of the provisional Austrian government in 1945:

> While all other territorial cessions caused or sanctioned by the Treaty of Saint-Germain ... were widely felt as natural, the entire Austrian nation, especially the people of Tyrol, perceived the separation of South Tyrol as a flagrant injustice and as rape.[33]

Nonetheless, the evaluation of the most frequently used adjectives in the corpus shows that the South Tyrol Question was first and foremost communicated as an economic issue and that Austria was not only a selfless protector. The adjective *wirtschaftlich* (economic) dominates the list, followed by *demokratisch* (democratic), and *politisch* (political). In April 1946, the newspaper *Das kleine Volksblatt*, for example, quoted Karl Renner as follows: "We hope that we [Austria] will be made strong enough by the restitution of South Tyrol and our economic heritage, which was stolen by the annexation."[34] The newspaper *Österreichische Volksstimme* reported: "Dr. Gruber compared South Tyrol with Alsace-Lorraine and pointed out the economic necessity of reattaching the area to Austria."[35] In the media – before the signing of the Gruber-De Gasperi Agreement in September 1946 – the idea was spread that South Tyrol could restore the Austrian economic balance and that the return of South Tyrol would not cause any damage to Italy.[36] In addition to Renner, who repeatedly affirmed that Austria needed South Tyrol for economic reasons,[37] Figl also treated the South Tyrol Question as an economic question. His aforementioned speech during the demonstration in Innsbruck 1946 read:

> I do not want to deny that the return of South Tyrol to its Austrian homeland is not only a political problem for South Tyrol itself as well as for Austria, but also an economic question …[38]

Figl referred to the importance of South Tyrol as the "tourist jewel of Tyrol" and emphasized the cultural importance of the lost province. Walter von der Vogelweide, Andreas Hofer, and sagas like *König Laurin und sein Rosengarten* were all considered "Austrian treasures" but have their origin in today's South Tyrol.[39] According to the *Wiener Kurier*, Figl had also declared:

> The return of South Tyrol to Austria is not the same as a confiscation of Italian interests in the hydroelectric power plants that Italy built. From an economic point of view, what Austria is most interested in is the fruit and vegetables that we lack, but of which Italy has enough.[40]

The political and economic question of whether Italy or Austria had greater claims on South Tyrol accompanied the discourse of the postwar years. Austria and especially politicians like Karl Renner or Karl Gruber, however, found itself in a generally ambivalent situation. On the one hand, the separation of South Tyrol was communicated as a great injustice and its repatriation as a necessity for both economic and political reasons, while, on the other hand, Italian interests were to be respected and protected. Thus, the claim to South Tyrol and the call for justice went hand in hand with the will to take full account of Italy's strategic fears or friendly relations with Italy.[41] The maintenance of the latter seemed to be essential (and probably more important than South Tyrol) for the attainment of the Austrian State Treaty.[42]

The media discourse on South Tyrol was therefore controversial and also changed considerably between 1945 and 1948. A bi-gram analysis, which examines a sequence of two adjacent elements, shows which combinations of words occurred repeatedly in the South Tyrol media discourse and how these combinations changed over the four years.[43] Generally spoken, keywords in n-grams (contiguous sequence of "n" words, e.g. a two word sequence is a bi-gram) can be seen as indicators of ideas and opinions in discourses and can uncover the most frequent linguistic patterns in a corpus, although they have always to be contextualized.[44]

Figure 2: Word clouds of bi-grams (1945 and 1946) within the Austrian newspaper corpus on South Tyrol.

As can be seen in Figure 2, in 1945, the Allied Powers (*Alliierten Mächte*) – who rejected the desire of South Tyrol for a free referendum (*freie Volksabstimmung*) as well as the reunification as a democratic solution (*demokratische Lösung*) – took an essential position in the Austrian media discourse on South Tyrol. In 1946 the focus shifted clearly to the *Vereinten Nationen* (United Nations), which became the new bearer of hope, accompanied by the desire to become a member and thus be able to actively participate.[45] Both in 1945 and 1946, the South Tyrol Question was a highly political issue, contextualized in a strongly historical way (First World War). Strategic, economic, and political considerations are also reflected in the bi-grams, especially in 1945 and in 1946, the finding of solutions dominated the discourse. Even though it has been Austrian politicians and their political actions printed in the media who clearly shaped the discourse on South Tyrol, frequently used statements like *ganze Welt* (whole world), or *ganze österreichische Volk* (the entire Austrian nation) should emphasize that the Austrian claims within the South Tyrol Question were not only a political matter but also the will of the whole (Austrian) population, or even the entire world.

As early as 1947, the South Tyrol Question was increasingly mentioned in the same breath as other Austrian affairs (see Figure 3). For example, the Yugoslavian demands (*Jugoslawische Forderungen*) for war reparations had nothing to do with South Tyrol. The implementation of the Paris Agreement, and its statutes on autonomy and the freest possible movement (*möglichst frei*) of people, were further areas of negotiation in 1947. In 1948, the South Tyrol Question seemed far less politically influenced and only a few two-word phrases were reminiscent of it. Travel offerings from and to South Tyrol point to a new normality, phrases like *endgültige Lösung* (final solution), or solution of the South Tyrol Question point to the desire for a final solution of this question.

Figure 3: Word clouds of bi-grams (1947 and 1948) within the specialized Austrian newspaper corpus on South Tyrol.

Hence, the results of the bi-gram analyses, as presented in graphs 2 and 3, show that the importance of the South Tyrol Question in public discourse in Austria was already declining in 1947, although most of the issues for South Tyrol had not yet been resolved. After the lost hopes for a possible reunification, however, other issues (e.g. economic questions about border traffic, etc.) took over the discourse. The bi-grams clearly show this shift in communication and interest in Austria.

From German to Austrian and Critique of Germany's Interference in the so-called South Tyrol Question

The controversial media discourse, which reflected the divergent attitudes (between emotional outbursts and strategic distance as well as between demands for justice and friendly affection for Italy) of the Austrian heads of state towards the topic of South Tyrol, show the difficulty of Austria to take a realistic view of itself. Although the South Tyrol Question was made a political and economic question of survival, the commitment to South Tyrol with its rich traditions and symbols also seemed to contribute to the national question of identity and identity building. In terms of foreign policy, the Austrian commitment to South Tyrol offered an opportunity for Austria to turn away from its orientation towards Germany and express its national independence.[46]

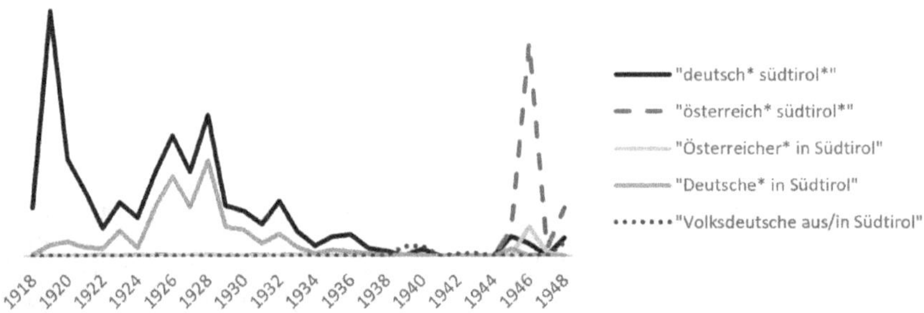

Figure 4: Relative frequency graph of the phrase searches: "deutsches Südtirol", "deutschen Südtirol", "deutsche Südtirol", "Deutsch-Südtirol", „deutsche Südtiroler", „deutschen Südtiroler", „deutschen Südtirolern", „Deutsche in Südtirol", „Deutschen in Südtirol", „Volksdeutsche in Südtirol", „Volksdeutsche aus Südtirol", „österreichisches Südtirol", „österreichischen Südtirol", „österreichische Südtirol", „österreichischem Südtirol", ‚österreichische Südtiroler", „Österreicher in Südtirol", Österreichern in Südtirol".

Figure 4 – which was created by counting relative frequencies[47] of selected phrases within the whole newspaper collection available in ANNO between 1918 and 1948[48] – shows clearly how German or ethnic German became Austrian for the designation of the German speaking population in South Tyrol, beginning in 1944 with its highest peak in 1946. The term ethnic German (*Volksdeutsche*) was mainly used between 1938 and 1942. While it seemed normal to speak of a "German South Tyrol" after the Italian annexation of the territory in 1919, this term was almost completely superseded by the term "Austrian South Tyrol" after 1945. In contrast, the terms "German-speaking South Tyrol" or "German-speaking South Tyroleans" established as the neutral, apolitical term as asked for by the Italians during the peace negotiations in 1946. As Figure 5 shows, this term only exceptionally occurred before 1946.

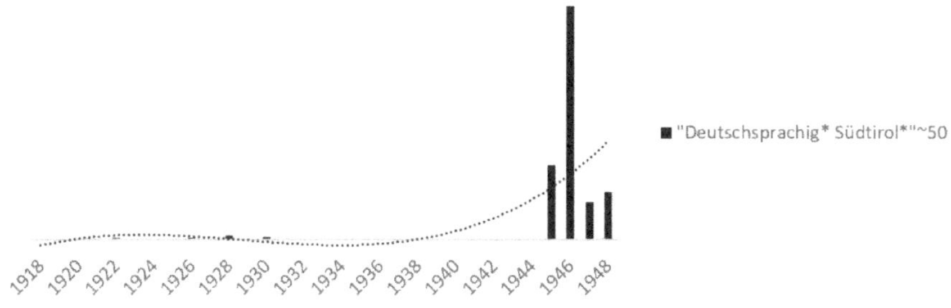

Figure 5: Relative frequency of the words "Deutschsprachig* and Südtirol* within a distance of 50 words.

Furthermore, the demarcation from Germany was found in Austrian newspaper reporting. The newspaper *Das kleine Volksblatt,* for example, reported in October 1945: "We put our pride in being able to say that Nazi Germany betrayed South Tyrol, Austria returned it." [49] In the same year, Gruber sought friendly relations with Austria's neighbors, especially Italy, but was cautious about Germany, which he described as a possible threat to Austria's independence:

> The traditional good relations with Switzerland will continue to be cultivated, and beyond that Austria hopes to come to friendly coexistence with a democratic Italy after the South Tyrol Question has been settled. Relations with Germany depend not only on its future status under international law, but above all on the abandonment of pan-Germanism in Germany. Austria does not want to be exposed to the threat to its independence again.[50]

Austria's new self-perception was based on the victim thesis –Austria was seen as the first victim of National Socialism – and so was the perception of South Tyrol. This also went along with the rejection and critique of Germany's interference in the South Tyrol Question. Austria, as a report in *Der Neue Mahnruf* stated, has always endeavored to "keep Germany out of this conflict: "South Tyrol is a specifically Austrian problem. Austria has honestly tried to orient Bozen to Innsbruck and Vienna, not to Munich, Stuttgart and Bonn."[51]

Outlook

South Tyrol was undoubtedly an essential pillar in the national re-orientation of Austria, or as Karl Gruber phrased it in 1946:

> After its rebirth, the new Austria had only one political program: to create all the conditions necessary to guarantee its independent existence and not to come back under foreign hegemony. The solution of the South Tyrolean question is undoubtedly an element that could significantly strengthen Austria's viability.[52]

But already after 1947, the interest of Austrian politics in South Tyrol had diminished considerably, which was clearly reflected in select daily newspapers. For the Austrian foreign minister Karl Gruber, the Austrian State Treaty had the highest priority and even after the failure of the conference on the State Treaty in 1947, an orientation towards the West and friendly relations with Italy for the attainment of the State Treaty seemed more important than the concerns of South Tyrol.[53] Only with the radicalization of the situation in South Tyrol did Austria actively resume its role as South Tyrol's protective power.[54] Since then, South Tyrol remained a place of remembrance of national relevance, even though the emotional connection to South Tyrol began to fade even more in early 1970, with the Second Autonomy Statute, and became nearly obsolete when Austria joined the EU in the mid-1990s.[55]

Acknowledgements

The author would like to thank Stefan Hechl for the provision of the post OCR corrected Austrian newspaper corpus.

This work was supported by the European Union's Horizon 2020 research and innovation programme under grant 770299 (NewsEye).

Endnotes

1 Max Haller, ed., *Identität und Nationalstolz der Österreicher: Gesellschaftliche Ursachen und Funktionen. Herausbildung und Transformation seit 1945. Internationaler Vergleich* (Vienna: Böhlau, 1996).

2 Rolf Steininger, *Südtirol: Vom Ersten Weltkrieg bis zur Gegenwart* (Innsbruck: Haymon, 2012); Georg Grote, *The South Tyrol Question, 1866-2010: From National Rage to Regional State* (Oxford: Peter Lang, 2012).

3 Eva Pfanzelter, *Option und Gedächtnis: Erinnerungsorte der Südtiroler Umsiedlung 1939*, (Bolzano: Raetia, 2015).

4 Rolf Steininger, *South Tyrol: A Minority Conflict of the Twentieth Century*, Studies in Austrian and Central European History and Culture (New Brunswick, NJ: Transaction, 2003).

5 Priska Bucher and Andrea Piga, "Medien und Migration - Ein Überblick," in *Medienrealitäten*, ed. Urs Dahinden and Daniel Süss (Konstanz: UVK, 2009).

6 Thomas Niehr and Karin Böke, "Diskursanalyse unter linguistischer Perspektive – am Beispiel des Migrationsdiskurses," in *Handbuch sozialwissenschaftliche Diskursanalyse. Bd. 2: Forschungspraxis*, ed. Reiner Keller et al., 3., 3rd ed. (Wiesbaden: Verlag für Sozialwissenschaften, 2008).

7 Sarah Oberbichler, "Argumentationsanalyse von historischen Migrationsdiskursen in Zeitungsberichterstattung mittels Atlas.ti," *Zeitgeschichte* 47, no. 4 (2020): 467–90.

8 "ANNO - AustriaN Newspapers Online," *anno.onb.ac.at,* accessed Sept. 7, 2020, http://anno.onb.ac.at/.

9 The corpus was processed by Stefan Hechl with the help of Transkribus, in order to improve the quality of the transcription by an average of 50 percent. See Stefan Hechl, "'Wir dürfen wieder Österreicher sein!' Die Rolle der Tagespresse in österreichischen Nation-Building-Prozessen 1945–1948" (Master's Thesis, University of Innsbruck, 2020).

10 The *Arbeiter Zeitung* could not be considered because of the poor quality of the scans.

11 For the sub-corpus, six lines before and six lines after a line containing the keyword "South Tyrol*" were extracted. This method has been chosen because no article separation was available.

12 Sarah Oberbichler, "Diachronic_ngram_clouds," *github.com*, accessed Sept. 5, 2020, https://github.com/soberbichler/Diachronic_ngram_clouds. The Notebook allows one to read the specialized corpus up close and from a distance, which is important when working with digital methods. Language and discourse can only be understood in the context of the entire text, which means data can never speak for itself. Results of digital analysis can be very helpful in finding patterns and act as starting points for further analysis but they cannot stand for themselves. See

also Paul Baker, *Using Corpora in Discourse Analysis*, Continuum Discourse Series (London: Continuum, 2006).

13 A Jupyter Notebook is an open-source web application which enables creating and sharing documents containing live code, equations, visualizations, and narrative text. See: "Project Jupyter," *jupyter.org*, accessed Jan. 24, 2022, https://jupyter.org.

14 Francisco Rowe et al., "The Potential of Notebooks for Scientific Publication, Reproducibility and Dissemination," *REGION* 7, no. 3 (2020): 1–5.

15 Peter Thaler, "National Reorientation, Habsburg Minorities, and the South Tyrol Question in Postwar Austrian," in *Dialogue against Violence: The Question of Trentino-South Tyrol in the International Context*, ed. Giovanni Bernardini and Günther Pallaver, Annali Dell'Istituto Storico Italo-Germanico in Trento Contributi 32 (Bologna: Società editrice il Mulino, 2017), 163–83 (here 170–76).

16 Steininger, *South Tyrol,* 80.

17 Thaler, "National Reorientation," 174.

18 "Der Weg nach Südtirol," *Tiroler Bauern-Zeitung*, April 25, 1946. Leopold Figl referred in this statement to the speech of the Austrian Chancellor, Kurt von Schuschnigg, who mobilized the Austrian people in 1938 with the exclamation "Mander, es isch Zeit." The phrase itself is attributed to Andreas Hofer. See Kurt Bauer, *Die dunklen Jahre: Politik und Alltag im nationalsozialistischen Österreich 1938 bis 1945* (Frankfurt am Main: S. Fischer, 2017).

19 Steininger, *South Tyrol.*

20 Hubert Mock, "'Bozen und Meran war immer Österreichs Gedankengut': Anmerkungen zur Geschichte des Südtirol-Bildes in Österreich," in *Memoria Austriae II. Bauten, Orte, Regionen*, ed. Emil Brix, Ernst Bruckmüller, and Hannes Stekl (Vienna: Oldenbourg, 2005), 370–411 (here 382).

21 Thaler, "National Reorientation," 176.

22 Thaler, "National Reorientation," 176.

23 Rolf Steininger, ed., *Akten zur Südtirol-Politik 1959-1969*, vol. 2: 1960: Vor der UNO (Innsbruck: StudienVerlag, 2006), 9, 552, 559, 560 and 590.

24 Hechl, "'Wir dürfen wieder Österreicher sein!,'" 32.

25 Teun A. van Dijk, "Eliten, Rassismus und die Presse," in *Die Vierte Gewalt: Rassismus und die Medien*, DISS-Studien (Duisburg: Duisburger Institut für Sprach- und Sozialforschung, 1993), 80–131 (here 88).

26 The data has been cleaned beforehand: Stop-words have been removed, tokens have been stemmed (reduction of inflected words) and lemmatized (grouping of inflected forms of words) as well as part of speech (POS) tagged (the tagging of nouns, adjectives, adverbs, and verbs).

27 "Südtirol," *Das Kleine Volksblatt*, April 10, 1945.

28 "Die günstigen Folgen der Wiedervereinigung," *Das Kleine Volksblatt*, Nov. 16, 1945.

29 "Die Grenzsorgen Österreichs," *Neues Österreich*, Dec. 10, 1945.

30 "Gespenster," *Neues Österreich*, Dec. 15, 1945.

31 "Vorbereitung für die Südtiroler Autonomie," *Das Kleine Volksblatt*, Nov. 21, 1946.

32 "Trotz des einheitlichen Willens des gesamten Volkes von Tirol nord- und südwärts des Brenners, trotz der 150.000 Unterschriften der Südtiroler Bevölkerung, trotz der Erklärung führender Männer, daß mit der Zerreißung Tirols nach dem ersten Weltkrieg dem Lande ein schweres Unrecht zugefügt und der Keim zu dauerndem Unfrieden gelegt wurde, trotzdem die ganze Welt genau weiß, daß das Recht auf unserer Seite steht, soll Südtirol neuerdings, ohne uns auch nur anzuhören, Italien zugesprochen werden." "Spontane Kundgebung in ganz Tirol," *Wiener Kurier*, May 3, 1946.

33 "Während alle übrigen durch den Vertrag von Saint-Germain bewirkten oder sanktionierten Gebietsabtretungen von der österreichischen Bevölkerung … weitgehend … als selbstverständlich empfunden wurden, empfand das ganze österreichische Volk, ganz besonders das Volk von Tirol, die Abtrennung Südtirols als flagrantes Unrecht und als Vergewaltigung." "Regierungskundgebung für Südtirol," *Österreichische Volksstimme*, Aug. 9, 1945.

34 "Wir hoffen, daß man uns durch die Rückgabe Südtirols und unseres [Österreichs] durch die Annexion geraubten wirtschaftlichen Erbgutes stark genug macht." "Bundespräsident Dr. Renner: Österreich in Erwartung eines Staatsvertrags," *Das Kleine Volksblatt*, April 6, 1946.

35 "Dr. Gruber verglich Südtirol mit Elsaß-Lothringen und wies auf die wirtschaftliche Notwendigkeit einer Wiederangliederung dieses Gebietes an Oesterreich hin." "Regierungskundgebung für Südtirol."

36 "Britische Stimmen für die Rückkehr Südtirols," *Das Kleine Volksblatt*, May 21, 1946.

37 "Dr. Gruber: Was ich von Paris erwarte," *Das Kleine Volksblatt*, Aug. 21, 1946.

38 "Ich will nicht leugnen, daß die Wiederheimkehr Südtirols in sein österreichisches Heimatland sowohl für Südtirol selbst wie auch für Österreich nicht nur ein politisches Problem, sondern auch eine wirtschaftliche Frage ist." "Petition von 155.000 Südtirolern," *Wiener Zeitung*, April 24, 1946.

39 "Petition von 155.000 Südtirolern," *Wiener Zeitung*, April 24, 1946.

40 "Die Rückgabe Südtirols an Österreich ist nicht gleichbedeutend mit einer Beschlagnahme der italienischen Interessen an den Wasserkraftwerken, die Italien erbaut hat. Woran Österreich vom wirtschaftlichen Standpunkt am meisten liegt, ist das Obst und Gemüse, das uns fehlt, von dem Italien aber Überfluß hat." "Der Bundeskanzler über Südtirol," *Wiener Kurier*, Jan. 28, 1946.

41 "Um die Heimkehr Südtirols," *Das Kleine Volksblatt*, Nov. 16, 1945; "Wirklicher Patriotismus kann nur demokratisch sein," *Österreichische Volksstimme*, Oct. 4, 1945.

42 Michael Gehler, ed., *Akten zur Südtirol-Politik, 1945-1958* (Innsbruck: Studienverlag, 2011).

43 Next to stop words, very frequent words like Austria(n) or Italia(n) have been removed, in order to be able to uncover less obvious word combinations.

44 Samia Touileb and Andrew Salway, "Constructions: A New Unit of Analysis for Corpus-Based Discourse Analysis," in *Proceedings of the 28th Pacific Asia Conference on Language, Information and Computing* (Thailand: Department of Linguistics, Chulalongkorn University, 2014), 634–43 (here 635).

45 "Im Spiegel der Zeit," *Wiener Kurier*, Oct. 16, 1945.

46 Mock, "'Bozen und Meran war immer Österreichs Gedankengut,'" 378–379.

47 It is not possible to create relative frequencies using the platform ANNO alone, since the necessary metadata is not available. In ONB Labs (https://labs.onb.ac.at/en/tool/sprachen-in-anno/), however, the information on the amount of digitized pages per year is available and can be manually connected with the search results from ANNO.

48 The complete alphabetical list of the digitized newspapers in ANNO can be found at the following link: http://anno.onb.ac.at/alph_list.htm, accessed Sept. 7, 2020.

49 "Wir setzen unseren Stolz darein, sagen zu können, das nazistische Deutschland hat Südtirol verraten, Oesterreich hat es wieder zurückgeführt." "Zwei Herzenswünsche unseres Volkes," *Das Kleine Volksblatt*, Oct. 23, 1945.

50 "Die traditionellen guten Beziehungen zur Schweiz werden weiter gepflegt werben, und darüber hinaus hofft Oesterreich, mit einem demokratischen Italien nach Regelung der Südtiroler Frage zu freundschaftlichem Zusammenleben zu kommen. Die Beziehungen zu Deutschland hängt nicht nur von dessen zukünftigem völkerrechtlichem Status ab, sondern vor allem auch von der Preisgabe des Pangermanismus in Deutschland. Oesterreich möchte nicht, daß es noch einmal der Bedrohung seiner Unabhängigkeit ausgesetzt ist." "Grundsätze unserer Außenpolitik," *Das Kleine Volksblatt*, Oct. 18, 1945.

51 "Österreich, das heißt Wien, unsere Regierung, war immer bestrebt, Deutschland herauszuhalten aus diesem Konflikt: Südtirol ist ein spezifisch österreichisches Problem. Man hat sich redlich bemüht, Bozen nach Innsbruck und Wien, nicht nach München, Stuttgart und Bonn zu orientieren." "Bonn hat in Südtirol nichts zu suchen," *Der Neue Mahnruf*, 1961.

52 "Das neue Oesterreich habe nach seiner Wiedergeburt nur ein politisches Programm: Alle Voraussetzungen zur Gewährleistung seiner unabhängigen Existenz zu schassen und nicht wieder unter fremde Hegemonie zu kommen Die Lösung der Südtiroler Frage bilde zweifelslos ein Element, das die Lebensfähigkeit Oesterreichs wesentlich stärken könne." "Unsere Vorschläge über Südtirol," *Das Kleine Volksblatt*, May 1, 1946.

53 Gehler, *Akten zur Südtirol-Politik, 1945-1958*.

54 Mock, "'Bozen und Meran war immer Österreichs Gedankengut,'" 380.

55 Mock, "'Bozen und Meran war immer Österreichs Gedankengut,'" 403–404.

Inclusion through Exclusion: Crafting Hegemony about the Deportability of "Economic Refugees" in 1990

Judith Welz

Introduction

The early 1990s marked a restrictive turn in migration politics in Austria, just like in many other European countries.[1] Fetching illegalized migrants and rejected asylum seekers from their homes in the middle of the night and forcibly removing them became a common instrument of national border control. The sudden rise in the use of force against non-citizens was perhaps not self-explanatory in the Austrian context. According to Patrik-Paul Volf, during the entire Cold War era, the accommodation of refugees constituted an important aspect of Austria's post-war nation-building process. "The refugee from Eastern Europe" stood as a symbol of the country's anti-communist stance and alignment with Western values and lifestyles.[2] Moreover, the continuous celebration of Austria's generosity toward asylum seekers also helped to paint an alternative self-image over the barbarism of the past.

This paper sets out to explore what the restrictive turn in Austria's border politics in 1990 meant for nation-building. If nation-building is approached from a biopolitical perspective, my findings suggest that restrictive border politics helped recalibrate migration and asylum politics to better meet the country's needs. This was achieved by creating the abject figure of the "economic refugee" who made the enlargement of the arsenal of border control instruments plausible. Once in place, it allowed for a migration and asylum regime much more selective than before.

Theory and method

Theoretical premises: The biopolitical construction of society and its abject other

According to Michel Foucault, the population politics of modern liberal states are no longer focused on eliminating undesirable ways of conduct but on encouraging desirable forms of behavior. In so-called governmental states, soft steering and governing have replaced force and violence as preferred political tools. The former require much less interference by the state since they come as quasi-automatic effects of the security dispositive, an ensemble of habitual practices, symbols, institutional arrangements, and ways of speaking that permeate society permanently, thereby providing more or less clear indications about what is normal, expected behavior and what is not. Subjects are drawn to perform in desired ways since only this promises a life of freedom and security. Conversely, failing to do so may lead to the exclusion of a subject from the realm of governmental steering and expose them to potential state violence.[3] According to Foucault, the language of the security dispositive follows a "racist"[4] logic as it categorizes people and behaviors into higher or lower value.[5] This hierarchy is highly productive, however, since the formation of a governmental society is constitutive of the construction of an abject other situated at its margins facing violence and repression.[6]

For Katrin Meyer and Patricia Purtschert, the national border is the primary location of contemporary biopolitics, since the question of who can become a member of society is permanently asked and answered. Therefore, an important feature of migration and asylum policy is to identify and thus produce more and less desired subjectivities. The boundary of social membership, therefore, not only constitutes a boundary for inclusion and exclusion but also for the use of governmental state technologies as opposed to state violence.[7]

Following these insights, I analyze deportation policy as an essential feature in constructing the governable body-politics as it marks the boundary between society and non-society and the point where governmental state technologies give way to repression and force.

Methodological reflections

I approach policy as a material product of political struggles for hegemony.[8] According to Antonio Gramsci, in liberal societies, political power requires consent.[9] Politics are, thus, hegemonic struggles over meaning, in the course of which different political and societal actors are trying to popularize their particular understanding of a "problem" and preferred solution. This is done by claiming one viewpoint as the only plausible, rational, or logical one and turning it into common knowledge. In the process, other perspectives are downplayed or selectively integrated into the own narrative to make it more robust.[10]

To reconstruct the dynamics of the political struggles relevant to my analysis, I opted for a process analysis as developed by Sonja Buckel.[11] The process analysis focuses on the different actors taking part in a struggle, their truth claims, argumentative strategies, alliances, and antagonisms, from the moment a debate is launched to the moment (a) specific knowledge(s) assert(s) hegemony and materializes in new legal norms.[12]

My case is the policymaking episode that pushed many immigrants and asylum seekers into illegality overnight and subjected them to the threat of deportation in 1990. Temporally, it stretches from December 1989, when members of the government parties filed a motion for a resolution at the Austrian National Assembly, to mid-March 1990, when the reform proposal developed by the Interior Ministry finally got adopted.

My sources comprise press coverage, material representing the policy-making process (motions and parliamentary debates), as well as the former and newly adopted policies. While the media analysis helped trace the political struggle, actors involved, strategies, and discursive positions, the analysis of the parliamentary debates gave insights into the crafting of hegemony in the last phase of the struggles.

Crafting hegemony about the deportability of "economic refugees" in 1990

Context

What happened before . . .

Until 1990, Austria's migration and asylum legislation were comparatively liberal, at least on paper, and deportation, even though it existed, was of little relevance. Between 1954 and 1990, non-citizens enjoyed a general entitlement "to take residence in Austria for an unlimited period of time,"[13] provided they met the criteria for legal entry. There were few entry requirements, with many nationalities exempted from requiring a visa for Austria, limiting the conditions for legal entry in many cases to the possession of a valid travel document. Since Austrian law did not specify how to deal with people who managed to enter the country despite the lack of such a travel document, they could not legally be expelled.[14] With regard to so-called guest workers, even though forced removal was inscribed into the bilateral agreements regulating this kind of foreign labor, it functioned more as a threat than something that occurred frequently.[15] Similarly, rejected asylum seekers, even though they could legally get deported, often managed to regularize their stay by taking up employment before Aliens' Police started the removal process. In fact, before 1990, non-citizens in Austria were expelled almost exclusively when found guilty of a crime if a court coupled the criminal sentence with a so-called "prohibition of stay" (*Aufenthaltsverbot*).

As hinted at in the introduction, contemporary historians attribute Austria's liberal approach to migration and asylum politics prior to the 1990s to the fact that they played a crucial role in post-war Austrian nation-building. Liberal entry and residence regulations should portray Austria as a "homeland of freedom,"[16] as Austrian parliamentarian Karl Czernetz (Social Democrats, SPÖ) put it on the day the National Assembly adopted the general right to residence. Furthermore, the generous attitude toward asylum seekers helped create the image of a country in full respect of human rights and liberal values and cover up the barbarity of the genocide during World War II.[17]

The beginning of change . . .

The first change in attitude and practice came about in the 1970s when the global economic crisis made employment opportunities scarcer. As a result, around one quarter of "guest workers" lost their jobs and, in turn, their right to reside.[18] Even though the Austrian government openly prompted them to leave the country, the administration did not resort to large-scale deportation.[19] And while some certainly left Austria, many more resisted the new policy of "guest worker reduction" and, on the contrary, stabilized their presence by bringing in family members through the right to family reunification. Consequently, immigration remained high in the aftermath of the oil crisis. Austrian policymakers reacted by adopting the Migrant Labor Act in 1975 as an apparent attempt to bring immigration under control via a rigid work permit and quota system.[20]

Changes in the general attitude to asylum followed in the 1980s, when the Soviet Union's growing dependency on Western capital and the easing of travel restrictions for its citizens were taken as signs of a dawning erosion of the "Eastern Bloc."[21] Refugees from communist countries, who had made up nearly one hundred percent of asylum claimants before 1998, lost their symbolic value in the clash of ideologies between East and West and began to be far less welcome than in previous years in Austria.[22] In 1988, Austrian Interior Minister Karl Blecha introduced a fast-track asylum procedure for asylum seekers from Hungary and Poland, which most often ended in a denial of the claim.[23]

Restrictive turn . . .

It was, however, only in the year after the fall of the Iron Curtain that the foundations of Austria's migration and asylum regime became turned upside down: As part of a legislative amendment to the Aliens' Police Act in March 1990, the general right of residence that had been valid for thirty-six years got replaced by a general obligation to acquire a residence permit.[24] Failing to obtain one, the applicant was illegalized. To deal with the new category of "illegal residents," border police were given new capacities regarding forced removals. Hence, the "administrative expulsion" (*Ausweisung*) could now be issued against anyone lacking a valid residence permit. Expulsion orders required a formal bureaucratic or judicial decision that could be appealed, although without postponing enforcement. Besides expulsion, the instrument of "push-back" (*Zurückschiebung*) was expanded. While its applicability had been limited to the spatial and temporal proximity of the attempted border crossing before, unlawful border crossers could now be apprehended up to seven days after entry anywhere in the country and be pushed back over the border. Since push-backs did not require a formal bureaucratic decision, appeals were not allowed.

The legislative changes in detail:

Right to reside
Formerly: § 2 (1) Aliens' Police Act of 1954 *Non-citizens are (...) allowed to take residence in Austria for an unlimited period of time.*
New: § 2 (1) Aliens' Police Act of 1954, version 1990 A legal presence of non-citizens in Austria requires 1. to have legally crossed the border 2. to have been issued a residence visa or permit.

Expulsion on grounds of illegalized presence
Formerly: Aliens' Police Act of 1954 *non-existent*
New: § 10 a. Aliens' Police Act of 1954, version 1990 Administrative expulsion:[1] Aliens, who have entered Austria avoiding border control and who cannot be pushed back, may be expelled within four months after entry, following an official notice.

1 § 10a Aliens' Police Act 1990

Push-back
Formerly: § 10 Aliens' Police Act of 1954 *Aliens, who have crossed the national border without authorization, may be pushed back in an informal manner if apprehended immediately after the crossing*
New: § 10 a. Aliens' Police Act of 1954, version 1990 Aliens, who have entered Austria avoiding border control and are apprehended by the police within the following seven days, may be pushed back without delay.

The effects . . .
Deportation numbers multiplied as a consequence of the reform: While during all of the 1980s, roughly 16,400 deportations were carried out, this number was surpassed in the single year after the amendment with 9,800 deportations and 9,800 push-backs. Moreover, forcible removals remained high throughout the decade, counting 85,800 deportations and 54,700 push-backs between 1991 and 1999.[25]

I will now turn to investigating the transformation of asylum seekers from subjects of protection to subjects highly vulnerable to exclusion and state violence and the political struggles accompanying it.

Struggles over deportability 1989/1990

The following analysis focuses on the struggles preceding the political construction of the economic refugee as deportable in 1990. The struggles were initiated when members of the Austrian parliament (MPs) filed a motion for a resolution at the national assembly on December 11, 1989, and came to its conclusion on March 14, 1990, when the reform proposal was adopted. The analysis is based on reporting by the daily newspaper *Der Standard* during this period. The choice of the newspaper is due to the fact that it reported relatively more than other daily newspapers about relevant topics and gave voice to the widest range of actors, thus making it best suited for an analysis of political struggles.[26] As one outcome of the analysis, four phases of the struggle could be identified.

Phase one: Proxy struggles: trafficking and undocumented work in focus (December 1989)

On December 11, 1989, some Austrian MPs filed a motion for a resolution at the National Assembly, requesting the government, or more specifically Interior Minister Franz Löschnak (Social Democrats), work out measures in the fight against human trafficking.[27] An initiative in this direction may have seemed peculiar since Austria was usually only crossed by traffickers to reach Germany or Switzerland. Nevertheless, the motion did not encounter any resistance because the moral objection to human trafficking was shared by all parties in parliament at the time. Since the MPs in question belonged to both coalition partners, namely the Social Democrats (SPÖ) and the People's Party (ÖVP), it may be assumed that the initiative had been accorded with the government. The contours of the problem as described in the motion were as such: First, human trafficking represented a deeply immoral business that involved the manipulation and violent exploitation of refugees, carried out by criminals operating internationally. Second, because of the trafficking, Austria's border was violated on two sides, by traffickers entering Austria from the east and by Austria's western and northern neighbors who "brutally" pushed back the trafficked into Austria in the case of apprehension.[28] In this context, Austria's border regulations were said to be too liberal and prone to exploitation and violation. However, when the MPs laid down their demands for reform, they remained confined to the topic of trafficking and did not touch upon other aspects of Austrian border law.[29] The interior ministry was charged with working out a legislative proposal to be discussed in the upcoming meeting of the National Assembly's Committee on Internal Affairs on January 16, 1990.

Briefly after, the cabinet met in an extraordinary meeting, and even though *Der Standard* covered the meeting in an article titled "Radical Change of Asylum Politics,"[30] no details were shared with the public as to how asylum law would be influenced by the upcoming reform and no public debate ensued. The discussion remained filled with the usual: Government members of both sides paying lip service to Austria's lasting commitment to international refugee protection and coalition partners fighting the scope and effects of undocumented foreign work: While the SPÖ discussed undocumented foreign labor as the root cause of wage dumping and joblessness in Austria, the ÖVP cited restricted access to the regular labor market as the origin of the problem, and called for liberalization.[31]

Phase two: Alarmism, decreeism, and an unintended revelation of the reform's contents (January and February 1990)

With the beginning of the new year, a shift in problematization could be observed originating in the interior ministry. The issue of trafficking became marginalized in favor of a problematization of high numbers of asylum seekers and an accommodation system on the brink of collapsing. Despite very alarming rhetoric, the media remained largely uninterested. Economic activities by Austrian companies in the transitioning countries, east–west day tourism, and the political developments in Romania following the murder of dictator Ceausescu remained the main topics at the beginning of the new year.[32] This disinterest notwithstanding, the ministry went from rhetoric into action in mid-January. The adoption of a visa requirement for Turkish citizens as a measure against trafficking or the dismissals of certain groups of asylum seekers from accommodation centers provided visible substance for claims about "full boats" or a dawning "migration of peoples" (*Völkerwanderung*) that had been envisioned by the entourage of the interior ministry. Due to the dismissals, refugees became homeless, which created the impression of chaos. For the first time in Austria's asylum history, the church stepped in to fill the humanitarian vacuum created by the government and provide shelter for asylum seekers.[33]

Thus, when the day of the committee meeting on internal affairs approached—in which the legislative proposal which had to be worked out by the interior minister in response to the motion was to be discussed—the minister had not only failed to mobilize consent about the necessity of a vast reform in terms of border politics. Worse still, he was under immense moral pressure not only from the church, which warned of the "sin of loveless rejection"[34] of refugees but also for drug and torture scandals at the heart of the Austrian police forces, which were about to be uncovered.[35] In this context, it seemed favorable to pass the reform as an initiative by MPs in order to evade the evaluation process, which was obligatory when reforms were proposed by government members. However, when members of the Green Party (Grüne) uncovered the plan, enough pressure could be mobilized to force the government to backpedal and schedule a proper evaluation process.[36] Following this, the contents of the proposal were made public and revealed an encompassing reform, only minor aspects of which pertained to the issue of trafficking. The majority of the legal changes touched upon entry regulations, residence rights, the asylum procedure, and police capacities for forced removal. The replacement of the general residence right with a general obligation to apply for that right and new possibilities for deportation, namely by introducing "administrative removal" and the expansion of capacities for push-backs, were also part of the reform.

Despite the immense scope of the reform proposal, the discussion following the revelation of its contents remained limited to a relatively small circle of experts. Nevertheless, they raised serious concerns about whether potential refugees were still sufficiently protected from deportation under the new regulations. The prominence of the authors of these concerns, which included the United Nations High Commissioner for Refugees and the international law office of the Austrian Ministry of External Affairs, resulted in the government accepting to adopt a few essential safeguards for asylum seekers to prevent their deportation before their claim was decided.[37] While these concessions appeased the institutionalized critics, they provoked civil society organizations, activists, and asylum lawyers to shift their criticism to another level, now voicing their mistrust of the institution charged with implementing the laws, namely the Austrian police forces. In the wake of previous scandals, police were deemed untrustworthy in protecting refugees, even if the law obliged them to. Additionally, the government was attacked for willingly ending the right to asylum in Austria and allowing police to make it happen. Thus, towards the end of this phase, the conflict became more pronounced even though it remained confined to a relatively small circle.[38]

In this phase, the discussion about foreign workers also entered the next level. While members of the ÖVP kept bemoaning the strict labor market regulations, the SPÖ expanded its problematization of undocumented foreign labor and foreign labor in general. By mid-February, a compromise between the coalition partners had apparently been found. Social Minister Walter Geppert from the SPÖ announced a revision of the Foreign Labor Act that would combine restrictive and liberal aspects by making access to the national labor market for newcomers harder while simultaneously strengthening the rights of laborers already residing in the country. The minister expressed his medium-term vision for the national labor market, the access to which should be stratified according to different types of residence status.[39]

Phase three: Escalation and "universalization" of the "refugee problem"(end of February to mid-March 1990)

By the end of February, two weeks before the National Assembly came together again, the perception of a refugee crisis that would legitimize the restrictive turn in Austria's migration and asylum politics as wished-for by the government was still not widely shared. Repeated calls to regions and communities to provide shelters kept being ignored, and the media still sidelined the topic.[40] Against this background, the action taken by the ministry next came as a surprise, although it would prove to be a game-changer.

At the end of February, Löschnak announced the transfer of eight hundred male Romanian asylum seekers to a former military base in a tiny village called Kaisersteinbruch in Burgenland. The villagers and their mayor, who had not been asked for consent, furiously objected with street blockages, demonstrations, and press conferences. Now, the media became interested and reported extensively on the conflict. News coverage of related topics increased three to ten times between February and March 1990. Quickly, masculinity and youth emerged as the features around which the objection against the refugees got centered. Moreover, while the tabloids reported happily about the villagers' fears of burglaries and rape for days, the minister remained suspiciously quiet. According to Peter Zuser, this short time frame was crucial in turning "the question of the foreigner" from a political non-issue into a critical one. Because even after the minister backpedaled and stopped the transfer of the eight hundred Romanians, the issue remained, never to go away.[41]

In the immediate aftermath of the incident, voices opposing the accommodation of refugees became bolder. The most widely-read Austrian tabloid *Neue Kronen Zeitung*, which had not shown much interest in the developments in migration and asylum politics before then, now acted as the "voice of the people" whom it claimed were naturally afraid of the "masses of foreigners" coming to Austria. The paper supported the interior ministry's course directly and indirectly by creating the impression that the reform reflected the people's will via numerous letters to the editor and opinion pieces voicing anti-refugee and racist opinions.[42] Simultaneously, local politicians now felt encouraged to justify their refusal to accommodate refugees with the fear of losing tourists. Backing for this argument at first came from the Minister of Economy, Wolfgang Schüssel, who threatened communities with a cancellation of public funding if they were to open accommodation centers for refugees. However, when a letter by the governor of Upper Austria Josef Ratzenböck to the interior minister became public, in which he called upon him not to send "people from countries whose origin is revealed by their appearance,"[43] the minister took a step back.[44]

During the entire phase, the right-wing Freedom Party (FPÖ) was curiously absent from the debates, and when party members spoke out, they usually seconded the minister's claims.

By the end of the phase, structural racism was revealed as an essential element of Austrian society. This provided opponents of stricter border control with plausibility for their argument that the reform was, in fact, founded on anti-refugee and racist motives. Some critics even went so far as to call the reform a fallback into the Nazi era.[45] Thus, in the runup to the National Assembly meeting where the laws were to be adopted, the government found itself confronted with allegations of racism.

Phase four: Crafting hegemony about the deportation of 'economic refugees' at the National Assembly (March 14, 1990)

On March 14, 1990, the draft law was on the agenda of the Austrian National Assembly for adoption. That day, the assembly was composed of four parties: The SPÖ and ÖVP in a coalition government headed by the SPÖ chancellor Franz Vranitzky, and the extreme right-wing FPÖ and the liberal to left-wing Green Party in opposition.

The three previous months had been characterized by gradually intensifying struggles over what the refugee-flight movements meant and what was to be done about them. Especially discussions about racism among the Austrian people and political representatives, economic implications of the rise in foreign residents and workforce, and the state of affairs concerning refugee protection in Austria had far-reaching impacts on the last phase of the struggle for hegemony, namely the one taking place within the national assembly.

The following in-depth analysis of the parliamentary debate on March 14, 1990, allows insights into how the fractions in favor of the reform—the SPÖ, the ÖVP, and the FPÖ—dealt with the relevant counter-hegemonic truth claims in their pursuit for a narrative about the problem and a solution that was robust enough to attain approval by a large segment of society.

The discursive strategies of members of the three parties were as such:

- Deportation for the protection of the nation: A very common discursive strategy to substantiate a claim that is challenged politically is to portray the problem as a fact that allows for a single interpretation only. MPs from SPÖ, ÖVP, and FPÖ used statistics to underline the necessity of legal change. Thus, some parliamentarians referred to the daily number of Romanians crossing the border, which was at several thousand, to suggest that Austria was too small a country to "accommodate one half of the population of Romania."[46] Others referred to data published by UNHCR estimating the number of refugees who were globally on the move in those days at five hundred million. MPs claimed that with the liberal asylum laws remaining in place, a majority of them would make their way to Austria.[47]

With this kind of framing of the problem, migration and asylum were moved to the realm of internal politics and policing. The Green Party attempted to provide more historical and transnational readings of the phenomena by claiming that Austria had a responsibility for the refugees due to its role in World War II, which resulted in the division of the world into two ideological blocks. However, such arguments were refuted as "foreign policy argumentation"[48] and thus irrelevant to a debate on border politics.

- Deportation in the service of refugees: Before the background of a national identity that had for decades drawn on the (purported) outstanding achievements in the field of refugee protection, and in an aim not to look hostile to refugees or racist, some MPs voting in favor of the amendment tried to portray the measures as not being harmful but instead beneficial for refugees.

MPs claimed that Austria's identity as an "asylum country" was not, as critics had claimed, threatened by the proposed reform but instead by bogus asylum seekers who were not fleeing from persecution but "simply" seeking better living conditions.[49] Those "economic refugees," as they were called, risked exhausting the resources and accommodation capacities desperately needed by actual refugees. Following this argumentative strategy, deporting bogus asylum claimants became necessary to save the asylum system.

A second argument followed the same logic: Thereby, deportation was claimed to be an essential instrument in the fight against the brutal, ruthless, and greedy business of human trafficking. If the trafficked were sent back, word would spread about the futility of trafficking, thereby destroying the traffickers' business and saving more people from falling into the hands of these "criminals."[50]

- Deportation makes for a better society: The question of racism figured prominently in the debates. This was due to loudly-voiced criticism prior to the parliamentary session accusing policymakers of racist motives. These allegations held more weight since Austria's national identity had been linked to being especially generous concerning refugee protection, ever since the late 1940s.

In order to save their image, policymakers introduced a distinction between the "legitimate fear of the people" and xenophobia when it came to reasons for rejecting non-citizens. While the former was placed in the realm of natural feelings and could not be controlled, the latter was claimed to be a product of political incitement. Unsurprisingly, the dominant political factions agreed that racism, in this particular struggle, was provoked by those who refused to take the "fear of the people" seriously. The Greens, in particular, were put in the spotlight. They were called "borderless," "brutal," and extremist.[51] Their reluctance to differentiate between true and false refugees was claimed to have augmented people's fear to the extent of inciting racist feelings in them.[52] By claiming too much anti-racism as the root cause of racism, accusations of racism directed at the government and the FPÖ could be deflected.

- Deportation in the service of national economics: The mutually exclusive viewpoints that the government parties held in the previous phases of the struggle concerning the meaning of the migration-flight movements for the national economy had not been consolidated before the National Assembly came together.

The SPÖ held on to its objective to tighten access to the labor market, presenting yet another argument: According to one MP, the "open border [was] xenophobic,"[53] since non-citizens risked getting shamelessly exploited by Austrian employers. Moreover, newcomers would replace long-term residents due to lower wages, thereby creating hardship for "fellow foreigners." ÖVP MPs, on the one hand, pointed to capacities in the national labor market and the newcomers' human right to work, while on the other hand, voicing fears about becoming an immigration country if the current regulations remained in place.[54]

However, coalition partners agreed on bringing the phenomena under control and gaining legislative power over the border. Tighter residence regulations and better instruments to expel and deport non-citizens were considered prerequisites for getting into a better place to select foreign workers according to the country's needs.

Summary and interpretation of findings

Common wisdom attributes the turning point in Austria's migration politics beginning in the 1990s to the rising numbers of immigrants and asylum seekers following the fall of the Iron Curtain. However, the fact that *Der Standard* reported a rise in first-time job permits for foreign workers by 19% in the same month that the restrictive reform was adopted proves that the situation is not that simple.[55]

It is thus more plausible that the activity at the border provided a good opportunity to gain control over immigration and foreign labor, something that had been attempted since the 1970s but without much success. Perhaps, what posed a problem at the turn from 1989 to 1990 were not so much the migrant refugees but the legal frameworks regulating their entry and residence. This is for several reasons: With the end of the ideological clashes between capitalism and communism, the "refugee from the East" lost the symbolic value it had had for the country's approach toward the global West.[56] Moreover, the decision to join the European Union came with the requirement to revise the regulations, especially since Austria's eastern borders were to become borders of the Union. Last but not least, the liberal entry laws fueled an already tense class situation. Since the 1980s, Austrian entrepreneurs and their political representatives had become more influential and more independent from the national workforce and their political representatives due to the growing financialization and internationalization of capital.[57] A massive expansion in the available workforce risked shifting power relations even more towards capital owners. Social Democrats, who were still strong with the electorate, back then heading the coalition government and the relevant ministries, had good reasons to use their political power to keep the changes to the current order as small as possible by gaining more control over the policy area. As outlined in the theory section of this article, a responsible minister cannot simply rewrite the parts of a law they deem problematic, since, in liberal societies, political power requires consent from a critical share of the people to last. On the contrary, they need to craft hegemony about what they see as a problem and the kind of solutions they prefer. Usually, they are challenged by societal actors who hold different viewpoints and interests. Which kinds of policies are adopted and—not less important—which truths about the "problem" they are designed to address are the outcome of "struggles over meaning."[58]

As the analysis of the political struggles fought out prior to the policy-making found, consent about the necessity to change the legal foundations of migration and asylum was not there from the beginning, and its crafting proved difficult. For one, a society that was made to believe for over forty years that their national identity depended on a generous attitude towards refugees could not easily be made complicit in restricting their access and residence in Austria. Sensing this, the government was reluctant to release the scope of the wished-for reform during the first phase of the struggle (December 1989), leaving the space for proxy discussions, namely about trafficking and undocumented foreign labor. In the second phase (January/February 1990), when the need for consent about the reform plans became pressing, the responsible interior ministry tried to mobilize support by claiming a refugee and accommodation crisis and creating the corresponding situation. Even after details about the reform were released, the media and the general public remained largely uninterested, and debates remained confined to a small circle of experts discussing the compatibility of some clauses with international obligations and the constitution. The situation changed only in phase three when the rather abstract claim of a refugee crisis suddenly became embodied by the young male Romanian asylum seekers. Following this, structural racism and widespread hostility towards refugees broke open, on the one hand giving supporters of the restrictive turn in migration and asylum politics a reason to claim that the reform was in the "interest of the people," on the other hand providing critics with substance for their claims about the racist foundation of the project.

Thus, in the last phase of the struggle for hegemony, the three parliamentary factions that made the reform pass, SPÖ, ÖVP, and FPÖ, needed to develop a narrative that would legitimize restrictive border laws, all while deflecting the accusations. The analysis of the argumentative strategies they applied the day the reform was adopted found that their most significant achievement was to assign the term "refugee" with a new meaning. Until then, refugees had widely been appreciated and praised in official political discourse as "brave anti-communist regime critics."[59] During the policy-making episode I analyzed, the concept of the refugee was broken in two and, from then on, signified both the real refugee worthy of protection and the false refugee to be targeted for deportation.

The introduction of the term "economic refugee" to name the false refugee proved a useful container to be filled with various, partly contradictory claims, all while combining them. Thus, the two coalition partners both used it as a buzzword while understanding different things: While the Social Democrats saw them as rivals in the job market, the People's Party disliked the great autonomy that migrant-refugees enjoyed under the then applicable regulations.

It was easy to observe how wary policymakers were in these days not to tarnish Austria's self-image as a state protecting refugees and human rights. For one, claiming that the legal changes did not touch upon the right to asylum for real refugees, the dominant political factions refuted reproaches about anti-refugee or racist motives. Moreover, much effort was put into portraying the legal changes as benefitting the refugees themselves. This is how deportation came to be presented as a way to save refugees from brutal traffickers, greedy employers, and even from bad individual choices like leaving their home country when it needed them most.

Conclusion

The question I set out to answer was whether the restrictive turn in Austria's migration and asylum policy ended the era in which these areas played an important role in nation-building for Austria. Applying a biopolitical approach to nation-building based on Michel Foucault[60] and further developed for the area of migration and deportation politics by Patricia Purtschert and Katrin Meyer,[61] I suggest that the multiplication of expulsion measures in 1990 was very relevant in terms of population politics.

The legal changes in the early 1990s constituted a first but crucial step in transforming the workings of the Austrian border by making entry requirements more selective. The introduction of the residence permit, for example, laid the groundwork for the Residence Act, adopted in 1992, which introduced a system of varying residence titles with different rights attached to them, especially regarding the labor market.[62] The introduction of the instruments concerning removal, push-back, and deportation in 1990 made the provisions of the new residence law enforceable.

The discursive construction of the "economic refugee" redefined the boundaries of belonging to Austrian society on two ends. By spelling out who among migrants and refugees was (no longer) desired and had to expect expulsion, desired migrant subjectivities also emerged on the inclusive side of this boundary. The force applied against the newly illegalized persons gave value to legal residence and helped make legal residents comply with desired ways of conduct, especially at the workplace. Deportation policy, thus, engendered inclusion and exclusion at the same time.

Endnotes

1 Matthew J. Gibney, "Asylum and the Expansion of Deportation in the United Kingdom," *Government and Opposition* 43, no. 2 (2008): 146–67 (here 146).

2 Patrik Paul Volf, "Der politische Flüchtling als Symbol der Zweiten Republik: Zur Asyl- und Flüchtlingspolitik seit 1945," *Zeitgeschichte* 22, 11-12 (1995): 415–36.

3 When using violence, the state acts in a sovereign as opposed to a governmental manner, according to Foucault: Michel Foucault, *In Verteidigung der Gesellschaft: Vorlesungen am College de France (1975–1976)*, (Frankfurt am Main: Suhrkamp, 1999), 304.

4 "Racist" is not to be understood in a race-theoretical way but refers to the general logic by which people and behaviors are classified into inferior and superior: Focault, *In Verteidigung*, 303.

5 Focault, *In Verteidigung*, 283–304.

6 Katrin Meyer and Patricia Purtschert, "Migrationsmanagement und die Sicherheit der Bevölkerung," in *Migrationsmanagement und die Sicherheit der Bevölkerung: Gouvernementalität und Sicherheit.* Zeitdiagnostische Beiträge im Anschluss an Foucault, ed. Katrin Meyer, Patricia Purtschert, and Yves Winter (Bielefeld: transcript, 2008), 149–72 (here 150–55).

7 Meyer and Purtschert, "Migrationsmanagement," 150.

8 Ulrich Brand, "State, Context and Correspondence: Contours of a Historical-Materialist Policy Analysis," Österreichische Zeitschrift für Politikwissenschaft 42, no. 4 (2013): 425–42 (here 434).

9 Antonio Gramsci, *Gefängnishefte: kritische Gesamtausgabe*, vol. 4, (Hamburg: Argument, 1991), 783.

10 Markus Griesser and Gundula Ludwig, "'Endlose Transaktionen': Eine hegemonietheoretische Aneignung Foucaults: Und deren Nutzen für die feministische Staatstheorie," *PROKLA: Zeitschrift für kritische Sozialwissenschaft* 38, no. 151 (2008): 271–88 (here 278–79).

11 Sonja Buckel, "'Managing Migration': Eine intersektionale Kapitalismusanalyse am Beispiel der Europäischen Migrationspolitik," *Berliner Journal für Soziologie* 22, no. 1 (2012): 82.

12 Lisa Grösel, "Die postfordistische Wende der politischen Regulation in Österreich im Bereich der Ausländer_innenpolitik: 1986 Bis 1992," (diploma thesis, University of Vienna, 2013), 43.

13 BGBI. Nr. 75/1954, "Aliens' Police Act" (*Fremdenpolizeigesetz*) 1954, §2(1).

14 The same was true for visa overstayers: cf. Manfred Srb (Grüne), Mar. 12, 1990, Abweichende persönliche Stellungnahme des Abgeordneten Srb zum Bericht des Innenausschusses über den Antrag 322/A der Abg. Elmecker, Burgstaller, Fister,

Kraft und Genossen, betreffend ein Bundesgesetz, mit dem das Paßgesetz 1969, das Grenzkontrollgesetz 1969 und das Fremdenpolizeigesetz geändert werden, Zu 1213 der Beilagen zu den Stenographischen Protokollen des Nationalrates XVII. Gesetzgebungsperiode,

Austrian Parliament, Vienna, 1-4 (here 4).

15 Kenneth Horvath, "Policing the Borders of the 'Centaur State': Deportation, Detention, and Neoliberal Transformation Processes. The Case of Austria," *Social Inclusion* 2, no. 3 (2014): 113–23 (here 117).

16 Karl Czernetz (SPÖ), Mar. 17, 1954, Stenographisches Protokoll, 35. Sitzung des Nationalrates der Republik Österreich, VII. Gesetzgebungsperiode, download service of the Austrian Parliament, Vienna, 1472–88 (here 1484).

17 Volf, "Der politische Flüchtling."

18 Dirk Rupnow, "Arbeitsmigration / "Gastarbeiter," House of Austrian History website, accessed Jan. 24, 2022, https://www.hdgoe.at/arbeitsmigration

19 Horvath, "Policing the Borders," 117.

20 Grösel, *Die postfordistische Wende*, 82–84.

21 Grösel, *Die postfordistische Wende*, 152

22 Volf, "Der politische Flüchtling," 419, 430.

23 Volf, "Der politische Flüchtling," 432–33.

24 The amendment also touched other aspects of migration and asylum law, like the treatment of flight passengers transiting Austria (Passport Act and Border Control Law), immigration detention, police capacities, institutional arrangements (Aliens' Police Act) as well as the asylum procedure (Asylum Act).

25 Own calculation based on official data.

26 Peter Zuser, "Die Konstruktion der Ausländerfrage in Österreich: Eine Analyse des öffentlichen Diskurses 1990," Insitute for Advanced Studies, Vienna, Political Science Series Working Paper 35, IRIHS Institutional Repository at IHS Vienna, accessed Jan. 23, 2022, https://irihs.ihs.ac.at/id/eprint/916/1/pw_35.pdf, 1–89 (here 80–82).

27 Dec. 11, 1989, 123rd meeting of the Austrian National Assembly, Stenographic Protocol, download service of the Austrian Parliament, Vienna, 14485-14582.

28 Franz Löschnak, Dec. 11, 1989, 123rd meeting of the Austrian National Assembly, Stenographic Protocol, download service of the Austrian Parliament, Vienna, 14485-14582 (here 14570); Alfred Fister (SPÖ), Dec. 11, 1989, 123rd meeting of the Austrian National Assembly, Stenographic Protocol, download service of the Austrian Parliament, Vienna, 14485-14582 (here 14579).

29 The demands included tighter border controls, legal penalties for traffickers and the conclusion of readmission agreements with Hungary, Yugoslavia, and Czechoslovakia: Fister, 123rd meeting, 14580.

30 "Asylpolitik im Umbruch: Mock: Visumfreiheit für CSSR-Bürger – Sonderministerrat," *Der Standard*, Dec. 14, 1989.

31 Lydia Ninz, "Peitsche für neue Gastarbeiter: Strengere Behandlung einreisender Arbeitswilliger in Diskussion," *Der Standard*, Dec. 12, 1989; "Sonder-Ministerrat beschließt Osteuropa-Paket: Die Regierung will östliche Schwarzarbeit regulieren," *Der Standard*, Dec. 16, 1989.

32 "Österreichs Engagement bei der wirtschaftlichen Aufholjagd der östlichen Staaten: Ökomillionen für Ostprojekte. Schüssel will Regierung zum Auffangen des politischen Risikos für Investitionen vergattern," *Der Standard*, Jan. 2, 1990; "Joint Ventures in Osteuropa," *Der Standard*, Jan. 9, 1990; "Rumänien/Tourismus: Reisefreiheit," *Der Standard*, Jan. 27–28, 1990.

33 Zuser, "Die Konstruktion der Ausländerfrage," 16–18, 20–21; "Kirche versteht sich als Anwalt der Flüchtlinge," *Der Standard*, Jan. 4, 1990; "Traiskirchen: Flüchtlinge delogiert," *Der Standard*, Jan. 10, 1990; "SP will wenige Ausländer, doch denen soll's Gutgehen," *Der Standard*, Jan. 20, 1990; "CSSR-Flüchtlinge sollen zurückwandern," *Der Standard*, Feb. 16, 1990; "Geppert, Löschnak und Amnesty in Sorge um Ausländer in Österreich: Arbeitsmarkt 'kontrolliert öffnen.' 'Sicherungsbescheinigung' soll Auslands-Schwarzarbeit fernhalten," *Der Standard*, Feb. 16, 1990.

34 *Der Standard*, Jan 4, 1990, 5.

35 "Folter und Mißhandlungen in Österreich: Amnesty International wartet mit einem Bericht über Elektroschocks- und Plasticksackerl-Verhören auf," *Der Standard*, Jan. 9, 1990; Franz Witzmann, "Ein Bauernopfer ist keine Polizeireform," *Der Standard*, Feb. 2, 1990.

36 Srb, Abweichende persönliche Stellungnahme, 1.

37 The non-refoulement principle for asylum seekers was taken up in §13a Aliens' Police Act 1954, version 1990. The right to file an asylum application at the border got inscribed in §2a Asylum Law, version 1990.

38 Jürgen Langenbach, "Gegen das neue Fremdenrecht formiert sich breiter Widerstand," *Der Standard*, Feb. 22, 1990; Heinrich Vana, "Abschieben ist keine Lösung: Plädoyer gegen die geplante Verschärfung des Ausländerrechts," Kommentar der Anderen, *Der Standard*, Jan. 25, 1990.

39 "AK zwischen Liberalisierung und Reglementierung des Arbeitsmarktes," *Der Standard*, Feb. 10, 1990; "Geppert, Löschnak und Amnesty in Sorge um Ausländer in Österreich: Arbeitsmarkt 'kontrolliert öffnen.' 'Sicherungsbescheinigung' soll Auslands-Schwarzarbeit fernhalten," *Der Standard*, Feb. 16, 1990.

40 "AK zwischen Liberalisierung und Reglementierung des Arbeitsmarktes," *Der Standard*, Feb. 10, 1990.

41 Zuser, "Die Konstruktion der Ausländerfrage," 80–82.

42 Zuser, "Die Konstruktion der Ausländerfrage," 59–61.

43 Own translation of "Leute aus Ländern, denen man die Abstammung eindeutig ansieht," "Empörung über Ratzenböck-Brief: 'Man sieht den Leuten die Abstammung eindeutig an' – Flüchtlinge aufteilen," *Der Standard*, Mar. 10, 1990.

44 "Empörung über Ratzenböck-Brief: 'Man sieht den Leuten die Abstammung eindeutig an' – Flüchtlinge aufteilen," *Der Standard*, Mar. 10, 1990; "Schüssel: Keine Sanktion für Flüchtlingsherbergen," *Der Standard*, Mar. 12, 1990.

45 Jürgen Langenbach, "Gegen das neue Fremdenrecht formiert sich breiter Widerstand," *Der Standard*, Feb. 22, 1990; "Flucht vor Flüchtlingen: Hearing über Paßgesetz," *Der Standard*, Mar. 9, 1990.

46 Paul Burgstaller (ÖVP), Mar. 14, 1990, Stenographisches Protokoll, 133. Sitzung des Nationalrates der Republik Österreich, XVII. Gesetzgebungsperiode, download service of the Austrian Parliament, Vienna, 15651–796 (here 15682).

47 Helene Partik-Pablé (FPÖ), Mar. 14, 1990, Stenographisches Protokoll, 133. Sitzung des Nationalrates der Republik Österreich, XVII. Gesetzgebungsperiode, download service of the Austrian Parliament, Vienna, 15651–796 (here 15695).

48 Felix Ermacora (ÖVP), Mar. 14, 1990, Stenographisches Protokoll, 133. Sitzung des Nationalrates der Republik Österreich, XVII. Gesetzgebungsperiode, download service of the Austrian Parliament, Vienna, 15651–796 (here 15699).

49 Fister, 133. Sitzung, 15705; Friedhelm Frischenschlager (FPÖ), Mar. 14, 1990, Stenographisches Protokoll, 133. Sitzung des Nationalrates der Republik Österreich, XVII. Gesetzgebungsperiode, download service of the Austrian Parliament, Vienna, 15651–796 (here 15719); Wendelin Ettmayer (ÖVP), Mar. 14, 1990, Stenographisches Protokoll, 133. Sitzung des Nationalrates der Republik Österreich, XVII. Gesetzgebungsperiode, download service of the Austrian Parliament, Vienna, 15651–796 (here 15706–707); Rudolf Parnigoni (SPÖ), Mar. 14, 1990, Stenographisches Protokoll, 133. Sitzung des Nationalrates der Republik Österreich, XVII. Gesetzgebungsperiode, download service of the Austrian Parliament, Vienna, 15651–796 (here 15708–709)

50 Fister, 133. Sitzung, 15706; Partik-Pablé, 133. Sitzung, 15694.

51 Ermacora, 133. Sitzung, 15700.

52 Frischenschlager, 133. Sitzung, 15718; Partik-Pablé, 133. Sitzung, 15693–94, 15695; Ettmayer, 133. Sitzung, 15707.

53 Fister, 133. Sitzung, 15705.

54 Burgstaller, 133. Sitzung, 15681; Michael Graff, Mar. 14, 1990, Stenographisches Protokoll, 133. Sitzung des Nationalrates der Republik Österreich, XVII. Gesetzgebungsperiode, download service of the Austrian Parliament, Vienna, 15651–796 (here 15684).

55 "Ostzuwanderer finden auch legale Jobs," *Der Standard*, Mar. 20, 1990.

56 Volf, "Der politische Flüchtling."

57 Otto Penz, "Vom Sozial- zum Wettbewerbsstaat: Arbeitsbeziehungen und politische Regulation in Österreich," in *Neoliberalismus in der Krise des Sozialen: Das Beispiel Österreich*, ed. Andrea Grisold, Wolfgang Maderthaner, and Otto Penz (Vienna: Böhlau, 2010), 139–78 (here 156).

58 Karin Bauer, "Asyl gibt es für viele nur mehr in der Kirche: Im überfüllten Lager Traiskirchen Verschärft sich täglich das Flüchtlingschaos," *Der Standard*, Jan. 13, 1990.

59 Volf, "Der politische Flüchtling."

60 Foucault, *In Verteidigung der Gesellschaft*.

61 Katrin Meyer, and Patricia Purtschert. "Migrationsmanagement."

62 Ilker Ataç and Albert Kraler, "Gewünschte, Geduldete und Unerwünschte: Klassifizieren, Selektieren, Stratifizieren. Migrationspolitik als Strategie des Filterns," *MALMOE*, no. 33 (2006): 25–26.

Leaving Siegfried Behind: Nibelung Monuments in the Cultural Infrastructure of Contemporary Austria

Alexandra Sterling-Hellenbrand

The figure of Siegfried has a long and conflicted reception history. We may immediately recall the doomed hero of Richard Wagner's *Der Ring des Nibelungen*. Alternatively, we may envision the dragon slayer of Scandinavian legend. Or perhaps we encountered excerpts from the thirteenth-century *Nibelungenlied* in school, learning about German literature or the European Middle Ages generally. This essay explores what we might consider a recovery of the Nibelung mythology for the developing ideals of contemporary Austria through an examination of recent Nibelung monuments. These monuments, whether new structures or older structures newly re-done, enable us to observe a long process in which the Second Republic has worked to rehabilitate and reimagine its cultural infrastructure for the twentieth century (and beyond) in a framework—however conflicted—of peace-making and hoped-for tolerance. After situating this discussion in the context of current memory studies, this essay will focus first on three Nibelung monuments: the *Nibelungendenkmal* in Pöchlarn (1987), the *Nibelungendenkmal* in Tulln (2005), and the *Siegfriedskopf* at the University of Vienna (1923; redesigned 2006).

The monuments are all based on the *Nibelungenlied*—or the Nibelung legend—yet they represent different aspects of its reception at discrete interfaces in individual communities. The first two examples were created around the turn of the twenty-first century. In their respective cities (Pöchlarn and Tulln), they demonstrate facets of the "local" display of medieval literature, embedding the literary past in the local landscape, where medieval texts and public memory intersect to form a new cultural interface. The third example, by contrast, shows the recontextualization of an older monument with a contentious past that extended from its dedication in 1923 through the twentieth century—until the university finally intervened to redesign and move it. Each of these installations, in ways unique to their environments, transforms the older Nibelung narrative not only into a new site of heritage and a new site of memory but also into a new site of imagination—imagination that can tell different stories to create a future that moves beyond the present and the past. The essay will conclude with a look at the most recent installations that represent medieval German literature from Austria and do not take up the *Nibelungenlied* or more well-known narratives at all. The *Steirische Literaturpfade des Mittelalters* (the Styrian Literature Pathways of the Middle Ages) reach back to the medieval literature of Styria to tell different stories by literally placing those stories in the landscape from which they emerged.[1] The Literature Pathways thus demonstrate an innovative twenty-first-century response from local and regional communities to the overwhelming attention paid to works like the *Nibelungenlied* on a national level. Taken together, these examples show a profoundly creative process that seeks new, forward-looking, and more sustainable narratives for older literature, made accessible for the modern Austrian public. Not only does this process shape the physical environment by establishing or remaking a tangible structure like a monument. It also shapes the more intangible cultural infrastructure of twenty-first-century Austria writ large, by extricating contemporary aspirations from the Nibelung mythology that had become so deeply embedded in nationalistic rhetoric from the nineteenth century onward. Combined, these projects make a unique contribution to current discussions in Austria and abroad regarding the future of difficult heritage.

Memory and Monuments

Narratives adapt and evolve; likewise, sites of memory do not remain static. Indeed, over time, the *Nibelungenlied* has become a fraught but resonantly potent site of memory (*Erinnerungsort*) in the German-speaking realm.[2] To be sure, the *Nibelungenlied* remains an odd narrative to inspire such veneration: essentially a family drama written by a thirteenth-century cleric in which courtly and Germanic values collide, it is a story of murder and betrayal, guilt and greed, and loyalty and honor that culminates in a spectacular bloodbath brought about by cold-blooded revenge born of long-festering hatred. This is scarcely a glorious tale to inspire feats of heroism. Nevertheless, the *Nibelungenlied* has long walked hand in hand with cultural identity and national sentiment. The tale captivated the imaginations of German-speaking intellectuals in the nineteenth century, as they sought to deploy the story for nationalistic or patriotic purposes, reading into the story grand dreams of building a unified German nation.[3] For Bismarck, Siegfried the smith became the symbol of the new nation.[4] Furthermore, it was not only in World War I that German and Austrian soldiers were called to demonstrate the same deep, unwavering loyalty toward comrades and country (*Nibelungentreue*) shown by the Burgundians (the Nibelungs) facing certain defeat in their last battle. Wapnewski muses that the *Nibelungenlied* is all too often cited but seldom read; as a site of memory, the narrative has spun a tale of its own independent of the text(s) from which it originated. In this process, we can see evidence of how the Middle Ages function consistently as a vehicle to reshape the past to conform to the needs of the present.[5] This process—called medievalism—sometimes occurs very uncritically. When thoughtfully deployed, however, medievalism can become a powerful mechanism for using the past to inspire cultural reflection and change in the present. The Austrian monuments at the center of this essay are a public expression of this desire for reflection and change, of a need to relegate the older story of Siegfried to history and move beyond it.[6] Monuments are "values made visible," says Susan Neiman in *Learning from the Germans: Race and the Memory of Evil.*[7] The reconfigured (Siegfried) or new (Pöchlarn and Tulln) monuments at the center of this study thus reveal much about the values their communities wish to express now.

In a broader context, we can see these monuments quite literally in the landscape of the culture of remembrance (*Erinnerungskultur*) that has impacted literary, cultural, and historical studies since the mid-twentieth century. Over time, the term has also come to refer not only to remembering the Holocaust—across Europe—but to remembering various other traumas of the German experience in the twentieth century. Memories do not exist as closed systems, says Aleida Assmann; in any given social reality, memories intersect, touch, strengthen, modify, and become polarized in connection with other processes of remembering and forgetting.[8] A dynamic dialogue between individual and collective memory takes place in the long shadow, as Assmann describes it, of a traumatic past. The events of 1989 infused this dialogue with new energy and purpose, as the dissolution of the bipolar political structure of Europe led "to an eruptive return of memories and a 'reawakening of history'"[9] Older national myths such as the Nibelungen, like conventional and previously accepted versions of history, came into question.

In such an environment of reawakening, the physical landscape and the objects of memory continue to play a significant role. Sharon Macdonald shows this not only in the context of Europe but also, as does Neil MacGregor, in the context of Germany. [10] As the political landscape has continued to change since 1989, inhabiting a physical landscape still indelibly marked by two world wars and forty years of division, we see that memorials change and are changed by those in power to shape public memory. Rudy Koshar describes this memory landscape (*Erinnerungslandschaft*) as "a topography steeped in memories and images," describing the way in which Germans have collectively processed their history since the nineteenth century through their monuments and dedicated public spaces.[11] Koshar emphasizes that memory work is reconstructive, ritualistic, and performative; it reveals stratified layers that have collected palimpsest-like over time, in what Koshar calls a "triadic relationship between humans, landmarks, and cultural meanings."[12] In this relationship, monuments resonate with ideas and metaphors, containing and perpetuating collective memory over time for the communities in which they are located. Koshar coins the term "emergent evolution" for this constantly replicable process.[13] The Austrian monuments under consideration here—the Nibelung monuments and the Styrian Literature Pathways—illustrate Koshar's concept of emergent evolution. They stand collectively in the *Erinnerungslandschaft* as artifacts that uniquely present the past, both literary and historical. Each monument demonstrates a unique intersection of memory, nostalgia, and visual culture in which a community seeks to adapt medieval literary heritage to reflect changing identities in the present. Memorials, suggests Neiman, "embody the ideals we choose to honor" and therefore, in choosing "to memorialize a historical moment, we are choosing the values we want to defend and pass on."[14] These monuments signal change, as they prompt a re-examination of the Nibelung narrative in particular and a re-evaluation of the values historically associated with it.

The Nibelung monuments are also unique memorials in that they commemorate fictional moments—in contrast to historical moments—that now have tangible form and physical presence. This aspect gives them and their audiences a unique opportunity to redirect and shape further discussions of values—and, to paraphrase Neiman, to choose differently. The newly (re) constructed Nibelung monuments show emergent evolution of identity in progress by exploiting this potential. This evolution taps into the ripples of affective memory that swirl around the *Nibelungenlied* as a site of memory, as the monuments instantiate the narrative and simultaneously redirect its reception, while the literature pathways offer entirely new opportunities for encounters with a less well-known literary past. In this context, we can perhaps also see these monuments as an example of prosthetic memory engaging with the Austrian nationalist/National Socialist past, as Gundolf Graml has recently used the term in his analysis of the Linz 09 exhibitions. The concept of prosthetic memory emphasizes the affective and subjective relationship to the past through the development of second-hand memory that differs from traditional historiography.[15] Such memory is generated through film, literature, museums—displays, in other words.[16] Graml, like Landsberg, focuses primarily on the artistic reception of historical moments or events. Nevertheless, the concept of prosthetic memory is useful here when we consider the Nibelung monuments and their function in the cultural landscape of their respective environments, as they participate in the construction of affective second-hand (i.e., prosthetic) memory through their implicit engagement with the reception history of the *Nibelungenlied* and their explicit creation of new narratives.[17] The monuments in question take narrative moments and instantiate them in the physical world—fiction becomes artifact, becomes history. We can paraphrase Graml, then, to say that attempts to make the *Nibelungenlied* and its reception tangible through tourist infrastructure can result in increased awareness and new narratives.[18] Thus, they foster a sense of distinctiveness and ownership, and investment in the narrative—this is an investment that reveals an Austrian sense of responsibility to transmute the older narrative into a foundation for future change. These monuments, as tangible adaptations of intangible yet deeply rooted cultural narratives, reflect unique Austrian contributions to the emerging memorylands of Europe.

Nibelung Monuments: Rehabilitating Memory

The Nibelungs are ever-present along the Danube through Upper and Lower Austria. In addition to numerous hotels, restaurants, and various small businesses from pharmacies to natural food stores and other organizations[19] that bear the name, we also find more prominent examples such as the Nibelungenbrücke in Linz, where the city has attempted to stake a positive claim to the legend to overcome its fraught history (and that of the bridge). There are also heavily-marketed tourist destinations, such as the entire section of the Wachau known as the Nibelungengau, with its wines and walking trails.[20] Three monuments stand out in this Nibelung-saturated landscape: the Nibelung monuments in Pöchlarn (1987) and Tulln (2005) and the *Siegfriedskopf* at the University of Vienna. Whereas the first two examples involve new monuments created around the turn of the twenty-first century, the third example shows the recontextualization of an older monument with its own contentious past. Each monument speaks to the values that respective communities wish to convey about themselves now.

Erected in 1987, the monument at Pöchlarn appears rather understated and traditional.[21] A stone structure provides the frame for a simple display of sixteen colorful mosaic shields with the coats of arms from the cities where the *Nibelungenlied* takes place, arranged from left to right (as the visitor approaches the monument) in the order that they appear in the narrative. We start in distant Metz and Xanten; the former is the home of Ortwin, nephew of Hagen, and the latter is the home of Siegfried himself. The visual journey then proceeds from Worms to Alzey, to Passau and Efferding on the first eight shields; the second set of eight begins at Pöchlarn and continues finally to Vienna and Esztergom (home of Etzel, king of the Huns), and ends with the insignia of Verona—home of Dietrich of Bern, loyal vassal of Etzel and one of the few survivors left standing after the disastrous battle with the Nibelungs. The monument does not engage any more specifically with the narrative that connects the places represented by their coats of arms; instead, the monument provides a kind of framework through the place names and the insignia on the shields. The audience must bring the story of the Nibelungs with them to fill out the frame; perhaps they recall what they might have learned in school, perhaps they are familiar with Wagner's *Ring* cycle, or perhaps they must create a narrative of their own. However, regardless of whatever knowledge visitors bring to the monument, the place names anchor them in the real geography of Germany and Austria.

Of course, the most important place name for this monument remains that of the location itself: the city of Pöchlarn (Bechelarn), which is the home of the margrave Rüdiger in the *Nibelungenlied*. Rüdiger is known for his hospitality, generosity, and honesty; his court at Pöchlarn stands out from the courts in Worms and Hungary as a place of peace, where the margrave seeks to bring people together and unite families. He argues for the common good when he presents Kriemhild with his lord Etzel's request for her hand in marriage. Not only does Rüdiger negotiate the match between Etzel and Kriemhild, but he also later arranges the betrothal of his daughter to Giselher, Kriemhild's youngest brother. Twice called upon to act as host for the Burgundians, Rüdiger exemplifies hospitality, loyalty, and honor. The first time, on the initial journey, Kriemhild is traveling with her entourage to meet and wed Etzel. Rüdiger again hosts the Burgundians later in the poem, when they stay at Pöchlarn as they journey to Hungary on the trip from which they will not return. Rüdiger's courtliness, the model hospitality of Lady Gotelint, and the generosity of Rüdiger's household also reflect Etzel's magnanimity, which we see on fine display in Etzel's welcome of exiled princes like Dietrich of Bern and others who have come to meet his bride.[22] These expressions of welcome in the *Nibelungenlied* contrast starkly with the deadly conflict that later unfolds at Etzel's hall. When Rüdiger falls at last in the 37th adventure, his death precipitates the final confrontation and the tragic conclusion of the epic. Rüdiger's fate notwithstanding, the monument in modern Pöchlarn stands as an expression of the margrave's legacy of hospitality and generosity; the city proudly offers the monument as a contribution to the European concept of peace in a clear statement on the city´s webpage.[23] We might consider this a prosthetic moment, where the monument creates a memory that should serve as an impetus for reflection or advocacy. The monument enhances the interface between narrative and place, as it underscores the reality of the places in which the story is set. This interface is further enhanced in a display called "Laute(r) Nibelungen," done around 2009. Four figures (*laute Nibelungen*) installed at intervals by the Danube tell of the hospitality found in medieval Bechelaren and thereby invite visitors to come and explore the modern town.[24]

While the Nibelung monument in Pöchlarn highlights the real places that anchor the narrative of the *Nibelungenlied*, the monument in Tulln goes further not only toward making the older story real but toward recontextualizing that older story and integrating it into a new narrative. Tulln's role in the Nibelungenlied is as significant as that of Pöchlarn, at least in terms of the narrative's arc in the second part of the poem. The poem tells us:

> There is a place that lies by the Danube in Austria which is called Tulln. There she [Kriemhild] became acquainted with a great number of strange customs which she had never seen before. Plenty of people welcomed her there who afterwards met with sorrow for her sake.[25]

This passage announces one of the most (in)famous meetings in German medieval literature: between Kriemhild, widow of the slain Siegfried and sister of the Burgundian kings, and Etzel (Attila), the king of the Huns, whom Kriemhild has agreed to marry. The city of Tulln provides the backdrop for this encounter that seals the later fate of the Nibelungs. In 2005, the city erected an imposing monument close to the Danube's edge, not far from the central pedestrian zone (Figure 1). Designed by artist Michail Nogin, it is a multi-layered installation with three primary parts. The larger than life-sized figures of Kriemhild and Etzel and their attendants (1) tower over a fountain (2) whose alternating water jets recall the turning of pages in the book (3) that we also see at the fountain's base. The book is open to a page that quotes a passage from this scene in the text from the nineteenth-century translation of the *Nibelungenlied* by Karl Simrock. The monument seeks to open a dialogue with a medieval literary past, engaging visitors in the present as they encounter the older narrative transformed from page to pedestal. As part of this dialogue, the monument also calls upon visitors to navigate between what is imagined and what is real; the location guides the negotiation of meaning, serving as a material reference to a "common imaginary world."[26] Placed physically (at the Danube's edge) at a location of importance to a twenty-first-century community (Tulln), the monument invites us to consider a medieval text (the *Nibelungenlied*) given tangible form in sculpture (the 2005 installation). The Tulln monument thus stands at the convergence of several spaces: an imaginative space that offers a threshold between literary past and real present; a creative space that mediates artistic forms, translating medieval verse into modern sculpture; a real space that marks the edge of the city, inviting visitors to enter a beautiful park and recreation area. These spaces combine to create a unique "place of imagination," a term used by Stijn Reijnders to describe physical ("authentic") locations that anchor a fictional creation shared in a collective imagination rather than in an experience of history.

More importantly, the monument supports what I have called a "new aspirational story" as a "moral anchor" for the cultural landscape in Tulln and arguably in modern Austria.[27] The monument attempts to redirect the nationalistic overtones of the Nibelung narrative as it reclaims but also refashions the older story. The Tulln monument drives this refashioning in its juxtaposition of east and west. Kriemhild, the Burgundian princess from the Rhineland, arrives from the west, walking eastward. Etzel faces west, having arrived from the land of the Huns in the east. Their costumes, like their physical features, highlight the different ethnic groups and cultural traditions from which the sculptor imagines that they come. On an individual level here, as well as on a cultural scale, the meeting of Kriemhild and Etzel is portrayed as the meeting of West and East; as the *Nibelungenlied* takes pains to remind us, it is also a meeting of Christians and pagans, characterized by a tolerance that the poet consistently finds remarkable.[28] All of the encounters on this particular journey are peaceful and celebratory; religious differences do not seem to matter—at least for a moment. The monument in Tulln enhances the city's tourist appeal, hoping to draw visitors with a creative visualization of the scene from the *Nibelungenlied* that took place at that spot. The scene itself invites the engagement of passers-by; they should wonder: who are these people? Where do they come from? What are they doing? Surrounded by a beautiful park, shimmering at times through the spray of the fountain water, the monument cultivates a playful mood. In this way, more consciously than the monument at Pöchlarn, the installation in Tulln prompts visitors to play with the memories they might have associated with the Nibelung legend over time: from required reading at school, from local history, from music and film, or from the political propaganda of two world wars. The monument implies that different memories can and should emerge in the twenty-first century from this story. In other words, the monument seeks to redirect the values we associate with the story; its physical anchor at this location in Tulln offers an opportunity to launch the story on a journey away from the ideological overtones that have hitherto confined it.[29]

Concerning the medieval narrative past and the Nibelung legacy, the monuments of Tulln and Pöchlarn clearly create a new site of heritage and memory for each community. The third Nibelung monument under consideration is not a new monument per se; instead, it is an older memorial that has taken a new form, a site of memory that has been reconfigured and perhaps rehabilitated. The sculpture, known as the *Siegfriedskopf*, was dedicated to the fallen heroes of the University of Vienna ("den Gefallenen Helden unserer Universität") and resided in the university's central entrance hall from its unveiling on November 9, 1923, until 2006.[30] In 2006, the sculpture was finally moved to the arcaded courtyard or *Arkadenhof* (Figure 2). Christoph Gnant also suggests that the Universities Act of 2002 played a significant role in giving the university the autonomy it needed to "consciously face up to its historical responsibilities."[31] The *Siegfriedskopf* had been a source of contention for decades: a meeting point for nationalist fraternities and student groups, and a magnet for both the Right (attraction) and the Left (repulsion). A proposal was made during the memorial year 1988 to commemorate the victims of the Nazi era with a plaque in the entrance hall, which would serve as a memorial for "the victims of war and violence with genuine grief."[32] In 1990, the university senate decided that the *Siegfriedskopf* be moved into the Arkadenhof. Progress on moving the sculpture stalled due to protracted debate in politics and the media, objections from the federal agency for historic preservation (*Bundesdenkmalamt*), and technical problems involving the actual physical transfer of the monument from one location to another.[33] It took an act of vandalism in 2002, an auspicious anniversary, and a renewed commitment by the university administration before the impetus finally came to realize the unfulfilled mandate and move the monument at last.

However, the monument was not only moved; it was reimagined and recontextualized in an innovative concept designed by the studio of Bele Marx and Gilles Mussard (Büro Photoglas). The artists extensively describe their work with textual references in their publication ("Kontroverse Siegfriedskopf").[34] A short summary will suffice here. The new installation dismantles the previous sculpture into three parts: the head, the pedestal, and the plinth. Text dominates the monument now. When one walks around the monument in its new form, one might experience a certain degree of frustration because one cannot clearly see the actual sculpture or take a photo, for instance. This difficulty is the purpose of the recontextualization, of course. The medium here is the message, to coin a phrase: in the new installation, the words obscure the image; these words now make unequivocally explicit that which has not always been as explicit or openly acknowledged as it should have been. Words have been a source of obfuscation, manipulation, and injury in the past—and the *Siegfriedskopf* only served to amplify those destructive messages in its previous incarnation.

Words now intentionally cover the sculpture and its components, literally recontextualizing them, and those words are then, in turn, encased in yet another story. The head displays text from articles in the *Arbeiter-Zeitung* from October and November 1923 regarding *Hakenkreuzterror* at the university. The pedestal has text from the 1990 debate about the monument in the context of right-wing extremism at Austrian universities. The plinth, finally, displays portions of another article that details the debates of the 1990s.[35] On the weather-resistant glass cube that contains the now tripartite display, we have a text by Minna Lachs, who describes an experience she had as a young female Jewish student at the university in the 1920s where a stranger helped her exit the Reading Room safely during a violent demonstration that had begun around the *Siegfriedskopf* in the entrance hall.[36] The emphasis on text reminds us of the power of language, as words and books are often the first victims of totalitarian regimes.[37] We are, however, reminded that words tell stories and record history; therefore, they have the power not just to damage or injure but also to resist.

The Styrian Literature Pathways: Creating Memory

Each of the previous installations interrogates recent history by embedding the literary past, represented by the troublesome *Nibelungenlied*, in the local landscape. Each monument provides evidence of how the Second Austrian Republic has come to tell different stories: the monuments create a new space where medieval texts and public memory can intersect and where prosthetic memory can be engaged. The new narratives transform the older narratives not only into new sites of memory but also into new sites of imagination—the imagination that can perhaps finally consign the Siegfried of the nineteenth and twentieth centuries to the archives and tell other stories better suited to the present and future.

The most recent representatives of such installations are the Styrian Literature Pathways (*Steirische Literaturpfade*); they deserve mention here because they do not take up the *Nibelungenlied* or other well-known narratives at all. Instead, the *Steirische Literaturpfade* reach back to the medieval literature of Styria to publicize different stories that are perhaps more closely connected to the local or regional landscape, and highlight the twelfth- and thirteenth-century literature that has been obscured by the *Nibelungenlied*'s long shadow. Initiated between 2009 and 2011, the *Steirische Literaturpfade* was designed as a ten-year project that would encompass eight communities across the province of Styria: Admont, Bruck an der Mur, Neuburg an der Mürz, Seckau, Stattegg, Unzmarkt-Frauenburg, Vorau, and Wildon.

The displays focus on texts produced in or near the communities where the pathways are situated. Each pathway has similar components: a walking path of short to moderate length that is marked at several intervals by five to seven metal stands that successively display various aspects of the literary text chosen to highlight that particular community[38] (Figure 3). The medieval German troubadour (or *Minnesänger*) Rudolf von Stadeck is rumored to have originated from the small town of Stattegg, located on the northwestern edge of the regional capital of Graz. Rudolf's words and verses take their place in the landscape of Stattegg in a unique display: five stations showing images from the Manesse manuscript, the single most comprehensive source of Middle High German troubadour poetry from the fourteenth century. The stations also display excerpts from the texts and offer brief interpretations of the poems and their themes. Located near the soccer field or the school, tucked into a neighborhood, or placed near a bus stop on the main road, the installations appear conspicuous—they are pink, after all—and yet understated due to their simplicity. They are metal stands that support a series of square panels, some of which are angled to suggest a piece of paper or parchment being unfolded. Finally, though the colorful structures seem a bit incongruous next to the athletic complex or by the historic limestone furnaces, they have been constructed to take the landscape into account; they invite curious visitors to walk up to or around the installations, to look through them, to read Rudolf's verses as part of the landscape in which he may have written them.

The Literature Pathways project features prominently in tourist information about Styria.[39] It prompts comparison with the Nibelung monuments as all of the installations share the impulse to engage with the medieval literary past in the present. Notably, however, the Pathways do not take up the *Nibelungenlied* or more well-known narratives; instead, they remain focused on the literature connected to or produced *from within* their local communities. The installations reach back to the medieval literature of the province of Styria to make the Styrian texts visible by placing them in their regional landscape. This initiative restores "real" medieval literature to the landscape in a way that gets back to the very clear literary, historical, and geographical roots of that literature. The Pathways certainly raise the profile of medieval texts that may have been ignored in the traditional canon. The project also demonstrates a local and regional response to the overwhelming attention paid to works like the *Nibelungenlied* on a national level. The installations of the *Steirische Literaturpfade* offer additional ways to construct new narratives firmly based on scholarly research and engagement with the texts. When one compares these installations to monuments like those in Tulln and Pöchlarn or museums like the Nibelung Museum in Worms, the Pathways clearly work toward a different goal. The goal is to focus and re-focus attention on the medieval texts themselves: their language (Middle High German and translation into modern German), their textual environment (manuscript and some bibliographical information), their message (in distilled and more expansive form), and their historical and geographical context. The unique strength of these Pathways is how they connect the physical environment of a text's inspiration and possible production with its message. These are small towns that have long celebrated, more or less publicly, the legacy of their medieval past—in poets, in structural landmarks such as castles, in narratives, in manuscripts, and in local names of towns and families. The project that led to the literary paths illustrates an exemplary partnership among various stakeholders to make the literature visible in the landscape. The project was supported by the University of Graz, the University of Applied Arts in Graz (FH Joanneum), the provincial government, and the state archives—as well as municipal governments in each location in collaboration with museums, schools, and tourist offices. The Pathways project is many things: outreach to the public from the university, the reinvigoration of medieval studies, the assertion of the importance and the relevance not only of literature but specifically of older literature, and the support of local and regional history. The project also reveals an intentional desire to eschew the politics, sensationalism, marketing, and commercialization that can accompany some of these endeavors. With a distinct element of consciousness-raising, the *Literaturpfade* provide a kind of counterpoint, an alternative way of displaying and deploying the Middle Ages in local communities that still wish to preserve and celebrate their history. This alternative is a significant component supporting a sustainable cultural infrastructure in the modern memory landscape. The audience's response to, and relationship with, this public display has a significant impact on how these monuments integrate into, and reflect the identity of, their respective communities. Current projects seek even larger audiences through updated digital formats.[40] This question of relevance and sustainability remains for the monuments in Tulln and Pöchlarn; it was actively addressed for the *Siegfriedskopf*, whose relevance was rearticulated by the new concept that informed the current display.

New Memorylands: Leaving Siegfried Behind

The Austrian installations presented above demonstrate a unique intersection of memory, nostalgia, and visual culture in which a community seeks to adapt an older narrative to define changing identities; in short, they propose new narratives for older literature. Either they rehabilitate old narratives to create new ones (Tulln and even perhaps Pöchlarn), or they are changed to reflect changed and changing circumstances (*Siegfriedskopf*), or they recover the older and still-existing narratives to bring them anew into contemporary consciousness (*Literaturpfade*). As these installations reimagine past (his)stories, they create fresh interfaces with the traditions that have perpetuated those stories over time. The medieval narrative past thus becomes reimagined as heritage for Austria today.

In this way, the installations reflect a uniquely Austrian contribution to the emerging "memorylands" of Europe where "land- and city-scapes have filled up with the products of collective memory work" that have only increased in recent decades.[41] In the newest Nibelung monuments particularly, the Danube communities of Pöchlarn and Tulln highlight Austria's geographical and ideological position not just in the middle of Europe but on a border between east and west, which has become increasingly significant. However, all the monuments prompt a re-examination of the values that they make tangible. The Austrian installations I have discussed here commemorate both historical and literary narratives; the installations mobilize those narratives to speak to modern audiences, to express the hope and the potential the texts embody. As the Second Republic has sought to walk the difficult line between fraught past and promising future since 1945, these monuments demonstrate Koshar's concept of emergent evolution in progress now. In their respective communities, the Nibelung monuments and the Styrian literature pathways foster a sense of identity and ownership based not only on a financial but also an intellectual investment, thereby reflecting a larger desire for renewal and cultural sustainability. If monuments are values made visible, then the Austrian installations inscribe those new values on the cultural landscape by turning the encounter with a fraught past into a foundation for cultural sustainability through productive dialogue into the future.

Such conversations are dynamic and ongoing in 2022, not only in Austria. Interestingly enough, a similar transformation occurred (ever so briefly) in Richmond, Virginia, during the summer of 2020, when demonstrations sparked by the Black Lives Matter movement turned a bright spotlight onto the statue of Robert E. Lee on the grand boulevard known as Monument Avenue. If the monuments to Confederate "heroes" in their "original placement and form" had previously insisted on the primacy of one historical and cultural narrative over another, then the spontaneous recontextualizations (and potential reconfigurations) of the Robert E. Lee statue that emerged during the 2020 demonstrations showed the strength of different narratives demanding to be heard.[42] Photographs show how the monument changed over the course of recent demonstrations—the ground around it became a colorful tapestry of signs and posters, as the statue itself was similarly covered. In those moments, the new images and words that enfolded the Lee monument recalled the reconfiguration of the *Siegfriedskopf*. The Lee statue has since come down, and many other Confederate monuments have been following in its wake. In Charlottesville, VA, the site of deadly right-wing violence in 2017, another statue of Robert E. Lee was dismantled and removed in 2021, and the city is now sponsoring an art campaign to "reimagine what belongs in the public square."[43] The *Siegfriedskopf* needed to be moved from the space it occupied at the institutional heart of the university; it had become the symbol of a legacy and past that had become increasingly contentious over time. Most Americans are not familiar with the *Nibelungenlied*—and even less so with Styrian literature of the Middle Ages. However, current US-American discussions of monuments to the Confederacy bring several contested issues to the fore as part of current culture wars, particularly concerning topics such as memory, commemoration, and memorials or public display. Like the myth of the Nibelungs, the myth of the Lost Cause in the US reverberates with overtones often amplified by a misappropriation of medieval narratives for social, cultural, or political purposes. The Middle Ages function consistently as a site of contention for those who would choose to re-imagine that period for their own purposes: nation-builders in the nineteenth century, the American South in its attempt to create a mythology to support racism, the Nazis in the early twentieth century, and white supremacists now.[44] The Austrian monuments at the center of this essay present dynamic interfaces between older narratives—sometimes obscured, sometimes illuminated by myth—and contemporary audiences as an invitation to reflect on other such interfaces between the medieval past and the modern present. A municipality like Tulln or Pöchlarn or any of the towns that host one of the Pathways—or a more multivalent community like the University of Vienna in the nation's capital—creates a new relationship with the older narrative of the *Nibelungenlied*, investing the new narrative with the significance that reflects how each community (city or university) wants to position itself with respect to its past in the present. The installations offer an opportunity to leave Siegfried behind, interrogate those other interfaces and engage in dialogue about reshaping them, and providing an imaginative model for deploying medievalism in a more plastic way that might allow for the incorporation of difficult conversations about the presence of the past.

Images

Figure 1. Tulln, Nibelungendenkmal (photo by author, taken June 2018)

Figure 2. University of Vienna, Siegfriedskopf (photo by the author, May 2019)

Figure 3 Stattegg, Steirische Literaturpfade des Mittelalters
(photo by the author, March 2020)

Endnotes

1 The project was designed in 2009 and implemented in 2012 by a creative team under the direction of Wernfried Hofmeister and Andrea Hofmeister Winter at the University of Graz. See Wernfried Hofmeister, "Altdeutsche Texts im Öffentlichen Raum. Projekt- und Forschungsbericht über das Netzwerk 'Steirische Literaturpfade des Mittelalters,'" *Zeitschrift für deutsches Altertum und deutsche Literatur* 143 (2014), 467–83. The project directors emphasize the aspect of sustainability as a key project goal. See also Wernfried Hofmeister and Andrea Hofmeister-Winter, "Alte Texte auf neuen Wegen: Gedanken zur literarhistorischen Nachhaltigkeit am Beispiel des regionalen Netzwerkprojekts 'Steirische Literaturpfade des Mittelalters,'" in *Literatur-Erlebnisse zwischen Mittelalter und Gegenwart: Aktuelle didaktische Konzepte und Reflexionen zur Vermittlung deutschsprachiger Texte. Unter Mitarbeit von Andrea Hofmeister-Winter*, ed. Wernfried Hofmeister and Ylva Schwinghammer (Frankfurt am Main: Peter Lang, 2015), 73–105. The project's website offers a visual overview: https://literaturpfade.uni-graz.at/de/.

2 Peter Wapnewski, "Das Nibelungenlied," in *Deutsche Erinnerungsorte*, ed. Etienne François and Hagen Schulze, vol. 1 (Munich: C.H. Beck, 2009), 159–70.

3 Friedrich von der Hagen, for example, passionately advocated for the *Nibelungenlied* as the German Iliad, as Wapnewski points out (Wapnewski, 162).

4 Volker Gallé, ed. *Siegfried: Schmied und Drachentöter* (Worms: Worms-Verlag, 2005).

5 This is one definition of medievalism. For an overview of the term and its history, see Elizabeth Emery and Richard Utz, eds., *Medievalism: Key Critical Terms* (Woodbridge: D.S. Brewer, 2014), here 2–3.

6 In Germany, a similar desire for reflection led to the design and construction of the Nibelungen Museum in Worms in 2001. See Alexandra Sterling-Hellenbrand, *Medieval Literature on Display: Heritage and Culture in Modern Germany* (London: Bloomsbury, 2020).

7 Susan Neiman, *Learning from the Germans: Race and the Memory of Evil* (New York: Farrar, Straus, and Giroux 2019), 266.

8 Aleida Assmann, *Der lange Schatten der Vergangenheit: Erinnerungskultur und Geschichtspolitik,* 2nd ed. (Munich: C.H. Beck, 2014), 17.

9 Assmann, *Der Lange Schatten*, 260.

10 See Sharon Macdonald, *Memorylands: Heritage and Identity in Europe Today* (London: Routledge, 2013) as well as Sharon Macdonald, *Difficult Heritage: Negotiating the Nazi Past in Nuremberg and Beyond* (London: Routledge, 2009). See also Neil MacGregor, *Germany: Memories of a Nation* (London: Trustees of the British Museum and the BBC, 2014).

11 The memory landscape (*Erinnerungslandschaft*) resonates both in personal and public spheres particularly due to "the collective meaning of certain buildings

or spaces." Rudy Koshar, *From Monuments to Traces: Artifacts of German Memory, 1870–1990* (Berkeley: University of California Press, 2000), 9.

12 Koshar, *From Monuments to Traces*, 13.

13 Koshar, *From Monuments to Traces*, 301.

14 Neiman, *Learning from the Germans*, 263.

15 Gundolf Graml, *Revisiting Austria: Tourism, Space, and National Identity, 1945 to the Present* (Berghahn, 2020), 110.

16 Alison Landsberg suggests that prosthetic memories are unique interfaces of individual and collective experience and "have no direct connection to a person's lived past and are yet essential to the production and articulation of subjectivity." See Alison Landsberg, *Prosthetic Memory: The Transformation of American Remembrance in the Age of Mass Culture* (New York: Columbia University Press, 2004), 20.

17 I paraphrase Graml's description of the function of the displays in Linz, as participating in "affective, prosthetic memory construction" (Graml, *Revisiting Austria*, 110).

18 Landsberg emphasizes the "usefulness" and the potential of prosthetic memory for consciousness raising and advocacy (Landsberg, *Prosthetic Memory*, 21). Graml applies this to the touristic infrastructure that "attempts to make history tangible and affective" and can perhaps "result in increased accessibility and new forms of knowledge" (Graml, *Revisiting Austria*, 107).

19 Such as sports clubs, like the bike club in Pöchlarn (accessed January 23, 2022, https://urc-nibelungen.at/).

20 Accessed January 23, 2022, https://www.donau.com/de/wachau-nibelungengau-kremstal/.

21 The present discussion of Tulln and Pöchlarn draws upon research that appears in an earlier article: Alexandra Sterling-Hellenbrand, "East Meets West? Heritage, Medievalism, and the *Nibelungenlied* on the Danube," *The Year's Work in Medievalism* 33 (2018), 1–11, accessed January, 23, 2022, https://sites.google.com/site/theyearsworkinmedievalism/all-issues/33-2018#h.p_ID_32.

22 Verses 1323–24. Citations from the *Nibelungenlied* are from *Das Nibelungenlied: Mittelhochdeutsch. Neuhochdeutsch. Nach der Handschrift B*, ed. Ursula Schluze and trans. Siegfried Grosse (Stuttgart: Reclam, 2010).

23 The city promotes this legacy to the public: "Das Nibelungendenkmal wurde von Heinz Knapp künstlerisch gestaltet und stellt einen Beitrag zum europaweiten Friedensgedanken dar." See "Nibelungendenkmal," accessed January, 23, 2022, https://www.poechlarn.at/Nibelungendenkmal.

24 The metal figures (Rüdiger, Hagen, Dietlinde und Giselher) were designed by artist Atanas Kolev and they speak with the recorded voices of Ursula Strauß and Prof. Klaus Behrendt. Accessed January, 24, 2022, https://www.poechlarn.at/Stadtrundgang.

25 Verse 1338. For the sake of expediency, I cite the English translation by Edwards here: *The Nibelungenlied: The Lay of the Nibelungs,* trans. Cyril Edwards (Oxford: Oxford University Press, 2010), 124.

26 Stijn Reijnders, *Places of the Imagination* (Burlington: Ashgate, 2011), 13–14.

27 Sterling-Hellenbrand, "East Meets West?," 7.

28 "Etzel's power was so widely known that at all times at his court the boldest of warriors ever heard of were to be found, be it among Christians or heathens—they had all made their way there with him. Those of the Christian faith, and also those of pagan beliefs, were about him at all times, all practicing their different ways of life—that may perhaps never come to pass again. The king's generosity saw to it that plenty was given to them all." See Schulze, *Nibelungenlied*, verses 1333–35; Edwards, *Lay of the Nibelungs,* 123.

29 Stijn Reijnders, "Stories that Move: Fiction, Imagination, Tourism," *European Journal of Cultural Studies* 19, no. 6 (2016), 672–89, 687.

30 For an earlier discussion of the updated Siegfriedskopf, see Alexandra Sterling-Hellenbrand, "Leaving Siegfried Behind: Reimagining Monuments in Austria and the American South," Botsbiberbiaas.org, accessed 23 January, 2022, https://botstiberbiaas.org/voices-reimagining_monuments/.

31 See Christoph Gnant, "The Refurbishment of the Main Building Aula and Arcaded Courtyard at the Beginning of the Twenty-First Century," in Julia Rüdiger, Dieter Schweizer, et al. eds., *Sites of Knowledge: The University of Vienna and Its Buildings: A History 1365 – 2015* (Vienna: Böhlau, 2015), 265–70, 265.

32 Gnant, "The Refurbishment," 266.

33 Gnant, "The Refurbishment," 268.

34 Accessed January 23, 2022, https://geschichte.univie.ac.at/de/artikel/kontroverse-siegfriedskopf.

35 See Margarete Grandner, Gernot Heiß, and Elisabeth Klamper, "Im Kampf um das Haupt des deutschen Helden Siegfried," *Forum* 444 (December 1990): 57–63.

36 Accessed January 23, 2022, http://www.photoglas.com/deutsch/buero_frameset.php?a=1&id=35.

37 This is a paraphrase of the dedication speech by Angelika Bäumer in July 2006. Accessed January 23, 2022, https://geschichte.univie.ac.at/de/artikel/denkmal-siegfriedskopf.

38 For the design background of the project, see Theresa Zifko's monograph *Literatur lokalisiert: museologische Überlegungen zur Präsentation von literarischen Texten mit besonderer Bezugnahme auf das Designkonzept des Projekts Steirische Literaturpfade des Mittelalters* (Frankfurt am Main: Peter Lang, 2013), here specifically 57–77.

39 The Pathways feature particularly in promotions for regional outdoor and cultural activities, as this for Stattegg: https://www.regiongraz.at/de/sport-und-freizeit/touren/stattegger-literaturpfad_tour_9001. Or as we see here on the

website for the monastery at Admont: https://www.stiftadmont.at/aussenanlagen/literaturpfad.

40 The Pathways are currently supported by the Universitätsverein "Steirische Literaturpfade des Mittelalters." For the Graz Museum of History (Museum für Geschichte) project director Wernfried Hofmeister recently collaborated with Anika Kronberger at the FH Joanneum to digitize the *Literaturpfad* at Unzmarkt as part of the Steiermark-Schau 2021: Accessed January 24, 2022, https://literaturpfade.uni-graz.at/de/neuigkeiten/detail/article/literaturpfad-im-digitalen-raum/.

41 Macdonald particularly places this memory work in the context of the dramatic changes in Europe since 1989, the re-unification of Germany and the collapse of the former Soviet Union (Macdonald, *Memorylands*, 1).

42 Regarding the Richmond demonstrations see Larissa Tracy, "Fascism and Chivalry in the Confederate Monuments of Richmond," *The Public Medievalist*, June 11, 2020, accessed September 7, 2020, https://www.publicmedievalist.com/confederate-monuments/.

43 National Public Radio journalist Debbie Elliott summarizes the developments: Debbie Elliot, "Confederate Monuments are Removed as Americans Consider How to Remember the Past," NPR.com, December 30, 2021, accessed January 24, 2022, https://www.npr.org/2021/12/30/1069027408/confederate-monuments-are-removed-as-americans-consider-how-to-remember-the-past.

44 See most recently, Amy Kaufman and Paul Sturtevant, *The Devil's Historians: How Modern Extremists Abuse the Medieval Past* (Toronto: University of Toronto Press, 2020).

The Formation of the Austrian Literary Field in the Post-War Period[1]

Christoph Leschanz

Introduction

Austrian literary life after 1945 is both separated from and connected to Germany. The question if there is something like "Austrian Literature" or not and how this kind of literature could be defined has been discussed for years and even decades[2] – without any final result. Austrian or German *Literaturgeschichte* sometimes uses terms like *Österreichische Literatur*, *Deutsche Literatur* and *Deutschsprachige Literatur* synonymously and it seems that while researchers of Austrian Studies speak and write – without any doubt – about Austrian Literature, colleagues in German departments without a focus on Austrian Studies will not hesitate to call Thomas Bernhard or Ingeborg Bachmann *German* rather than *Austrian* writers more often than not. This paper argues that a shift of perspective could help solving the problem: If we look at an Austrian literary field instead of something like *Österreichische Literatur* there are parameters which allow to distinguish between different literary fields in different countries without the need of concepts such as *Nationalliteratur* that will always be linked to some sort of national identity or concept.

An Austrian literary field is not the same as Austrian Literature would be. The field of production of literary value at a specific time and in a specific territory – which could be a state, a nation, a language area and so on – are the most important aspects of field theory. For the analysis of such a literary field not only writers and their texts are important but also publishers, the media and academia or political and socioeconomic circumstances. They form the *space of possible*.[3] This sociological approach helps to integrate essential parts of literary production and literary life that are not addressed by classical literary studies and *Literaturgeschichte*. It is neither the text nor the author that is most important, but the whole literary field with its own history, hierarchy and rules. Every utterance in the literary field – such as a novel, a play, an interview et cetera – is only meaningful in connection with this history, hierarchy, and these rules. The interconnection between field and text is crucial for the analysis of literary work. The literary field (like any other social field) only exists due to the struggle of the different agents over (literary) legitimacy: "One of the central stakes in literary (etc.) rivalries is the monopoly of literary legitimacy."[4]

To survive as an author in a given literary field one must establish oneself in this field, knowing what is possible and what is impossible to do and to write at a certain point of time. If an agent does not possess these abilities he*she simply will not achieve a certain position in the literary field.[5] This kind of *Zeitgenossenschaft* for different agents and texts *can*, together with the specific rules and history of a literary field, be responsible for similarities of texts normally described by the *Literaturgeschichte*. They can be misunderstood and interpreted as something typically *Austrian* even though it is just the *Zeitgenossenschaft* and the literary field that are responsible. The specific "Austrianness" of "Austrian Literature" is an effect of the literary field and a label supporting specific strategies and position-takings of agents both in the literary and the scientific field.[6] Instead of looking at something like "Austrian Literature" it is necessary to reconstruct the Austrian literary field to understand the similarities and differences in texts that were produced from agents in this field. A field is constructed only by the constant struggle for power of its parts and therefore exists only if such a struggle exists. For the distinction of different literary fields, it is important to separate different struggles as they are indicators for different literary fields. Unfortunately, the works of Bourdieu do not describe suitably enough how to separate different (literary) fields in detail but there are possibilities to do so as I have described earlier.[7] If we take a closer look at something called the *effects of the fields* it is possible to separate different fields from another:

> We may think of a field as a space within which an effect of field is exercised, so that what happens to any object that traverses this space cannot be explained solely by the intrinsic properties of the object in question. The limits of the field are situated at the point where the effects of the field cease. Therefore, you must try by various means to measure in each case the point at which these statistically detectable effects decline. In the work of empirical research the construction of a field is not effected by an act of imposition.[8]

In the case of Austria and West Germany for example it is noticeable that on the one hand the *Gruppe 47* was not a major player in Austrian literary life after 1945 while on the other hand the conflict of the Austrian P.E.N. and the *Grazer Autorenversammlung* in 1973 was irrelevant for the Western German literary field. These are only two examples of such effects but if we dig deeper, we can find a lot more of them. A few of these *effects of the field* will be described in this article.

A closer look at the Austrian literary field in the period after World War II shows that there are very specific conditions and influences that separated the Austrian literary field from the German ones, especially the literary field of West Germany which is the one "closer" to Austria as both were democratic "Western" countries and not in the sphere of influence of the Soviet Union. These specific conditions and influences enabled and supported the construction of an independent Austrian literary field. There are of course interconnections between different literary fields as well (e. g., between the fields in Austria, West and East Germany) and agents can be part of more than just one field which is the case with many Austrian writers like Thomas Bernhard, Peter Handke or Elfriede Jelinek. They all held different positions in the different fields they are and were part of. The example of Robert Menasse in the late 1990s and early 2000s shows clearly how different these positions may be. Menasse was one of the most famous and important writers and intellectuals in Austria at that time and as an intellectual involved in different discourses – beside literary mainly political ones. In the German literary field, his role or position as either writer or intellectual were not comparable. The particular positions of agents in the Austrian and the (Western-)German literary field can be observed in many other cases as well. All these different *effects of the field* point towards an independent Austrian literary field in the given time period. Some examples for such effects are described in this article to present a first brief overview.

Characteristics of the Austrian Literary Field after the Second World War

The end of World War II marks a new beginning for the Austrian literary field although a lot of continuities existed between the new literary field and the preceding times of the *Austrofaschismus* and the NS regime.[9] In contrast to Germany, Austria received a milder treatment of the four allied forces due to the fact that they regarded Austria as the so called "first victim" of German aggression in the Moscow Declarations in 1943. This had effects also on literary life, but the biggest impact of course was the constitution of the Second Austrian Republic and therefore the separation from Germany. The Austrian literary market was isolated especially from the German one. Import and export of books and journals were restricted.[10] This fostered the emergence of an independent literary field. What is more, the Austrian state as well as the four occupying powers tried to stabilize the new Austrian independence to prevent a second *"Anschluss"*. This was to be achieved by strengthening a new "Austrian identity" based on Austrian history and high culture – especially classical music (*Wiener Staatsoper*, *Wiener Philharmoniker*, *Salzbuger Festspiele*) but also literature (*Burgtheater*) – and traditional *Heimat*-idyll. All that led to specific "Austrian circumstances". In addition, many of the famous pre-war generation of Austrian writers belonging to the autonomous pole of the literary field did not survive the time of the war: Robert Musil, Stefan Zweig, Karl Kraus, Ödön von Horvath or Joseph Roth are just some examples. Franz Werfel – honorary president of the Austrian P.E.N. in London exile – died shortly after the war had ended. Writers like Robert Neumann, Hermann Broch, Erich Fried, Theodor Kramer or Ernst Waldinger decided to stay abroad while writers like Friedrich Torberg, Hilde Spiel, Felix Braun or Berthold Viertel returned only years after the war had ended.[11] It is not only a singular event or factor that led to an independent Austrian literary field but an interplay of different circumstances. Some of them shall serve as an example in this article to highlight some of the most important ones:

1) The Austrian field of power
2) Cultural Policy of the *Große Koalition*: Österreich-Ideologie
3) The cultural policies of the occupying forces
4) The separation of the Austrian literary market

The Austrian Field of Power

The first step of the reconstruction of any (literary) field is to "analyze the position of the field vis-à-vis the field of power".[12] It is necessary to define the relevant agents, institutions, and forms of capital that are important in the struggle for power in a specific field. All these factors vary according to the type of field, period of time and where the field is situated: "The field of power is the space of relations of force between agents or between institutions having in common the possession of the capital necessary to occupy the dominant positions in different fields (notably economic and cultural). It is the site of struggles between holders of different powers (or kinds of capital)."[13]

Unfortunately, the concept of the field of power and its interaction with the literary field is only vaguely defined by Bourdieu in his work and was both criticized and reworked to be suitable for a globalized world.[14] Nevertheless his analysis of the state nobility[15] can serve as a foundation for the theoretical basis of the analysis of both the field of power itself and the position of the literary field in the field of power. Bourdieu's work on French elite schools and the reproduction of social hierarchy are a blueprint for further research in other social spaces at different times and therefore also for the Austrian case. All participants in the struggle for social dominance in the field of power are always trying to legitimate their personal source of power – whatever sort of capital that may be – to naturalize their power:

> This struggle over the power to dictate the *dominant principle of domination*, which leads to a constant state of equilibrium in the partition of power, in other words, to a *division in the labor of domination* [...], is also a struggle over *the legitimate principle of legitimation* and, inseparable, the legitimate mode of reproduction of the foundations of domination.[16]

Hence it is necessary to define the relevant players in this struggle and, depending on the social space and the specific period of time, these players may vary significantly. The French field of power in the 1960s and 1970s is not comparable with the contemporary field of power in the United States and the Austrian field of power in the post-war period is not identical with the present one – even though there will likely be continuities and overlaps.

For our case of the Austrian field of power and its influence on the literary field we therefore must define the relevant players of the Austrian social space in the post-war period. For this time the power of the political field in Austria is striking. The influence of both of the grand parties in Austria, the ÖVP and the SPÖ was not limited to the political sphere but extended to nearly all areas of social space, covering economy (*Verstaatlichte Industrie*), media (Öffentlicher Rundfunk: RAVAG, ORF) and cultural life (*Bundesmuseen* and *Bundestheater*) to name just a few. For example: "Management positions in the nationalized industries and in the nationalized big banks with their own industrial complex [were] sometimes meticulously regulated."[17] Since the mid-1950s, a rigid *Proporz* had established itself within the state broadcasters. Even the personnel of the *Austria Wochenschau* was linked to the two parties. There were two directors and the exact screen-time of politicians of each of the two parties were clocked for equal publicity.[18] Besides that the ÖVP as well as the SPÖ owned different newspapers and magazines with a significant circulation and different publishing houses. The conservative Catholic publishers also have to be taken into account.[19] If we take a closer look at public funding of literary life through individual grants, we find that nearly all of them were issued by the official state bureaucracy and therefore highly connected to the ruling parties and the responsible ministers for education and cultural affairs.[20]

With the exception of a brief period in 1945 the ÖVP was responsible for the *Bundesministerium für Unterricht* where all cultural decisions were made from 1945 until 1970. The Austrian field power in the post-war period was mainly controlled by the two ruling parties ÖVP and SPÖ whose combined percentage at elections never fell below eighty percent between 1945 and 1980 and repeatedly reached even ninety-five percent.[21] From the end of the Second World War until 1966 both parties ruled together, forming the Austrian "consociational democracy, often fancied as *Proporz* democracy."[22]

Due to the overarching influence of the political field in the postwar period the position of the literary field in the field of power is mostly defined by its relation to the political field and to state bureaucracy (at a wider scale, including e.g. the *Bundestheater*) which were closely tied to it. The cultural policies of the Austrian administrations between 1945 and 1970 are crucial for the literary field in that period. Together with the cultural policies of the four occupying forces that will be addressed later, they constitute the main influence on the Austrian literary field in that period.

Cultural Policy of the *Große Koalition*: *Österreich-Ideologie*

The cultural policy of the early Second Republic focused primarily on the creation and stabilization of something like a "new Austrian identity" in opposition to Germany and any form of *Deutschtum*. While the official state policy in the time of the *Austrofaschismus* tried to combine these two ideologies—as with Engelbert Dollfuß in his *Trabrennplatz* speech in 1933[23]—the postwar agenda was very clear: "Austrian" from 1945 onwards was above all one thing and namely *not German*.[24] The four occupying forces supported these efforts. Tradition, *Heimat*, imperial Austro-Hungarian high culture—especially classical music but also literature—and traditional Catholic virtues were the main parts of the construction of this new "Austrian identity" that was presented as something that dated back centuries. The responsibility for war crimes and the Holocaust, committed by Austrians as well as by Germans and the fascist regime of Dollfuß and Schuschnigg in the time of *Austrofaschismus* were ignored. It would take until the 1980s and the Waldheim Affair to change that. Until then the past offered salvation as Alexander Lernet-Holenia—who would become president of the Austrian P.E.N. nearly 25 years later—wrote in 1945:

> Indeed, we need only continue where a madman's dreams have interrupted us; indeed, we need not look ahead, only look back. To put it perfectly clearly: we do not need to flirt with the future and

> do nebulous projects, we are, in the best and most valuable sense, our past, we only have to remember that we are our past - and it will become our future.[25]

In similar words the Austrian chancellor Leopold Figl after the first postwar elections after spoke in November 1945 about "our old culture" and "our cultural mission".[26] Hans Pernter – vice chairman of the ÖVP in 1945 and responsible for their cultural program – wrote in 1945:[27]

> The Austrian person is a reality, a product of Austrian nature and Austrian culture. It must be a lofty goal of Austrian cultural policy, through the formation of the Austrian people, to consciously commit to the Austrian nation, which should take a place of honor among the cultural nations of the world.[28]

These are just a few examples for the cultural guidelines of the Second Republic but they show quite clearly which kind of culture – and therefore literature – was suitable for the newly formed state. Everything should be "Austrian" and the worst accusation in that time in regard to cultural activities was that something is "German". The school subject *Deutsch* was changed to *Unterrichtssprache* and "no worse accusation could be made against a textbook than that of being German-friendly." School books were "cleansed" of "German heroism."[29] In contrast to the "typical German" with his characteristics – as Hofmannsthal already wrote in 1917 – "state-mindedness (*Staatsgesinnung*) as something that holds us together, more virtue, more proficiency," the Austrians should be characterized through "Love of the *Heimat* as something that holds us together, more piety, more humanity."[30] These stereotypes were used from the beginning of the Second Republic onwards and continued to transform into auto-stereotypes of Austrian identity until today.

The implementation of this new "Austrian identity" was common practice throughout the whole social space. If we take a closer look at the Austrian *Jungbürgerbuch* of the year 1961, which each young citizen who attained legal adulthood received, we can find a definition of literature that defines very well the goals of cultural policy at that time:

> Every book lives from the soil from which it grows. Thus we experience gripping human destinies in *Heimat* books, this is how we get to know our country and love it with the help of the poets of our *Heimat*. And there are books in which there is not a word about

> Austria, in which no province, no mountain, no lake of our homeland is named, which are therefore not „*Heimat* books“ - and in which every word, every sound, every motif is genuinely Austrian.[31]

In this official book for young Austrians, Grillparzer is also quoted: "Proclaiming Austria is a service to humanity"[32] and Austria was above all a traditional Catholic *Heimat* and the legacy of the Imperial Austro-Hungarian Empire. The *Sissi*-Trilogy of Ernst Marischka stands as a good example for the propagated image of Austria.

Official literary prizes followed the same alignment and, in addition, strong continuities existed between award recipients from the time of the *Austrofaschismus* and even the NS-regime and the Second Republic. Erna Blaas, Bruno Brehm, Arthur Fischer-Colbrie, Robert Hohlbaum, Franz Karl Ginzkey, Paula Grogger and Max Mell received several official literary awards after 1945, including the *Großer österreichischer Staatspreis für Literatur* or different awards of Austrian states and cities. All of them also had published during the time of the NS Regime in the *Bekenntnisbuch österreichischer Schriftsteller (1938)* or *Die Ostmark erzählt (1941)*.[33] While these ties did not go unnoticed and were criticized in the contemporary literary field (for example in the literary journal *PLAN*), other ties – mostly to the *Austrofaschismus* seldom or never raised any opposition. A lot of the involved agents of that time held important positions in crucial parts of the state and media. Rudolf Henz for example, before and after the German annexation the director of the public broadcasting station *RAVAG* and co-founder of the Austrian P.E.N.-Club after the war, also writer and *Staatspreisträger für Literatur 1953*, important figure in post war literary life in Austria also was the author of the *Dollfußlied* in 1935.[34] He was also publisher of the important literary journal *Wort in der Zeit* and head of the Austrian *Kunstsenat* from 1967 until 1980.[35] Henz is just another example for the entanglement of pre- and postwar Austria as well as for the entanglement between the literary field and the field of politics in Austria at that time.

To sum up, it is not surprising that this conservative focus on something like *Heimat* and "Austrian tradition" fostered a specific environment for the Austrian literary field of that time that was very different from the circumstances in West and East Germany and therefore helped to stabilize an independent Austrian literary field. Everything "German" was banished from the official Austrian agenda and that also benefited the independence of Austrian literary life.

The Cultural Policies of the Occupying Forces

Beside the cultural policies of the Austrian administrations the four occupying powers also had an interest in stabilizing the newly formed republic. They wanted to strengthen an independent Austria to prevent a second "Anschluss" and thereby weaken Germany.[36] After tensions increased between the United States and the United Kingdom on the one hand and the Soviet Union on the other hand at the beginning of the Cold War from 1947 onwards an independent Austria also served geopolitical and geostrategic purposes for the opposing great powers. While in the beginning and the direct aftermath of the war their main focus lay on denazification and a so called "re-orientation" of the population[37] this changed abruptly after the conflict between the "West" and the "East" gained momentum. The Cold War also left its marks on Austria and the cultural fields:

> Almost everything, from sports to ballet, from radio and comics to space travel, acquired political significance and could be used as a potential weapon to undermine opinion formation at home and in hostile societies abroad.[38]

The Soviet Union, France, the United Kingdom, and the United States all engaged in cultural politics in the time of occupation between 1945 and 1955. They funded several guest performances of artists, different exchange programs, had their own publishing houses as well as media and broadcasting stations or libraries.[39]

The Soviet Union began right after their conquest of Vienna in April 1945 with the reconstruction of cultural life. This of course was intended to influence the population in their favor but also strengthen the autonomy and independence of the new Austrian state. Already on 27 April the *Wiener Philharmoniker* performed their first concert and operas and theaters opened shortly afterwards. All that happened before the official surrender of the Wehrmacht and the end of the war.[40] Just a few weeks later, in May 1945, the *Gesellschaft zur Pflege der kulturellen und wirtschaftlichen Beziehungen zur Sowjetunion* (sometimes called the Österreichisch-Sowjetische Gesellschaft, *ÖSG*) was founded. The Soviet troops also supported the reconstruction of the *Staatsoper* – a very important symbolic act[41] and funded the *Scala Theater* in Vienna. Besides that the two Austrian writers and members of the KPÖ Ernst Fischer and Viktor Matejka both received important positions in the political field: Fischer became *Staatssekretär* in the Provisional State Government (until the end of 1945) and Matejka *Stadtrat* in the city council of Vienna (until 1949). Both of them were responsible for cultural affairs and therefore had much influence on the literary field.

While the resources of France and the United Kingdom were limited, the United States funded many different cultural institutions and programs between 1945 and 1955. They even had their own theatre, the *Kosmos-Theater* in Vienna. Their broadcasting station *Rot-Weiß-Rot* helped young Austrian artists like Ingeborg Bachmann, Milo Dor, Reinhard Federmann, Herbert Eisenreich or Jörg Mauthe with their first steps in the literary field through employment in the cultural sector. Other important figures of Austrian literary life like Hans Weigel also worked for *Rot-Weiß-Rot*.[42] Because of the lack of interest of the Austrian audience in politics, *Rot-Weiß-Rot* started different "typically Austrian" programs and radio-shows like *Unsere Radiofamilie* (Bachmann wrote some scripts for that serial) and *1000 Worte Österreichisch*.[43] Especially the latter shows how the policies of the Information Service Branch (ISB) of the United States also supported the already mentioned attempts to boost the new Austrian identity. The ISB recruited its personnel mainly from the local population. In 1947 the ISB employed only 67 US citizens but 707 Austrians.[44] Some of them were or would later become important figures in the Austrian literary field. A few already have been mentioned, others where Marcel Prawy or also Ernst Haeusermann, program director at *Rot-Weiß-Rot* and later head of the *Kosmos-Theater*, afterwards the *Theater in der Josephstadt* and finally, after the *Staatsvertrag* and when the occupying forces had already left, director of the *Burgtheater* from 1959 until 1968.[45]

The example of Ernst Haeusermann shows very clearly how the Austrian cultural fields were entangled with the cultural policies and cultural initiatives of the occupying powers. Other agents who were part of the literary field like Ernst Fischer or Viktor Matejka even held political positions. For a lot of writers the newspapers, theaters, (literary) journals or broadcasting stations of the United States, France, the United Kingdom and the Soviet Union offered employment and the possibilities to establish themselves in the literary field. It is necessary to mention that all these institutions were led separately from East or West German ones as the policies for Austria and Germany differed, due to the already mentioned Moscow Declarations from 1943. In contrast to Germany, the Allies only intended "reorientation"policies for the Austrians instead of "re-education-policies" as they were implemented in Germany.[46] The separation from Germany and the efforts to foster an Austrian identity independent from any kind of "*Deutschtum*" not only stabilized the newly formed Second Republic but also led to a somewhat isolated state in different areas. The literary market

– which depended to a high degree on the sales potentials in Germany – was one of them.

The Separation of the Austrian Literary Market

After the end of the war in 1945 the supply of goods for everyday needs in Austria was highly limited which had also effects on the literary field as, for example, the supply of paper was scarce.[47] In addition, the separation of Austria from Germany led to the isolation of the Austrian book market from the German, which historically used to be the most important export market for Austrian publishers and a source of income for Austrian writers. The Austrian publishing house Zsolnay for example sold 68 percent of its books before the war in Germany and only 12 percent in Austria and this case was no exception but rather typical.[48] Furthermore most of the writers had strong ties with Germany as well:

> Many of them maintained very close ties to German publishers; working for German magazines and newspapers was also an important source of income for many, and hardly anyone could have made a living from selling their books in Austria alone.[49]

The isolation after 1945 led to several problems: first of all, the obvious problem of the impossibility of selling Austrian editions in Germany but also more extensive ones like copyrights or import of books, newspapers and journals. Many writers who had fled to exile between 1933/34 and 1945 had signed contracts with publishers in exile for the rights of their works. Because the import and export and the exchange of foreign currencies was strictly regulated after the war it was impossible to acquire these rights for Austrian publishing houses even when the publishers abroad were willing to sell them, which was not always the case.

Although it was possible to reach agreements with different countries like Switzerland[50] or France,[51] regarding the import and export of books in the following years, it took until 1948 for the first agreements with Germany.[52] Even then it took another five years until 1953 for a full liberalization of book trade with West Germany. Only then did import and export properly function with the most important export market for Austrian publishers. In the meantime, a lot of regulations and problems remained: "The mailing of pamphlets to Germany [was] still forbidden by the Allies in 1949."[53] And still in 1951 German publishers were not allowed to send review copies or advertisement material worth more than 100 Schilling to Austria by post without the approval of the Austrian Foreign Trade Commission.[54]

As a consequence of the isolation from the German market the Austrian literary field had no choice but to develop their own mechanisms and hierarchies. Beside the effects for publishers, the situation also affected writers directly. Exchange with German colleagues was limited, reading tours impossible. A proper positioning in the German literary field where the payment for literary articles or scripts for broadcasting stations significantly exceeded the Austrian ones was impossible. The isolation even was a problem for writers in exile who were willing to return to their home country and wanted to return to Austria. They faced various difficulties after the war had ended:

> The fact is that in the immediate post-war period only American government officials or military personnel were allowed to cross the Atlantic, so-called „Austrian Refugees" - Austrians who had retained Austrian citizenship – could travel from the spring of 1946, those who had accepted American citizenship were also allowed to do so only if they represented special American interests.[55]

It is therefore not surprising that the highest and most prestigious positions of the newly forming literary field were held by either the few writers belonging to the autonomous pole of the literary field that did return early like Hans Weigel, Ernst Fischer or Ernst Lothar (who wrote one of the rare Austrian bestsellers in 1947: *Der Engel mit der Posaune*) or the writers that had not left the country at all like Heimito von Doderer or the more conservative ones like Rudolf Henz or Alexander Lernet-Holenia.

Another limiting factor for the literary field in the immediate post-war period was the shortage of paper even though the Austrian paper industry had not suffered that much during the war and the paper mills and printing houses were mostly intact. While 18,000 tons of paper had been produced in Austria in 1937, in 1946 production only reached 7,200 tons. Moreover, a significant share of that amount – approximately half of it – was exported to acquire foreign currencies for foreign trade.[56] The domestic allocation of paper was limited and the demands of the publishing houses could not be met. In March 1948 only 200 tons were distributed to the printers while more than six times that amount had been requested. In 1946 the situation had been even worse. The publishers received on average only 200 kilograms of the 2,500 kilograms they had requested.[57] Therefore many of the publishers tried to cover their needs through the black market which further reduced the available official supply.[58]

The paper shortages of the years 1945-48 led to conflicts in the publishing scene and affected the literary field. Books were one of the goods that were relatively easy to produce to cover the needs of consumer goods after the war, but they were in short supply: "They could not have produced as many books as they could have sold."[59] The practice of paper rationing led to heated discussions of that topic:

> The most unbelievable impertinence that the bureaucratization of the paper sector places on a publishing company, apart from a few 'favorites of fate,' is that a newly founded committee, the so-called Paper Commission, decides in a secret and authoritarian manner who will be blessed with a paper allocation and who will not. […] Instead, according to a key that only God knows who came up with, only certain favorite children are taken into account in, as I said, secret and authoritarian commission decisions, while the publishing programs of other companies are unhesitatingly and autocratically dropped.[60]

Othmar Helwich, at that time managing director of the *Papierkommission der österreichischen Buch-, Kunst- und Musikalienverleger* countered:

> Finding so much nonsense crammed into such a small space is almost no longer humorous. […] First it says a: "...newly created body, the so-called Paper Commission..." A telephone call would have been enough to ascertain that the "newly created body, the so-called paper commission" has existed for two years! The publishing house of the author of the letter cannot be older than two months if the establishment of the paper commission is so new to him that he only now found out about its existence. Secondly, it says: "... In book publishing it is well known that the publishing programs have to be submitted to the Federal Ministry for Education for approval of the paper allocation..." Well, in book publishing it is not like that! And it never was! Publishing programs have never had to be submitted to the Federal Ministry of Education „for approval of paper allocation" and the Federal Ministry of Education has never given „paper allocation approval". But every real publisher knows that. Thirdly, it says: "...one would think that the commission set up for the allocation of paper would

> have the duty to distribute the quotas allocated to the individual publishers accordingly . . ." It does! Namely: distribute the paper to the individual publishers as required. Fourth, it says: ". . . Instead, they're working from a key that God knows who came up with. . ." A simple telephone inquiry would have shown that no key, which God knows no one could have thought up, was distributed. Fifth, it says: „Instead, only certain favorite children are taken into account in secret and authoritarian commission decisions..." Secret? Naturally and self-evidently and thank God! Authoritarian? The Commission is made up of publishers' representatives! (This, too, could easily have been ascertained from a telephone inquiry.) And: „Only certain favorite children?" In response to a telephone inquiry I would have informed you that the January 1948 contingent of 300 tons included 351 favorite children! That wouldn't have been a secret at all.[61]

The reprint of some of Karl Heinrich Waggerl's books in the *Otto-Müller-Verlag* also led to discussions. Waggerl had published in the already mentioned *Bekenntnisbuch* that had honored the *"Anschluss"* in 1938 and had already been a famous author at the time of the *Austrofaschismus*. Therefore and because there was such a limited paper supply, the plan of issuing reprints of his works was criticized. Among others Viktor Matejka wrote about that case and also pointed to the problems that some antifascist writers had publishing at that time while books from people like Waggerl received new editions. In the end the *Otto-Müller-Verlag* did not receive the requested paper for the print run, but the revised edition was published anyway – most likely with the help of the black market.[62]

The statements in the *Anzeiger* and the *Causa Waggerl* are just two examples of the internal conflicts in the literary field that took place over the distribution of paper quotas. Like the other *effects of the field* already presented they were also strictly bound to Austria and the Austrian literary field without any connections to the German occupation zones which exemplifies the seclusion of the Austrian case once more.

Conclusion

The formation of the Austrian literary field after the end of the war in 1945 was influenced by a lot of different factors like the cultural policies of the new Austrian administrations as well as the policies of the four occupying powers. The isolation from Germany and the German book market as well as the shortage in paper supplies are additional aspects that have to be taken into account when reconstructing the literary field of that time. The examples presented have shown that there are several circumstances that were very specific for the Austrian case without any connection to Germany or German literary life. The situation in Germany, with the formation of West and East Germany, was utterly complex on its own. The Austrian literary field with its internal struggles and quarrels like the debates about the re-formation of the Austrian P.E.N.-Club focused primarily on national affairs.[63] The influences from Germany (mainly West Germany) were marginal and the *Gruppe 47* for example until 1950 nearly unknown.[64] Together with the strong focus of the official Austrian administrations until the 1960s on the construction and implementation of something like a new "Austrian identity" that should not appear "new" at all but rather as something very old, conceived through centuries, forming the *Österreichische Menschen*,[65] literature should play and played its part in supporting the newly formed state.[66] The literary field therefore both acted as a companion in this process of stabilizing the new Austrian state and received invaluable support in constructing an independent literary field in return. The value of cultural capital increased throughout the whole social space of the nation because the main focus of Austrian identity – beside the myth of *Heimat* and *Tradition* – lay on the so called "Austrian high culture" of which literature and the *Burgtheater* as its most important symbol were an integral part. This enhancement of the value of cultural capital should not be underestimated because it formed the basis of legitimacy of the high value of culture and literature throughout the Austrian social space. So called "Austrian high culture and literature" therefore needed to be supported and funded by the state because national identity was based on it. That led directly to extensive funding of literature in the following decades – until today. The postwar period and the formation of the Austrian literary field at that time, therefore, are also crucial for the understanding of the course of events in the following decades and the rise of a new generation of writers that today are summarized under the label *Österreichische Literatur* including Thomas Bernhard, Ingeborg Bachmann, Ernst Jandl, or the two Nobel Prize winning authors Elfriede Jelinek and Peter Handke. This new generation was able to present itself as the new *Avantgarde* because an independent Austrian literary field had been established in the years before. The inner-Austrian conflict was also crucial for their accumulation of symbolic capital but this topic has to be explored somewhere else.

Endnotes

1 This article presents some results of the ongoing research project "Das österreichische literarische Feld in der Nachkriegszeit" at the Department of Comparative Literature of the University of Vienna, funded by the Austrian Academy of Sciences.

2 Albrecht Schöne et al., eds., *Kontroversen, Alte Und Neue: Akten Des VII. Internationalen Germanisten-Kongresses, Göttingen, 1985: Band 10: Vier Deutsche Literaturen? Literatur Seit 1945 – Nur Die Alten Modelle? Medium Film – Das Ende Der Literatur?* (Tübingen: Max Niemeyer, 1986).

3 Pierre Bourdieu, *The Rules of Art: Genesis and Structure of the Literary Field* (Stanford: Stanford University Press, 1995), 234–39.

4 Bourdieu, *The Rules of Art*, 223–27.

5 Bourdieu, *The Rules of Art*, 236, 261–64.

6 Bourdieu, *The Rules of Art*, 231–34; Pierre Bourdieu and Loïc J. D. Wacquant, *An Invitation to Reflexive Sociology* (Cambridge: Polity, 1992), 98–99.

7 Christoph Leschanz, "Der Nationalstaat als überholte Ordnungskategorie im Zeitalter der Weltliteratur? Ein methodischer Vorschlag zur Abgrenzung verschiedener literarischer Felder als Alternative," in *Vom Sammeln Und Ordnen*, ed. Paul Ferstl et al., Internationale Forschungen zur Allgemeinen und Vergleichenden Literaturwissenschaft 211 (Berlin: Weidler, 2022).

8 Bourdieu and Wacquant, *An Invitation to Reflexive Sociology*, 100.

9 Joseph McVeigh, *Kontinuität und Vergangenheitsbewältigung in der österreichischen Literatur nach 1945,* Untersuchungen zur österreichischen Literatur des 20. Jahrhunderts 10 (Vienna: Braumüller, 1988); Uwe Bauer, "Kontinuität – Diskontinuität: Die Zäsuren 1933 – 1938 – 1945 im österreichischen literarischen Leben. Zum Problem des Begriffs 'Literarische Epoche,'" in *Literaturgeschichte: Österreich: Prolegomena und Fallstudien*, ed. Wendelin Schmidt-Dengler, Johann Sonnleitner, and Klaus Zeyringer, Philologische Studien und Quellen 132 (Berlin: E. Schmidt, 1995).

10 Heinz Lunzer, "Der literarische Markt 1945–1955," in *Literatur der Nachkriegszeit und der Fünfziger Jahre in Österreich*, ed. Friedbert Aspetsberger, Norbert Frei, and Hubert Lengauer, Schriften des Instituts für Österreichkunde 44/45 (Vienna: Österreichischer Bundesverlag, 1984), 25–32.

11 Peter Eppel, "Bemerkungen zur Frage der Rückkehr österreichischer Emigranten aus den USA," in *Eine schwierige Heimkehr: Österreichische Literatur im Exil 1938–1945*, ed. Johann Holzner, Sigurd P. Scheichl, and Wolfgang Wiesmüller, Innsbrucker Beiträge zur Kulturwissenschaft Germanistische Reihe 40 (Innsbruck: Institut für Germanistik, University of Innsbruck, 1991).

12 Bourdieu and Wacquant, *An Invitation to Reflexive Sociology*, 104.

13 Bourdieu, *The Rules of Art*, 215.

14 Larissa Buchholz, "What Is a Global Field? Theorizing Fields Beyond the Nation-State," *The Sociological Review* 64 (2016), https://doi.org/10.1111/2059-7932.12001; Christian Schneickert, Andreas Schmitz, and Daniel Witte, *Das Feld der Macht: Eliten – Differenzierung – Globalisierung* (Wiesbaden: Springer Fachmedien, 2020).

15 Pierre Bourdieu, *The State Nobility: Elite Schools in the Field of Power* (Stanford: Stanford University Press, 1996).

16 Bourdieu, *The State Nobility*, 265.

17 Oliver Rathkolb, *Die paradoxe Republik*: Österreich 1945 bis 2015 (Vienna: Zsolnay, 2015), 78–79.

18 Rathkolb, *Die paradoxe Republik*, 78-79.

19 Hans P. Fritz, "Buchstadt und Buchkrise: Verlagswesen und Literatur in Österreich 1945–1955" (PhD diss., University of Vienna, 1989), accessed February 21, 2022, https://www.wienbibliothek.at/sites/default/files/files/buchforschung/fritz-peter-buchstadt.pdf, 98.

20 Hans Temnitschka, "Die Rolle der Kulturbürokratie: Der Entscheidungsnotstand des Beamten im Förderungswesen," in *Kulturlandschaft Österreich: Analysen und Kritische Beiträge*, ed. Otto Staininger (Vienna: Europaverlag, 1977); Reingard Rauch-Keller, *Kunstförderung: Die Subventionierung zeitgenössischen Kunstschaffens durch den Bund,* Maske und Kothurn: Internationale Beiträge zur Theaterwissenschaft, Beiheft 10 (Vienna: Böhlau, 1981).

21 Bundesministerium für Inneres, "Nationalratswahlen: Historischer Rückblick," accessed Feb. 21, 2022, https://www.bmi.gv.at/412/Nationalratswahlen/Historischer_Rueckblick.aspx.

22 Rathkolb, *Die paradoxe Republik*, 77.

23 A short excerpt from Dollfuss' speech shows very clearly how Austria was understood as a "German nation" by the Austrofascists: "Wir wollen den sozialen christlichen deutschen Staat Österreich. Ja, wir sind deutsch, so selbstverständlich deutsch, daß es als überflüssig vorkommt, das eigens zu betonen. (Bravo!) Wir haben deutsche Kultur in diesem christlichen Teil Mitteleuropas zu erhalten und in österreichischer Form für die christlich-deutsche Kultur zu gestalten. Wir überlassen das Urteil, wer schließlich dem Deutschtum besser gedient haben wird, nachkommenden Generationen." (We want the social Christian German state of Austria. Yes, we are German, so naturally German that it seems redundant to emphasize that specifically. (Bravo!) We must preserve German culture in this Christian part of Central Europe and shape it in Austrian form for Christian-German culture. We leave it to future generations to judge who will ultimately have served German culture better.) "Die Kundgebung der Vaterländischen Front," *Neue Freie Presse*, September 12, 1933, accessed February 21, 2022, https://anno.onb.ac.at/cgi-content/anno?aid=nfp&datum=19330912&seite=3.

24 Werner Suppanz, Österreichische Geschichtsbilder: *Historische Legitimationen in Ständestaat und Zweiter Republik,* Böhlaus zeitgeschichtliche Bibliothek 34 (Vienna: Böhlau, 1998), 32.

25 Alexander Lernet-Holenia, "Gruß des Dichters," *Der Turm: Monatsschrift für österreichische Kultur* 1, 4/5 (1945). "In der Tat brauchen wir nur dort fortzusetzen, wo uns die Träume eines Irren unterbrochen haben, in der Tat brauchen wir nicht voraus-, sondern nur zurückzublicken. Um es vollkommen klar zu sagen: wir haben es nicht nötig, mit der Zukunft zu kokettieren und nebulose Projekte zu machen, wir sind, im besten und wertvollsten Verstande, unsere Vergangenheit, wir haben uns nur zu besinnen, daß wir unsere Vergangenheit sind – und sie wird unsere Zukunft werden."

26 "Stenographisches Protokoll: Sitzung des Nationalrates, 2. Sitzung des Nationalrates der Republik Österreich," accessed Feb. 21, 2022, https://www.parlament.gv.at/PAKT/VHG/V/NRSITZ/NRSITZ_00002/imfname_141045.pdf, 26.

27 The concept of the Österreichischer *Mensch* was mainly developed in the interwar period from various writers and intellectuals – most of them part of the literary field of that time. To name just a few of them: Hugo von Hofmannsthal, Hermann Bahr, Robert Müller, Richard Schaukal, Anton Wildgans, or Robert Musil (Johnston, *Der österreichische Mensch*). Not all of them used the term Österreichischer Mensch but their works and thoughts about a typical "Austrianess" were used as important parts for the construction of an Austrian identity after World War II.

28 Hans Pernter, "Oesterreichische Kulturpolitik," Österreichische Monatshefte: *Blätter für Politik* 1 (1945): 8–9. "Der österreichische Mensch ist eine Realität, ein Produkt österreichischen Wesens und österreichischer Kultur. Es muß ein hohes Ziel österreichischer Kulturpolitik sein, über die Formung des österreichischen Menschen zum bewußten Bekenntnis zur österreichischen Nation zu kommen, die einen Ehrenplatz unter den Kulturnationen der Welt einnehmen soll."

29 Suppanz, Österreichische Geschichtsbilder, 33.

30 Hugo von Hofmannsthal, "Preusse und Österreicher: Ein Schema," in *Reden und Aufsätze 2: 1914–1924*, Hugo von Hofmannsthal: Gesammelte Werke in zehn Einzelbänden 9 (Frankfurt am Main: Fischer Taschenbuch Verlag, 1979), 459–61.

31 Österreich, unser Vaterland: *Jungbürgerbuch*, 4th edition (Vienna: Österreichischer Bundesverlag; Verlag für Geschichte und Politik; Verlag für Jugend und Volk, 1961), 127–28. "Jedes Buch lebt von dem Boden, dem es entwächst. So erleben wir packende Menschenschicksale in Heimatbüchern, so lernen wir unser Land kennen und lieben durch die Hilfe der Dichter unserer Heimat. Und es gibt Bücher, in denen kein Wort von Österreich steht, in denen kein Land, kein Berg, kein See unserer Heimat genannt ist, die also keine "Heimatbücher" sind –, und in denen doch jedes Wort, jeder Klang, jedes Motiv echt österreichisch ist."

32 *Österreich, unser Vaterland*, 10.

33 Michaela Judy, "Literaturförderung in Österreich: Untersuchungen zum Verhältnis von Literratur und staatlicher Förderungspolitik" (PhD diss., University of Vienna, 1984), 81.

34 "Rudolf Henz (1897-1987)," kunstsenat.at, accessed February 21, 2022, https://www.kunstsenat.at/preistraeger/CV/henz.htm.

35 Friedbert Aspetsberger, *Literarisches Leben im Austrofaschismus: Der Staatspreis*, Literatur in der Geschichte, Geschichte in der Literatur 2 (Königstein im Taunus: Hain, 1980), 113.

36 Oliver Rathkolb, "Kalter Krieg und politische Propaganda in Österreich 1945–1950," in *Kalter Krieg in Österreich: Literatur – Kunst – Kultur*, ed. Michael Hansel and Michael Rohrwasser, 11–34 (here 12–14).

37 Siegfried Beer, "Die Besatzungsmacht Großbritannien in Österreich 1945–1949," in Österreich unter alliierter Besatzung 1945–1955, ed. Alfred Ableitinger, Siegfried Beer, and Eduard G. Staudinger, 58; Reinhold Wagnleitner, *Coca-Colonisation und Kalter Krieg: Die Kulturmission der USA in Österreich nach dem Zweiten Weltkrieg*, Österreichische Texte zur Gesellschaftskritik 52 (Vienna: Verlag für Gesellschaftskritik, 1991), 82.

38 Stefan Maurer, Doris Neumann-Rieser, and Günther Stocker, *Diskurse des Kalten Krieges: Eine andere österreichische Nachkriegsliteratur*, Literaturgeschichte in Studien und Quellen 29 (Vienna: Böhlau, 2017), 464.

39 Wagnleitner, *Coca-Colonisation und Kalter Krieg*; Barbara Porpaczy, "Die französische Besatzung und die österreichische Nachkriegsidentität," in *Freiheit und Wiederaufbau: Tirol in den Jahren um den Staatsvertrag*, ed. Christian Fornwagner and Richard Schober, Veröffentlichungen des Tiroler Landesarchivs 14 (Innsbruck: Wagner, 2007); Johannes Feichtinger, "Die Kulturpolitik der Besatzungsmacht Großbritannien in Österreich," in Österreich unter Alliierter Besatzung 1945–1955, ed. Alfred Ableitinger, Siegfried Beer, and Eduard G. Staudinger.

40 Michael Wimmer, *Kultur und Demokratie: Eine systematische Darstellung von Kulturpolitik in Österreich* (Innsbruck: StudienVerlag, 2011), 93; Rathkolb, *Die paradoxe Republik*, 322.

41 Evelyn Deutsch-Schreiner, *Theater im "Wiederaufbau": Zur Kulturpolitik im österreichischen Parteien- und Verbändestaat* (Vienna: Sonderzahl, 2001), 101–7.

42 Joseph McVeigh, "'Ohne dass der Hörer kapiert…': Der Sender Rot-Weiß-Rot im Kalten Krieg," in Hansel and Rohrwasser, *Kalter Krieg in Österreich*, 265–79.

43 McVeigh, "'Ohne dass der Hörer kapiert,'" 273.

44 Oliver Rathkolb, "Die Entwicklung der US-Besatzungskulturpolitik zum Instrument des Kalten Krieges," in *Kontinuität und Bruch, 1938 – 1945 – 1955: Beiträge zur österreichischen Kultur- und Wissenschaftsgeschichte*, ed. Friedrich Stadler, Emigration – Exil – Kontinuität: Schriften zur zeitgeschichtlichen Kultur- und Wissenschaftsforschung 3 (Münster: LIT, 2004), 45; Wagnleitner, *Coca-Colonisation und Kalter Krieg*, 87.

45 Stadt Wien, Wien Geschichte Wiki, "Ernst Haeusermann," accessed February 21, 2022, https://www.geschichtewiki.wien.gv.at/Ernst_Haeusserman.

46 Beer, "Die Besatzungsmacht Großbritannien in Österreich 1945–1949," 58; Wagnleitner, *Coca-Colonisation und Kalter Krieg*, 82.

47 Lunzer, "Der literarische Markt 1945–1955," 27–28.

48 Norbert Bachleitner, Franz M. Eybl and Ernst Fischer, *Geschichte des Buchhandels in Österreich,* Geschichte des Buchhandels 6 (Wiesbaden: Harrassowitz, 2000), 301–4.

49 Bachleitner, Eybl, and Fischer, *Geschichte des Buchhandels*, 306.

50 Fritz, "Buchstadt und Buchkrise," 122–28.

51 Verein der Österreichischen Buch-, Kunst- und Musikalienhändler, *Anzeiger für den Buch-, Kunst- und Musikalienhandel* 1, January 1, 1947, 7.

52 Lunzer, "Der literarische Markt 1945–1955," 28.

53 Fritz, "Buchstadt und Buchkrise," 132.

54 Joseph McVeigh, "Lifting the Paper Curtain: The Opening of Austrian Literary Culture to Germany after 1945," *German Studies Review* 19/3 (1996): 482.

55 Eppel, "Bemerkungen zur Frage der Rückkehr österreichischer Emigranten aus den USA," 121.

56 Fritz, "Buchstadt und Buchkrise," 61.

57 Verein der Österreichischen Buch-, Kunst- und Musikalienhändler, *Anzeiger für den Buch-, Kunst- und Musikalienhandel. 7,* April 1, 1948, 4.

58 Christoph Kepplinger-Prinz and Elisabeth Prinz, "Kampf ums Papier: Literarische Produktion in Österreich um 1950," *Journal of Austrian Studies*, 48/3 (2015): 43.

59 Lunzer, "Der literarische Markt 1945–1955," 26.

60 Verein der Österreichischen Buch-, Kunst- und Musikalienhändler, *Anzeiger 7*, 3.

61 Verein der Österreichischen Buch-, Kunst- und Musikalienhändler, *Anzeiger 7*, 3–4.

62 Kepplinger-Prinz and Prinz, "Kampf ums Papier," 48–52.

63 Klaus Amann, *P.E.N: Politik, Emigration, Nationalsozialismus: Ein österreichischer Schriftstellerclub* (Vienna: Böhlau, 1984), 83–93.

64 McVeigh, "Lifting the Paper Curtain," 486–87.

65 William M. Johnston, *Der österreichische Mensch: Kulturgeschichte der Eigenart Österreichs,* Studien zu Politik und Verwaltung 94 (Vienna: Böhlau, 2010).

66 Birgit Scholz, *Bausteine österreichischer Identität in der österreichischen Erzählprosa 1945–1949* (Innsbruck: StudienVerlag, 2007).

"Musikland Österreich" and the Second Republic – A Myth to Create a Nation and Its Identity

Vanessa Maria Carlone and Bernhard Alexander Achhorner

Introduction

... Musik – ob dieses Land im Licht, im Schatten liegt,
Mit seiner Tonkunst hat es stets gesiegt.
So breitet sich der Töne Fülle aus:
Beethoven, Haydn, Mozart, Schubert, Strauß.[1]

The collective memory is particularly susceptible to politicized forms of recollection, because every society reconstructs and interprets its history backwards in relation to the present. Certain points of reference from the past often appear to be responsible for the determination of values, ideas, patterns of thought, or even images of the self or the other within communities. Furthermore, these points of reference function as a tool for self-definition and the assurance of identity.[2] The nostalgic heroization of important figures from the musical past is of central importance in the instrumentalization of the myths of Austria as a "cultural nation" and "land of music," which serves as a foundation of national identity, but also for the image construction and positioning of Austria in international political discourse.

Particularly after World War II, efforts to re-establish Austria politically through specific cultural and identity policy measures were the focus of political leaders, which is why decisive emphasis was placed on the musealization of the country's musical heritage. In this context, Austrian cultural policy was mainly oriented towards a so-called "culture of representation," which understood itself as "apolitical" and encouraged the passing on of clichés and well-established traditions from the "unburdened" period prior to 1945. At the same time, this political strategy served the normalization of social life, for which the "Habsburg myth," as well as the State Opera, festivals, Vienna Philharmonic Orchestra, and Sängerknaben, was adapted, which functioned in favor of tourism and was adapted to the respective political needs. The recourse to musical heroes such as Mozart, Haydn,

Schubert, and Strauß, as well as to a cultural heritage that has evolved over time essentially originated in the time of the Austro-Hungarian Empire. This trend was not, however, conveyed as a result of the political, social, and economic development of the small state of Austria after 1945, but rather as the remaining culture of a powerful political entity that had not existed since 1918.

This article will discuss the question of how the political functionalization and heroization of Austrian musical heritage has acted as a mediating instrument to enforce idealized, stylized, and mythologized forms of collective "Austrian" identity, and how it has contributed to the formation and establishment of the Second Republic. Therefore, after a brief introduction to Austria's self-perception and image as a "cultural superpower," the concept of cultural memory and its significance in the construction of (national) identity will be discussed. These identified mechanisms will be examined based on the example of the myth of "Musikland Österreich," with its processes of canonization, heroization, and the invention of traditions as nation building tools dissociated from the failures of the First Republic and the 1938-1945 period.

The concept of Austria as a "cultural superpower"

The cultural nation of Austria – with its reputation as a small state with great culture – takes advantage of an historically grown "Austrian heritage," which today determines the generally legitimized cultural identity of Austria on a national and international level.[3] By drawing on the extraordinary cultural achievements of the past, Austria's self-representation as a cultural superpower was intended to compensate for its political inability to act, and to emphasize the state's political independence in solving the country's identity crisis.[4] When looking back throughout the history of Austria, it becomes clear that the permanent search for identity can largely be explained by the continuously changing forms of state and government. Additionally, the various political and cultural parameters from the Habsburg Monarchy, the First Republic, the authoritarian *Ständestaat*, and the annexation to the Greater German Reich up to the Second Republic are further reasons for the protracted search for the essence and development of the Austrian self-identity.[5] For this reason, the relevant literature often refers to Austria as a "delayed" nation, since the nation-building process itself began relatively late, in contrast to Austria's neighboring countries.[6]

With the beginnings of the Second Republic post World War II, efforts to politically re-establish and position Austria in international political affairs by means of the stylization of Austria's "cultural heritage" were a strong focus of the country's political agenda. This ideology is expressed in the governmental declaration of Federal Chancellor Leopold Figl on December 21, 1945:[7] "Durch die Repräsentanz österreichischer Kultur [sollte Österreich] nicht nur als eigenständiger Staat, sondern auch als ernst zu nehmender Akteur im internationalen Umfeld wahrgenommen [...] werden."[8] Consequently, this strategy determined both Austria's image, which had been constructed for the international community, and the efforts to bring Austrian culture back into the international spotlight after 1945, as well as the inner (patriotic) self-perception of the Austrian population.[9] According to ambassador Emil Brix, every cultural policy measure implemented in Austria is evaluated according to its significance for the country's cultural identity, which makes cultural policy, to a certain extent, also educational policy.[10] As a result, the recourse to Austrian traditions and cultural heritage, as well as to extraordinary cultural merits and achievements of the past, became the identity-establishing elements of the young republic.[11]

Another central point of Austrian cultural policy after 1945 is the genesis of an institutionalized Austrian foreign cultural policy, which is closely related to the beginnings of the Second Republic. Both in domestic and foreign policy, responsibilities and competencies were newly regulated and standardized by the constitution of institutional frameworks, thus creating a modern transdisciplinary policy field.[12] This aspect also became apparent in Austria's efforts, which began in 1947, to establish an official institution for international cultural diplomacy.[13] For a long time, Austrian cultural policy and its cultural representation abroad were mainly oriented towards the great achievements of Austrians in the past. This seemingly nostalgic focus on the idealized period before 1945 in Austrian cultural self-representation was a strongly limiting element, causing Austrian (foreign) cultural policy to focus increasingly on the staging of this "historical" identity.[14] This becomes particularly obvious in the selectivity of cultural transmission and in the shaping of Austrian commemorative culture, which is consequently a determinant for the manifestation of a society's identity.[15] Thus, on the one hand, a stylized "cultural memory" that was not based on recent events, but on important occurrences in a mythologized and absolute past, functioned domestically as a fundamental basis for the creation of a specifically Austrian identity. Cultural policy, on the other hand, was also in connection with activities of cultural representation within the frame of Austria's foreign policy.

Cultural memory and cultural identity

The theoretical basis of the subsequent analysis provides the concept of "cultural memory" as developed by Jan Assmann. A common connection to the past in the form of identity-generating knowledge functions in this form of memory constellation as a fundamental component of collective identity formation. However, Assmann also assumes that there is a significant and qualitative difference between a collective memory based on everyday communication and a collective memory reliant upon cultural objectifications full of symbolism.[16] While other theorists stop at the border of everyday communication and interactions, Assmann distinguishes a structure of memory on the level of objectified culture. By his observations, he postulates that there must be a guiding difference between both a "communicative" and a "cultural" memory. In this configuration, the communicative memory purports experiences of history within the frame of individual biographies. Its fundamental media are living recollections in organic memories. It tells a story of daily routines, a "history from below"[17] characterized by "a high degree of formlessness, willfulness, and disorganization."[18] In opposition to this, cultural memory is characterized by its distance from the everyday.

> Distance from the everyday (transcendence) marks its temporal horizon. Cultural memory has its fixed point; its horizon does not change with the passing of time. These fixed points are fateful events of the past, whose memory is maintained through cultural formation (texts, rites, monuments [, and of course music]) and institutional communication (recitation, practice, observance). We call these 'figures of memory'.[19]

Briefly worded, one could say, that within the cultural memory, in contrast to the communicative memory, the official and institutionalized transmissions "from above" function as a "specialized carrier [...] of memory"[20].

Living memory implies continual tangibility. Meanwhile, symbolic encoding and materialization of recollection imply the question of how stored cultural meanings are getting reflexive again. In this context, ritual staging within the frame of fests, religious celebrations, or mass events in general, right up to concerts, come into the focus of research because of their constantly recurring components and sequences of events, which ensure the maintenance of cultural continuity. In this process, cultural meanings are actualized and, thus, circulate within the members of the community. In other words, a performative reproduction and actualization of cultural meanings, stored and subjectivized in rituals as a form of shared symbolic worlds, is necessary to constitute a degree of increase from the everyday to the extra-ordinary. This "temporal increase" is necessary to ensure the genesis of individuals into collective communities. Assmann even calls human beings two-dimensional entities, who live in two different temporal structures: a festive extraordinary time structure on the one hand and everyday life on the other.[21] In between these two time structures, there is a "floating gap" shown by Jan Vansina in his study about the historical awareness of nonliterate societies: "Historical consciousness works on two registers: time of origin and recent times. Because the limit one reaches in time of reckoning moves with the passage of generations, I have called the gap a floating gap."[22] What Vansina tries to describe with his term "floating gap" is "a tripartite structure"[23] on which societies – in his case, nonliterate – rely upon within the process of generating identity-foundational knowledge. In this tripartite structure, the first frame of memory affects reports about the recent past, which initially contain a high volume of information, but this volume continuously decreases with the progression of time. "Concerning a more remote past, there is either a total lack of information or one or two names are produced with great hesitation. For the most remote past, however, there is again a profusion of information dealing with traditions about the origin of the world and the early history of the tribe."[24] Vansina's "floating gap" describes precisely the point of demarcation used by Assmann for his two different frames or constellations of memory. The communicative memory is based on everyday life and the recent past, while the cultural memory relies on the time of origin and an absolute past. Through recurring rituals, a society or group actualizes a form of memories that are not instantaneously available, since they relate to information of the origin of the community; thus, they are not stored in the communicative memory. Rituals have recourse to information stored in the cultural memory, and through the actualization of this information, the group or community makes their unity and uniqueness certain. Consequently, ritual utterances care – due to their regularity of recurrences – for the imparting and transferring of identity-establishing knowledge and, thus, for the reproduction of cultural identity. In other words, ritual repetition ensures the coherence of communities in space and time.[25]

Two out of the three questions to be answered should be clarified by now: First, the question of how identity-foundational knowledge of communities gets stored in certain "figures of memory," and second, the manner of how this information becomes actualized and reflexive again. The third main aspect, which is important for the understanding of the way collective identity arises, is the question about the origin of the knowledge that gives a community its uniqueness. Therefore, we have to ask for the mythical urtexts[26] of a society, which have a particular motoric mode of operation, as Assmann demonstrates in his article "Frühe Formen politischer Mythomotorik."[27] The term "Mythomotorik"[28] implies a collective action-leading effect of foundational narratives. According to Assmann, myths of origin generate an archive of texts that drive communities in their cultural practices. Furthermore, they try to legitimize current social conditions as given by nature, or they try to question these conditions. In other words, this complex of narrative symbols, and foundational and mobilizing stories function for a group of human beings as a way of interpreting their present and looking ahead into their future.[29] In the course of history, numerous examples of such founding myths can be observed; for example, the Exodus of Egypt as an essential form and foundation of Israelite collective identity.[30]

For Austria and the Second Republic, the *Opfermythos*, in addition to the myth of Austria as the "land of music" with all its representatives, such as Mozart and Strauß, the Salzburg Festival, State Opera, and Burgtheater, as well as the Vienna Philharmonic Orchestra, can certainly be regarded as one of the main identity-establishing texts of the Austrian nation. As formative texts, they provide answers to the question: "'Wer sind wir?' Sie dienen der Selbstdefinition und Identitätsvergewisserung. Sie vermitteln identitätssicherndes Wissen und motivieren gemeinschaftliches Handeln durch Erzählen gemeinsam bewohnter Geschichten."[31] The political and cultural leaders of the Second Republic exploited the potential of such an archive of shared mythical stories, and politically instrumentalized the traditional cultural institutions for the reconstruction of a re-established Austrian nation. The concept of an Austrian "cultural superpower" also made it possible to conceal the close involvement of Austrians in the machinery of Nazi terror, including their artists and other cultural administrators. Therefore, it was further necessary to communicate that Austrian culture and politics have to be seen as two completely separate fields.[32] In reality, this aspect did not correspond to the truth, since the connection between music and politics in the creation of a national identity proved to be particularly successful, making the Second Republic of Austria appear as the "land of music" par excellence, particularly in the last third of the twentieth century.[33]

The myth of Austria as the "land of music"

Austria's image and the cultural identity of Austrians is strongly influenced by music. The term "land of music" is used to describe a (territorial) proximity of Austria to music: The lively musical activity as a cultural habit is associated with a certain characteristic feature of the country's inhabitants, in the sense of a natural collective talent. The fact that a significant number of the most famous composers and interpreters of classical music were born in Austria is understood as testimony to the fated musical mission of the country.[34]

Already, in the first verse of the current Austrian national anthem, which was introduced in the Second Republic, the line "Volk, begnadet für das Schöne"[35] refers to an aesthetic-artistic talent that is supposedly innate to Austrians, with music playing a central role. The pride of Austrians in being defined as the descendants of certain outstanding personalities and heroes functions also as a factor that separates them from the "non-gifted" people due to a related sense of superiority.[36] The idea of a kind of "national music" can serve as an answer to essential social and identity-politics questions, since music, as a form of socio-cultural practice, bears the possibility of being able to function as a medium of communication of political content, and to achieve certain effects of belonging on the recipient.[37] The stylization and staging of such an image as Austria as the "land of music" is, thus, of central importance, both for the foundation of national identity and for the tourism industry, in addition to Austria's role in international political discourse.[38] Since the aesthetic experiences of a population are of great importance for the formation of a country's collective identity, the selectivity of cultural transmission, which bears the central potential for the political instrumentalization of art and culture, for example, by eliminating dubious details of various artists' biographies, the way in which the nation's culture of remembrance is shaped, and the formation of a certain cultural canon, are particularly powerful tools to overcome political and identity crises.[39]

Canonization and conservatism: Austria's "Tonheroen"

According to Aleida Assmann, canonization processes take place through the specific selection of objects and subjects that are accorded the highest recognition and significance within a community of (shared) memory, and are, therefore, permanently stored in active cultural memory:[40] "Indem sich eine Nation zu ihrer Musik bekennt, konstruiert sie [also] nicht nur einen eigenen Kanon von Klassikern, sondern auch sich selbst."[41] Thus, the canon represents an important component of the individual society's festive culture of staging, which ensures the continuous existence of a shared past that is interpreted, presented, and adapted to current cultural and political needs. In this process, forms of organized human coexistence become effective, which are often based on inclusion and exclusion mechanisms in which the familiar, as opposed to the foreign, is continuously labelled with the identity-constituting attributes as "authentic" and "exclusive."[42] This aspect forms a central factor of cultural memory, which Jan Assmann describes as "identitätskonkret,"[43] and which makes the unambiguous demarcation between belonging and not belonging actually possible.[44] As a result, the concept of culture is often territorialized in accordance with the idea of national unity, leading powerful political actors to draw rhetorically created boundaries and differences, conveying the impression of (national) cultural territories.[45] Consequently, canonization processes contribute to the formation of politically instrumentalizable (musical) spaces of memory.[46]

"Österreich [...] ist ein Land, in dem sich jeder Veränderungen wünscht, aber nur unter der Prämisse, dass alles so bleibt wie es ist und wie es immer war."[47] Particularly during the Second Republic, significant efforts were made to preserve the country's musical heritage, ranging from the adherence to certain musical forms and historical performance practices to the nostalgic heroization of certain historical musical personalities.[48] Austria's cultural canon is largely based on high culture and on musicians and composers from the so-called period of "classical music" with their associated virtuosity. As a result, contemporary, folk, traditional, and popular (e.g. "Austro-Pop") music, which are equally prominent in the musical landscape of Austria, have often received comparatively little attention in the country's (foreign) cultural policy. Consequently, the social reception of cultural activities often seems to have remained rooted in earlier centuries, with the result that even today the capital city of Vienna conveys an image that is essentially the same as that of around 1900.[49] According to the Austrian musicologist Manfred Wagner, this aspect entails that Haydn, Schubert, Strauß, Mozart, and Beethoven will remain permanent contemporaries for centuries to come.[50] Through this nostalgic heroization of certain musical characters of the past, attempts are made to create a harmonizing, ostensibly depoliticized Austrian identity, which basically transforms aesthetics into political moments.[51] Thus, the instrumentalization of the relevant facets of music history played an essential role in the formation of Austria's national identity and within the attempts to shape the Second Republic after World War II, which is particularly evident in the cultural-political disruption between tradition and innovation.

Remembering, inventing and forgetting – tools for national distinction

Specific identity-political efforts to construct an Austrian national consciousness for the young Second Republic led, especially after 1945, to a special emphasis on Viennese musical tradition, which was presented as an extraordinary art form in cultural political objectives.[52] Therefore, identification is recognized as a context-dependent process linked to concrete material and symbolic conditions, in which music, as a non-linguistic art form, was particularly successful as a unifying medium in the multilingual Habsburg Empire.[53] However, although the Austrian post-war identity, as far as it is related to music, is based on the multicultural vision of historical multi-ethnic musical diversity, it paradoxically functions, from the Second Republic onwards, primarily as a vehicle and medium for national distinction.[54]

Austria's self-perception as the first victim of National Socialism, in an attempt to detach itself from its own Nazi past and to relinquish all joint responsibility for the crimes of World War II, as well as the country's supposed musical affinity, led to an intensified attempt to create a kind of positive national connotation by emphasizing its own differences to Germany.[55] This fact is also reflected in the minimal efforts to repatriate the Austrian artists and intellectuals who had been expelled by the National Socialists during World War II, causing Austria to lose an enormous amount of creative potential after the war, which once again entailed that contemporary movements in all cultural sectors were largely ignored.[56] Moreover, this approach of course did not contribute to a critical historical examination of the country's own National Socialist past, since Austria actually wanted to liberate itself from its own (dark) history.[57] Instead, artists, including numerous composers and musicians who played leading roles in National Socialist cultural policy and the cultural public from 1938-1945, were denazified immediately after the end of World War II and honored with (state) prizes and awards. Without any critical reappraisal, they were able to continue their careers unhindered and to the full extent, which resulted in composers being able to incorporate hidden anti-Semitic quotations and allusions in their works written after 1945.[58] Additionally, for example, the New Year's Concert of the Vienna Philharmonic Orchestra, which was originally introduced as a medium of National Socialist cultural policy, was cleverly reinterpreted and productively misunderstood as part of the conscious foundation of an Austrian cultural nation.[59] Thus, the orchestra itself became one of the most important representative institutions of Austrian musical culture. This example of a so-called "invented tradition"[60] becomes effective through the instrumentalization of the concept of tradition as something naturally innate, which showcases its potential for the foundation of a cultural identity and the communication of a collective memory, particularly in its exclusionary efforts, for which Austria strived in relation to Germany.[61] Through a multitude of small references, a continuity with the past is established, which is a prerequisite for legitimizing and continuing certain practices in the future, or in other words, musical practices and repertoires can also be ritualized in a modified way and adapted to new purposes.[62]

In the course of self-heroization after World War II, an identity transition was intended to promote the retransformation from Germanness to Austrianness in both national and cultural terms; therefore, the Viennese classical composers, such as Mozart, Haydn, Brahms, and Beethoven had to be further Austrianized. These composers were supposed to bring the navel of music – in terms of a cultural relict, saved from the other [German] side – back to Vienna, although nobody wanted to remember that, for example, Brahms and Beethoven were strictly speaking only "Austrians-by-choice."[63] Particularly through Mozart, who was promoted as a "Genius austriacus"[64] – thus, becoming a central figure in the construction of a national memory – it was to be shown that Austria possessed an uninterrupted tradition of cultural identity without any space for hatred or coercion.[65] This aspect can be similarly applied to Anton Bruckner, who was also a subject of this retransformation from a German to an Austrian musical identity:[66] Although Bruckner himself never made any comment on the Germanism of his music, political and academic entities identified the serious and pure character of his compositions as such, making him particularly German in terms of an aesthetic-moral quality. From 1945, however, Bruckner was labelled as "Austrian" – an attribute that has remained until today:[67] "Wenn somit die Diskussion um den 'deutschen' oder 'österreichischen' Bruckner überhaupt etwas aussagt, dann wohl am ehesten über die, die sie geführt haben und führen: über 'uns Österreicher' selbst und unsere Suche nach Identität."[68]

Conclusion

In summary, it can be stated that an idealized, stylized, and mythologized form of collective "Austrian" (national) identity was created and established in the Second Republic through the political functionalization and heroization of the country's musical heritage. Usually, a common connection to the past functions as the substrate of all sorts of collective identity. Most commonly, these connecting points of reference contain the officially transmitted – or in other words, the institutionalized – knowledge of mythical and primordial times of societies. The Austrian identity conveyed by the political elite is composed of numerous mythical components, with the *Opfermythos*, the "Habsburg myth," and the "Musikland myth" playing a decisive role, especially in the Second Republic. Those formative texts function as handed-down wisdom from an "absolute" past, which has the potential to provide answers to the question: "Who are we?" By maintaining or constructing a cultural canon on the basis of invented traditions, mechanisms of inclusion and exclusion become effective, which are most clearly evident in Austria's efforts to disassociate itself from Germany following World War II. Austria's cultural canon is predominantly focused on high-culture events and characterized by an idealized and ostensibly depoliticized past, which essentially corresponds to the world of Vienna around 1900. This "floating gap" addressed by Jan Assmann (in relation to Jan Vansina) in his concept of cultural memory, is central to the cultural and identity policy-shaping and building of the Second Austrian Republic, which is essentially based on the exclusion of occurrences in the immediate past. Instead, the idea of national unity culminates in the cultural canon of earlier times and in the self-perception of a cultural superpower.

Endnotes

1 (Music - whether this country lies in the light, in the shadow, It has always triumphed with its musical art. This is how the fullness of tones spreads: Beethoven, Haydn, Mozart, Schubert, Strauss) Rudolf Henz, *Festliche Dichtung – Gesammelte Sprüche und Spiele*, Schriften für den Volksbildner 30 (Vienna: Österreichischer Bundesverlag für Unterricht, Wissenschaft und Kunst, 1935), 50.

2 Maurice Halbwachs, *Das Gedächtnis und seine sozialen Bedingungen* (Frankfurt am Main: Suhrkamp, 1985), 390; Christian Jansen and Henning Borggräfe, *Nation – Nationalität – Nationalismus*, Historische Einführungen 1 (Frankfurt am Main: Campus, 2007), 98; Heidemarie Uhl, "Warum Gesellschaften sich erinnern," in *Erinnerungskulturen*, Informationen zur Politischen Bildung 32, ed. Forum Politische Bildung (Innsbruck et al.: Studien-Verlag, 2010), 5.

3 Heinz Rögl, *Kulturpolitik: Kulturverwaltung in Österreich* (Vienna: Österr. Kulturdokumentation, Internat. Archiv für Kulturanalysen, 1998), 9; Emil Brix, "'Volk begnadet für das Schöne.' Anmerkungen zur österreichischen Kulturpolitik," in Österreichische Identität und Kultur, Österreich-Studien Szeged 1, ed. Károly Csúri and Markus Kóth (Vienna: JATEPress Szeged – Praesens Verlag, 2007), 42–43, 46; Susanne Breuss, Karin Liebhart, and Andreas Pribersky, eds., *Inszenierungen: Stichworte zu Österreich* (Vienna: Sonderzahl, 1995), 172; Marion Knapp, *Österreichische Kulturpolitik und das Bild der Kulturnation: Kontinuität und Diskontinuität in der Kulturpolitik des Bundes seit 1945*, Politik und Demokratie 4 (Frankfurt am Main: Peter Lang, 2005), 69, 72.

4 Domokos Kosáry, "Entwicklungstypen von Kleinstaaten in Europa," in *Kultur und Politik in Österreich und Ungarn*, Begegnungen an der Donau, ed. Peter Hanák et al. (Vienna et al.: Böhlau, 1994), 12; Sozialwissenschaftliche Arbeitsgemeinschaft, *Der österreichische Kulturdienst im Ausland* (Vienna: SWA, 1954), 34–35; Breuss, Liebhart, and Pribersky, eds., *Inszenierungen*, 14; Wolfgang Gratzer, "Österreichische Literaturmusik als Opposition: Drei Thesen," in *Die Künste der Nachkriegszeit: Musik, Literatur und Bildende Kunst in Österreich*, Wiener Musikwissenschaftliche Beiträge 23, ed. Stefan Schmidl (Vienna et al.: Böhlau, 2013), 252–53; Martina Nußbaumer, "Musik im 'Kulturkrieg': Politische Funktionalisierung von Musikkultur in Österreich 1914–1918," in *Aggression und Katharsis: Der Erste Weltkrieg im Diskurs der Moderne*, Studien zur Moderne 20, ed. Petra Ernst, Sabine A. Haring, and Werner Suppanz (Vienna: Passagen-Verl., 2004), 312.

5 Frederic Morton, "Die Lust und der Drang," *Die Presse*, October 25, 1996.

6 Anton Pelinka, "Vorwort: Österreich ist nicht gleich Österreich ist nicht gleich...," in *Inszenierungen: Stichworte zu Österreich*, ed. Susanne Breuss, Karin Liebhart, and Andreas Pribersky (Vienna: Sonderzahl, 1995), 9; Breuss, Liebhart, and Pribersky, eds., *Inszenierungen*, 23.

7 Vanessa Maria Carlone, *Das "Musikland Österreich" und seine kulturpolitische Mission in Italien: 80 Jahre ÖKF und ÖHI Rom als Mittel musikalischer Repräsentation einer Kulturnation*, Beiträge zur Kulturwissenschaft 46 (Oberhausen: Athena 2019), 123.

8 (By representing Austrian culture, Austria should not only be perceived as an independent state, but also as a serious player in international affairs). Elke Atzler, "Vom Österreichischen Kulturinstitut zum Österreichischen Kulturforum: Eine Zeitreise durch die österreichische Auslandskulturpolitik am Beispiel Roms," in *Austria in Urbe: 1938–2018*, ed. Elke Atzler and Andreas Gottsmann (Rome: Edition Lammerhuber, 2018), 118.

9 Alexander Burka, *Was blieb vom Fenster in den Westen? Zur Auslandskulturpolitik Österreichs in Ostmitteleuropa seit 1945 am Beispiel Polens und der Tschechoslowakei/ Tschechiens*, Politik und Demokratie 23 (Frankfurt am Main et al.: Peter Lang, 2012), 45–46; Rögl, *Kulturpolitik*, 10.

10 Brix, "'Volk begnadet für das Schöne,'" 49; Knapp, Österreichische Kulturpolitik und das Bild der Kulturnation, 92.

11 Atzler, "Vom Österreichischen Kulturinstitut zum Österreichischen Kulturforum," 118.

12 Burka, *Was blieb vom Fenster in den Westen?*, 17–19.

13 The Institute building in Rome was returned by the Ministry of Education in 1949 at the request of the Italian government to its established provisions for "cultural purposes" in accordance with the Austrian-Italian Cultural Convention of February 2, 1935; (Atzler, "Vom Österreichischen Kulturinstitut zum Österreichischen Kulturforum," 118–19).

14 Michael Wimmer, *Kultur und Demokratie: Eine systematische Darstellung von Kulturpolitik in* Österreich (Innsbruck et al.: Studien-Verlag, 2011), 72; Brix, "'Volk begnadet für das Schöne,'" 41.

15 Jan Assmann and Tonio Hölscher, *Kultur und Gedächtnis* (Frankfurt am Main: Suhrkamp, 1988), 16, blurb; Astrid Erll, *Kollektives Gedächtnis und Erinnerungskulturen: Eine Einführung* (Stuttgart: J.B. Metzler, 2017), 168.

16 Astrid Erll, "Kollektives Gedächtnis und Erinnerungskulturen," in *Einführung in die Kulturwissenschaften: Theoretische Grundlagen – Ansätze – Perspektiven*, ed. Ansgar Nünning and Vera Nünning (Stuttgart: J.B. Metzler, 2008), 171.

17 Jan Assmann, *Das kulturelle Gedächtnis: Schrift, Erinnerung und politische Identität in frühen Hochkulturen* (Munich: C. H. Beck, 2013), 51, 56.

18 Jan Assmann and John Czaplicka, "Collective Memory and Cultural Identity," *New German Critique* 65 (1995): 125–33 (here 127).

19 Assmann and Czaplicka, "Collective Memory," 128–29.

20 Jan Assmann, "Communicative and Cultural Memory," in *Cultural Memory Studies: An International and Interdisciplinary Handbook*, ed. Astrid Erll and Ansgar Nünning (Berlin et al.: De Gruyter, 2008), 117.

21 Jan Assmann, "Der zweidimensionale Mensch: das Fest als Medium des kollektiven Gedächtnisses," in *Das Fest und das Heilige: Kontrapunkte des Alltags*, Studien zum Verstehen fremder Religionen 1, ed. Jan Assman and Thomas Sundermeier (Gütersloh: Gütersloher Verlagshaus G. Mohn, 1991), 17.

22 Jan Vansina, *Oral Tradition as History* (London: J. Currey, 1985), 24.

23 Assmann, "Communicative and Cultural Memory," 112.

24 Assmann, "Communicative and Cultural Memory," 112.

25 Assmann, *Das kulturelle Gedächtnis*, 57.

26 Further fertile myth theories for the analysis of identity foundational texts would be Rene Girard, *The Scapegoat* (London: Athlone, 1986); Max Horkheimer and Theodor W. Adorno, *Dialectic of Enlightenment* (New York: Herder & Herder, 1972); Roland Barthes, *Mythologies* (New York: Hill & Wang, 1972).

27 (Early forms of political "Mythomotorik"). Jan Assmann, "Frühe Formen politischer Mythomotorik: Fundierende, kontrapräsentische und revolutionäre Mythen," in *Revolution und Mythos*, ed. Dietrich Harth and Jan Assmann (Frankfurt am Main: Fischer Taschenbuch Verlag, 1992), 39–61.

28 (A motoric mode of operation of myths).

29 Assmann, "Frühe Formen politischer Mythomotorik," 40.

30 Assmann, "Frühe Formen politischer Mythomotorik," 40–41.

31 ('Who are we?'They serve the purpose of self-definition and identity reassurance. They impart identity-securing knowledge and motivate collective action by sharing common stories). Assmann, *Das kulturelle Gedächtnis*, 142.

32 Michael Wimmer, "Reflections on a Special Case: What Makes Cultural Policy Truly Austrian?," *The Journal of Arts Management, Law, and Society* 35, no. 4 (2006): 265–76 (here 269–70).

33 Gerhard Anselm, "Weit mehr als nur 'deutsch-italienische Musikbeziehungen': Die Musikgeschichtliche Abteilung als Vorreiterin eines Paradigmenwechsels in der Musikgeschichtsschreibung," in *Von der Geheimhaltung zur internationalen und interdisziplinären Forschung: Die musikgeschichtliche Abteilung des Deutschen Historischen Instituts in Rom 1960–2010*, ed. Sabine Ehrmann-Herfort and Michael Matheus (Berlin et al.: De Gruyter, 2010), 131.

34 Ernst Marboe, *Das Österreich-Buch* (Vienna: Österreichische Staatsdruckerei, 1948), 108; Theophil Antonicek, "'Österreichisches' in der Musik?," in *Was heißt Österreich? Inhalt und Umfang des Österreichbegriffs vom 10. Jahrhundert bis heute*, Archiv für österreichische Geschichte 136, ed. Richard G. Plaschka, Gerald Stourzh, and Jan Paul Niederkorn (Vienna: Verlag der Österreichischen Akademie der Wissenschaften, 1995), 337, 339; Anita Mayer-Hirtzberger, "Musikstadt Wien," in *Wien: Geschichte einer Stadt – Band 2: Die frühneuzeitliche Residenz (16. bis 18. Jahrhundert)*, ed. Karl Vocelka and Anita Traninger (Vienna et al.: Böhlau, 2003), 14; Nußbaumer, "Musik im 'Kulturkrieg,'" 301; Carlone, *Das "Musikland Österreich" und seine kulturpolitische Mission in Italien*, 15, 44–47, 123.

35 (people, blessed for the fine arts). Bundeskanzleramt Österreich, "Bundeshymne," Geschichte und Wissenswertes (n.d.), accessed Sept. 3, 2020, https://www.bundeskanzleramt.gv.at/bundeshymne.

36 Helmut Brenner, "Versuch einer Theorie der politischen Verwendung von Musik," in *Musik und Politik*, 235. Available online at https://www.uibk.ac.at/peacestudies /downloads/peacelibrary/musiktheorie.pdf.

37 Rüdiger Ritter, "Neuer Wein in alten Schläuchen: Gedanken zu den Konzepten 'Nationalmusik' und 'nationale Musik' am Beispiel des Komponisten Stanisław Moniuszko," *Archiv für Musikwissenschaft* 61 (2004): 19–37 (here 35–36); Peter Stachel, "Politische Musik," Österreichisches Musiklexikon (May 6, 2001), accessed Aug. 28, 2020, https://www.musiklexikon.ac.at/ml/musik_P/Politische_Musik.xml.

38 Carlone, *Das "Musikland Österreich" und seine kulturpolitische Mission in Italien,* 15, 44–47, 123.

39 Uhl, "Warum Gesellschaften sich erinnern," 5; Assmann and Hölscher, *Kultur und Gedächtnis*, 16, blurb; Erll, *Kollektives Gedächtnis und Erinnerungskulturen*, 168.

40 Aleida Assmann, "Canon and Archives," in *Cultural Memory Studies: An International and Interdisciplinary Handbook*, ed. Astrid Erll and Ansgar Nünning (Berlin et al.: De Gruyter, 2010), 100; Federico Celestini, "Musik und kollektive Identitäten," in *Historische Musikwissenschaft: Grundlagen und Perspektiven*, ed. Michele Calella and Nikolaus Urbanek (Stuttgart: J.B. Metzler, 2013), 325–26.

41 (By professing its music, a nation [thus] constructs not only its own canon of classics, but also itself). Carlone, *Das "Musikland Österreich" und seine kulturpolitische Mission in Italien,* 46.

42 Bernhard Alexander Achhorner, *Musik und kulturelles Gedächtnis: Zur musikalischen Instrumentalisierung von Heimat, Kultur und Identität im Tiroler Nationalsozialismus* (Bielefeld: Aisthesis, 2019), 76; Albert Bergesen, "Die rituelle Ordnung," in *Ritualtheorien: Ein einführendes Handbuch*, ed. Andréa Belliger and David J. Krieger (Opladen et al.: VS Verlag für Sozialwissenschaften, 1998), 49; Jansen and Borggräfe, *Nation – Nationalität – Nationalismus*, 10–11.

43 ("concretion of identity"). Assmann and Czaplicka, "Collective Memory," 130.

44 Jan Assmann, "Kollektives Gedächtnis und kulturelle Identität," in *Kultur und Gedächtnis*, ed. Jan Assmann and Tonio Hölscher (Frankfurt am Main: Suhrkamp, 1988), 13.

45 Gerhard Hauck, *Kultur: Zur Karriere eines sozialwissenschaftlichen Begriffs*, Einstiege 16/17 (Münster: Westfälisches Dampfboot, 2006), 161.

46 Achhorner, *Musik und kulturelles Gedächtnis*, 132.

47 ("Austria […] is a country where everyone wants change, but only under the premise that everything stays the way it is and always has been.") Gregor Auenhammer, "Austria in Urbe: 1938–2018," moderation of the book presentation, January 18, 2018, Rome.

48 Antonicek "'Österreichisches' in der Musik?," 340.

49 Manfred Wagner, *Musikland Österreich*, Österreich – Zweite Republik. Befund, Kritik, Perspektive 14 (Innsbruck et al.: Studien-Verlag, 2005), 64; Gratzer, "Österreichische Literaturmusik als Opposition," 254.

50 Stefan Seigner, quoted in Martina Nußbaumer, *Musikstadt Wien: Die Konstruktion eines Images*, Rombach Wissenschaften – Edition Parabasen 6 (Freiburg im Breisgau et al.: Rombach, 2007), 355.

51 Stachel, "Politische Musik"; Carl Dahlhaus, *Die Musik des 19. Jahrhunderts*, Neues Handbuch der Musikwissenschaft 6 (Wiesbaden: Laaber, 1980), 32; Antonicek, "'Österreichisches' in der Musik?," 340.

52 Wolfgang Gratzer, "'Rein geistiger Imperialismus?' Die Salzburger Festspiele 1951 als Ort der Identitätsstiftung," in *Die Künste der Nachkriegszeit. Musik, Literatur und Bildende Kunst in Österreich*, Wiener Musikwissenschaftliche Beiträge 23, ed. Stefan Schmidl (Vienna et al.: Boehlau, 2013), 182; Nußbaumer, *Musikstadt Wien*, 10.

53 Mayer-Hirtzberger, "Musikstadt Wien," 19; Nußbaumer, *Musikstadt Wien*, 10, 20, 359–60.

54 Albrecht Riethmüller, "1933 und das Fiasko der kulturellen Identität in der Musik," in *Nationale Musik im 20. Jahrhundert: Kompositorische und soziokulturelle Aspekte der Musikgeschichte zwischen Ost- und Westeuropa. Konferenzbericht Leipzig 2002*, ed. Helmut Loos and Stefan Keym (Leipzig: Schröder, 2004), 387.

55 Karl Müller, "Der Stein der Republik," in *Begnadet für das Schöne: Der rot-weiß-rote Kulturkampf gegen die Moderne*, Beiträge zur Kulturwissenschaft und Kulturpolitik 2, ed. Gert Kerschbaumer and Karl Müller (Vienna: Verl. für Gesellschaftskritik, 1992), 8; Uhl, "Warum Gesellschaften sich erinnern," 5; Breuss, Liebhart, and Pribersky, *Inszenierungen*, 15, 108.

56 Knapp, Österreichische Kulturpolitik und das Bild der Kulturnation, 100, 102–105, 122; Rögl, *Kulturpolitik*, 10–11; Michael Wimmer, *Kulturpolitik in Österreich: Darstellung und Analyse 1970–1990* (Innsbruck et al.: Österr. Studien-Verl., 1995), 28–29.

57 Wimmer, *Kultur und Demokratie*, 74, 87; Gert Kerschbaumer, "Oliver Rathkolb: Austriakischer Kulturexport," in *Begnadet für das Schöne. Der rot-weiß-rote Kulturkampf gegen die Moderne,* Beiträge zur Kulturwissenschaft und Kulturpolitik 2, ed. Gert Kerschbaumer and Karl Müller (Vienna: Verl. für Gesellschaftskritik, 1992), 68, 73.

58 Kurt Drexel, "'Melodic Commitment to Racially Pure Joy': Musical Policy and Identity Concepts in Tyrol during the National Socialist Regime," in *MUSICULT'16. III. International Music and Cultural Studies Conference Proceedings*, ed. Burçin Ercan (Istanbul: n.p., 2016), 96.

59 Stachel, "Politische Musik"; Wiener Philharmoniker, "Die Geschichte des Neujahrskonzerts," Neujahrskonzert der Wiener Philharmoniker (n.d.), accessed Sept. 3, 2020, https://www.wienerphilharmoniker.at/neujahrskonzert/geschichte; Hauck, *Kultur*, 143.

60 Eric Hobsbawm and Terence Ranger, *The Invention of Tradition* (Cambridge: Cambridge University Press, 1983).

61 Hauck, *Kultur*, 151; Achhorner, *Musik und kulturelles Gedächtnis*, 53.

62 Hobsbawm and Ranger, *The Invention of Tradition*, 1–6.

63 Gert Kerschbaumer, "Das musikalische Riesenrad: Die Philharmoniker sind wir," in *Begnadet für das Schöne: Der rot-weiß-rote Kulturkampf gegen die Moderne*, Beiträge zur Kulturwissenschaft und Kulturpolitik 2, ed. Gert Kerschbaumer

and Karl Müller (Vienna: Verl. für Gesellschaftskritik, 1992), 12; Carl Dahlhaus, *Allgemeine Theorie der Musik I: Historik – Grundlagen der Musik – Ästhetik,* Gesammelte Schriften in 10 Bänden 1 (Laaber: Laaber Verlag, 2000), 288; Markus Kóth, "Österreich: Einleitende Anmerkungen zur Alpenrepublik und ihrer Identität," in Österreichische Identität und Kultur, Österreich-Studien Szeged 1, ed. Károly Csúri and Markus Kóth (Vienna: JATEPress Szeged – Praesens Verlag, 2007), 9; Breuss, Liebhart, and Pribersky, *Inszenierungen,* 208; Antonicek "'Österreichisches' in der Musik?," 348.

64 Kerschbaumer, "Das musikalische Riesenrad: Die Philharmoniker sind wir," 14.

65 Cornelia Szabó-Knotik, Österreichisches Musiklexikon 3, s.v. "Musikland Österreich" (Vienna: Verlag der Österreichischen Akademie der Wissenschaften, 2004), 1537; Kerschbaumer, "Das musikalische Riesenrad: Die Philharmoniker sind wir," 20.

66 Riethmüller, "1933 und das Fiasko der kulturellen Identität in der Musik," 386–87.

67 Thomas Leibnitz, "Anton Bruckner: 'Deutscher' oder 'Österreicher'? Deutungen, Vereinnahmungen, Hintergründe," in Österreichische Musik – Musik in Österreich*: Beiträge zur Musikgeschichte Mitteleuropas; Theophil Antonicek zum 60. Geburtstag,* Wiener Veröffentlichungen zur Musikwissenschaft 34, ed. Elisabeth Theresia Hilscher (Tutzing: H. Schneider, 1998), 463, 466–69, 473–74.

68 (If the discussion about the 'German' or 'Austrian' Bruckner says anything at all, then it is most likely about those who have led and are leading it: about 'us Austrians' ourselves and our search for identity). Leibnitz, "Anton Bruckner," 476.

Continuity in the Electricity Supply of the Second Republic: The Case of Kaprun

Marc Landry

Introduction

On the occasion of the completion of the main stage of Austria's *Tauernkraftwerk Glockner-Kaprun* in 1951, Prof. Dr. Hermann Grengg (1891–1978) penned an article detailing the history of the landmark facility and his involvement in its construction. Grengg's viewpoint on the subject was of some import. As one of Austria's most prominent hydraulic engineers and a manager in Styria's provincial electrical utility in the interwar years, he had participated in the debates surrounding the Kaprun facility from the beginning.[1] Grengg, who had joined the Austrian Nazi Party in March 1933, had also been appointed the technical director in charge of constructing the Kaprun complex after the *Anschluss*. In this role, Grengg took a number of key decisions that determined the future of the project beyond the National Socialist period.

Highlighting these decisions, in fact, was the main purpose behind his commemorative missive. Grengg explained that as the engineer responsible for planning and commencing construction on Kaprun, he had stood before the "grotesque necessity" of having to refight a battle he had believed long over. The engineer referred to the conflict over the ultimate shape of the Kaprun power plant and the role it would play in the electricity supply. First plans to build dams in the Kaprun valley had surfaced in the mid-1920s. They had emerged as part of an effort to systematically develop the waterpower potential of Austria's mightiest mountain range—the Hohe Tauern. The climax of this early conceptual phase came with a scheme designed by the German electrical giant AEG on behalf of the Salzburg provincial government. Instead of placing several power stations throughout the Hohe Tauern, AEG wanted to capture all high-altitude runoff from throughout the entire mountain range and divert it all to the steep Kaprun valley, where it would generate unheard-of amounts of electricity. Grengg had belonged to a group of—primarily Austrian—engineers that had criticized this idea as outsized and even utopian in scale. The Styrian himself characterized it as a "propagandistic derailment."[2]

Instead, Grengg and others argued for a smaller-scale, "decentralized" solution to developing the energy of the Tauern. Instead of concentrating all

Tauern water and energy production in Kaprun, it foresaw a series of dams and power plants placed throughout the range. Kaprun would be the first in this sequence. This variant, Grengg argued, not only showed greater sensitivity to the peculiarities of the Alpine environment—something Reich German engineers ostensibly did not understand as deeply as their Austrian counterparts. It would also utilize the waterpower in a manner that would most benefit the electricity supply of the Austrian urban and industrial heartland in the east of the newly annexed country. In his time at the *Alpen-Elektrowerke* (AEW) Grengg explained, he had ensured that this decentralized variant was the "final solution" by literally setting some of the project's dimensions in stone. His article, then, was intended to remind at least the engineering community of the "up and down" history of Austria's most important dam.[3]

At least one Austrian energy expert agreed about the critical role Grengg had played in defending Austrian concerns. Oskar Vas, one of the most prominent hydroelectric authorities in the country since the interwar years, had this to say about Kaprun as the dam neared completion:

> If today the concept adopted in the past era can be completed without essential changes, because it wholly meets the needs of the Austrian energy supply, then this is not least the merit of Hermann Grengg, who, together with his coworkers, knew to defend Austrian thinking and Austrian necessities in the choice of the system.[4]

Kaprun stands as perhaps the most important infrastructure project in the early history of the Austrian Second Republic. One meaningful measure of its significance is the amount of funding it received in a time of scarcity. All told, the Austrian electricity supply claimed nearly forty percent of Marshall Plan investment from 1948 to 1954. Kaprun alone received about half of these funds.[5] Not only did the dams go on to play a critical role in supplying the rebuilding society with electricity, but the new state and its elites instrumentalized Kaprun as the outstanding symbol of Austrian reconstruction. Particularly in the 1950s and 1960s, textbooks, newsreels, feature films, cigarette advertisements, and numerous stamps commemorated the achievement.[6] These media representations portrayed the dam's completion as a result of Austrian hard work and ingenuity. That the idea for the project had emerged in the time of the First Austrian Republic, that the project had actually commenced when Austria was a part of Nazi Germany, and that construction had depended upon the heavy use of forced laborers and prisoners of war, usually went unaddressed. In this manner, "Kaprun" attained mythical status for the new republic.

Given the outsized role that the project has played in the postwar period, it has naturally attracted the attention of scholars. Researchers have done much to illuminate the mythical aspects of the dam's history.[7] Along these lines, scholarship has also revealed the important role that forced labor played in the construction of the dam during the Nazi period.[8] Others have shown the centrality of Kaprun in the context of the Austrian Marshall Plan.[9] The myth of Kaprun has also been challenged in the cultural sphere. Notably, the Nobel-prize-winning Austrian author Elfriede Jelinek wrote a play, *Das Werk* (*The Plant*), that engaged with the icon of Kaprun at the turn of the twenty-first century. At the beginning of the play, washing machines and refrigerators in glass cases are stacked upon the stage. Both appliances stand for the consumption made possible, in part, by Kaprun. The washing machine, in particular, suggests how the history of Kaprun has been laundered up until the present.[10]

The Kaprun project is less well understood from an energy perspective. Since the 1980s, historians have shown an increased interest in how past societies have provisioned themselves with energy. The belief that the analysis of energy systems contributes to fundamental insights into a society's basic structures has motivated this scholarship.[11] In order to take active advantage of free energy, humans have to get it into the right form, in the right place at the right time. Broadly speaking, this requires technology, infrastructure, and social organization. Analyzing the energy choices a society makes and how it understands them, as this essay seeks to for Austria, can tell us much about who has the power to determine what power is used for. Another way of thinking about Kaprun is as part of an "envirotechnical landscape."[12] This concept developed by environmental historians is useful in analyzing the significance of the hybrid landscapes that emerge when societies fuse technology with nature. It helps to illuminate views about nature and the technology—dams, canals, power plants—deployed to take advantage of it. This essay is an attempt to understand Kaprun from an energy and envirotechnical standpoint, particularly as it relates to questions of Austrian identity.

Looking at the complete history of plans for dams in the Kaprun valley, we can see that from the emergence of the idea, a battle has raged about the facility's dimensions and very purpose. Would Kaprun be one of several sites where the abundant hydropower of the Hohe Tauern would be harnessed, or would it be the only place? Should the waterpower of the Hohe Tauern be harnessed to serve the interests of industry in the *Altreich*, that is, within the borders of Germany prior to the annexation of Austria? Or would it be exploited primarily to store as much energy as possible for the benefit of the territory of Austria as delineated in the boundaries of the First Republic? By paying attention to the engineering debates and the actual concrete dam that impounded specific waterways for specific reasons, we can see a continuity in "state-building" efforts beginning in the 1920s, through the Nazi period, and into the Second Republic. Historian Ernst Hanisch has argued that Kaprun largely mirrored changes in Austrian identity: it started as an Austrian-German undertaking, became a German one, and ended as an Austrian monument. This is mostly correct, but a closer look at Kaprun suggests that, thanks to the existence of a strong Austrian sensibility among engineers, Austrian influence has always been fundamental at Kaprun.[13]

This paper looks at the long-term planning history of Kaprun. The Kaprun case shows that even with infrastructure completed in the postwar period, we must also consider its broader historical contexts. The realization of the Kaprun project was the culmination of conflicts over three decades. With large-scale engineering projects, it is exceedingly rare that they are implemented out of the blue. Instead, plans often sit in desk drawers for years until opportune political and social moments.[14] If the Kaprun case is exemplary, we should expect other key infrastructures of the early Second Republic to have similar origins. Nation-building in Austria after 1945, in other words, owed much to the political entities that preceded the Second Republic. Economic development in the Second Republic was, in some cases, neither reconstruction nor a new beginning but a continuation.[15]

The Power of the Tauern

The idea to build hydropower dams in the Kaprun Valley preceded their actual completion by nearly three decades. In this respect, Kaprun resembles many large-scale infrastructure projects. From an energy history perspective, the deeper context of the Kaprun dams reveals that the initial conflict over the project concerned the role that Kaprun would play in the electricity supply. Would this be a scheme to provide electricity to the industrial zone in what was then central Germany? Or would Kaprun instead become the foundation of an Austrian regional electricity grid?

To understand the function of the Kaprun dams, it is first necessary to consider the environmental circumstances of their surrounding region. Austria's Hohe Tauern mountain range is remarkable in many ways. The Tauern form the continuation of the main crest of the Alps as it passes from the western provinces of Austria. Comprising an area of some 6,000 square kilometers, the range is home to Austria's two highest mountains, the Grossglockner (3,797 meters) and the slightly smaller Grossvenediger (3,674 meters). Just below the Grossglockner sits Austria's (and the Eastern Alps') largest (though rapidly shrinking) glacier: the Pasterze. Two characteristics of the Tauern, in particular, attracted the attention of hydraulic engineers. First was the incredible water bounty of this mountain range, drained by the Salzach River to the north and the Drau to the south. Second, the Hohe Tauern is composed of several high, steep valleys whose form is a result of glacial scouring since the last ice age. High altitude and great relief lend great potential energy to Alpine torrents, and glaciated valleys often contain ideal spots to store water behind dam walls. Since the late nineteenth century, Europeans had begun to spy "white coal" in Alpine water and the Hohe Tauern represented as large a reserve of this energy as existed anywhere in the mountains.[16]

In the mid-1920s, Württembergische Elektrizitätswerke AG (WEAG), a smaller state utility in the nominal southern German province, developed a project to tap the energy of the Hohe Tauern with a series of dams in multiple valleys, including Kaprun. WEAG, like many German utilities at the time, was preoccupied with expansion strategies to meet the continually-rising demand for electricity in that country. For several years, the company had been exploring the possibility of developing the rich waterpower of the Austrian Alps. Since the amount of power slumbering in Alpine waterways was far too great to be fully utilized by the smaller Austrian economy, the WEAG planned on exporting power to Germany. The WEAG became convinced, however, that making this energy competitive with the cheap electricity generated by German lignite required a completely new approach to hydro. Instead of simply attempting to harness the power of individual rivers, WEAG considered the prospect of developing the power of entire mountain ranges. This could be achieved by finding suitable high-Alpine valleys to serve as power reservoirs and then concentrating water from throughout the mountain group in these basins. WEAG believed it had found an ideal setting to do this in the Hohe Tauern range.[17]

The WEAG plan called for concentrating a significant portion of the water draining off the northern slope of the Tauern range in reservoirs located in three separate valleys (see Figure 1). The centerpiece dams would be located in the watersheds of the Grossglockner and the nearby Grossvenediger. It recommended diverting water to these two reservoirs by piercing watersheds, crossing Austrian provincial borders, and transferring water considerable distances if necessary. Water from the Grossvenediger catchment area was to be stored in the Krimmler Ach valley, while the Grossglockner dams would be located in the steepest valley of the entire range, the Kaprun valley. WEAG calculated that the turbines of their *Tauernwerke* would generate some two billion kilowatt-hours of electricity, running twelve hours a day, the whole year round. Of the three separate Tauern projects, WEAG deemed the Venedigerwerk (see Figure 2) to be the most promising and envisioned beginning the development of Tauern hydro there. The plan's architects argued that the energy of the Tauern would be a salve for both countries' economic woes and a means of "tightening the bonds" between the two.[18]

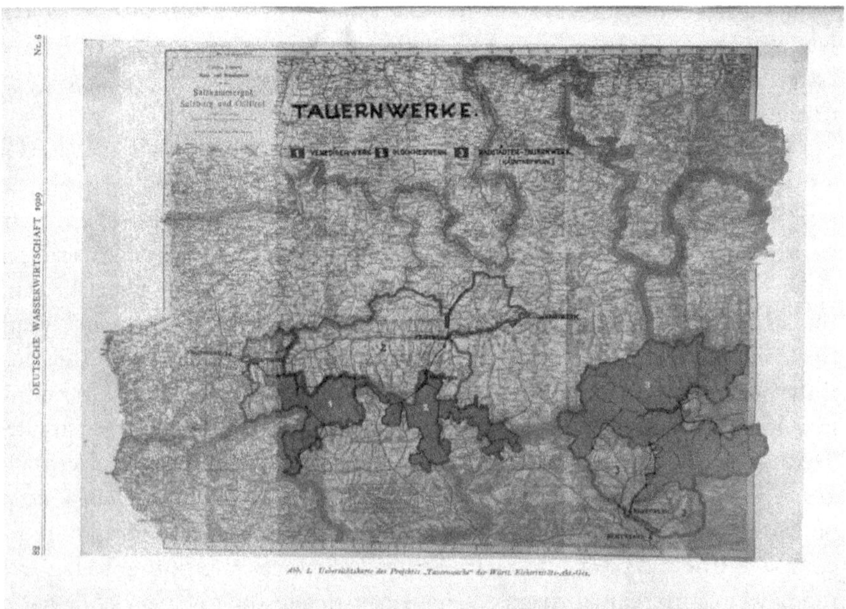

Figure 1: "The Tauern Works," *Deutsche Wasserwirtschaft.*

Soon thereafter, the giant German General Electric Company (AEG) publicized its own plans for an even more ambitious "super" Tauern project. AEG was an electrical trust of world renown. It had been the first company in Germany to acquire the license to construct Thomas Edison's renowned illumination systems. The Berlin company also had the backing of the Creditanstalt, one of Austria's foremost banking houses. Instead of constructing dams in multiple Tauern valleys, the AEG project envisioned centralizing as much Tauern water as possible in one single valley: Kaprun. Of all the Tauern valleys, Kaprun was the steepest. Therefore, AEG argued, it was best suited for generating the maximum amount of waterpower possible in the Hohe Tauern. Their engineers calculated that to provide the necessary storage, the water level of the highest Kaprun dam would have to lie at an altitude of just above 2000 meters. However, this meant it would be higher than the sources of numerous waterways in the mountain range that might be drawn upon for additional power. To get as much water as possible to Kaprun, AEG foresaw building a network of high-altitude "slope canals" totaling 1,200 kilometers in length. The slope canals, an unproven technology, would capture water before it collected into torrents and deliver it to Kaprun. Another novel feature of the plan was to transfer water across the main ridge of the Alps to the Kaprun valley via tunnel. While AEG's designs boasted greater dimensions, both companies promised that their Tauern projects would generate enough electricity to satisfy all Austrian demands and leave plenty of electricity left over for export to Germany.

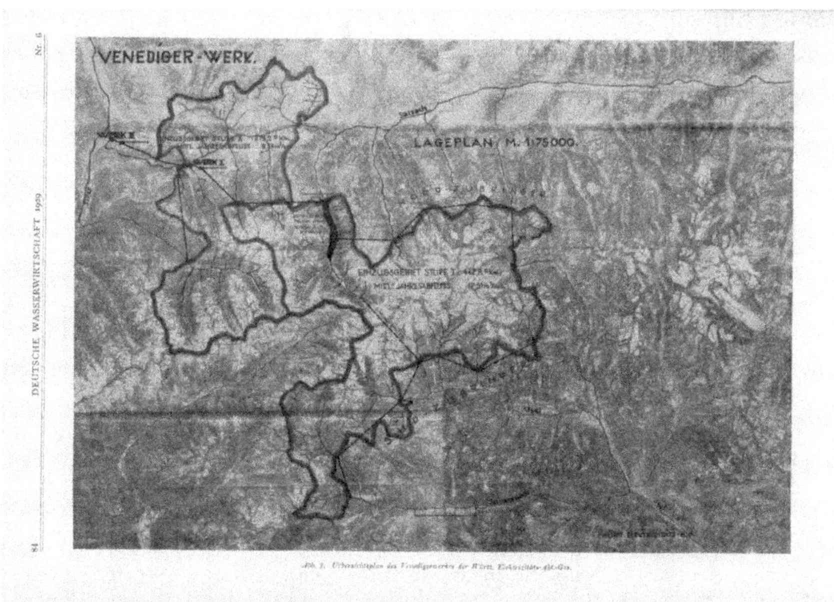

Figure 2: "Venediger Works," *Deutsche Wasserwirtschaft.*

The AEG project had been comissioned at the behest of Salzburg governor Franz Rehrl. Rehrl argued that Austria needed to move from the erection of "middling" hydropower plants to those "of the greatest dimension with the widest radius of action." And nowhere else in the entire Alpine area, he claimed, was there the possibility to exploit such a high-lying area in so few stages, with such a steep gradient. In the AEG project, Rehrl saw a unique opportunity to animate the sluggish economy of his mostly agrarian province. Besides the benefits that would come from selling electricity to Germany, the project would provide an enormous boost to the local construction industry. The AEG project would create thousands of jobs building new roads and performing the numerous hydraulic engineering tasks such an undertaking would require. Some of Rehrl's support may also have derived from a sense of competition with other provinces of Alpine Austria. Rehrl noted that Salzburg's western neighbor Tyrol had been transporting and selling its hydroelectricity to nearby Bavaria for several years. And tiny Vorarlberg in westernmost Austria had recently become the first Alpine province to send its waterpower hundreds of kilometers north to the heartland of German coal-fired utilities in the Rhineland.[19]

At this point, Hermann Grengg entered the debate. Grengg evidently viewed himself as an authority compelled to defend what he perceived as Austrian energy interests. He took to the pages of the trade journal *Die Wasserwirtschaft* to explain how the AEG plan violated these concerns. This was the mouthpiece of several groups, most notably the Water Management Association of Austrian Industry (*Wasserwirtschaftsverband der österreichischen Industrie*), and the central forum for Austrian hydropower. Already in this first response, Grengg established the outlines of his critique. Any project in the Hohe Tauern that conformed to Austrian interests would have to obey two broad conventions. First, it would have to be based upon established methods of high-altitude Alpine dam-building that had been employed in the 1920s. That Austrians, as citizens of a mountainous country, better understood the peculiarities of engineering in this environment, was implicit. Second, it would have to respect the interests of the relevant Austrian *Länder*. Up until that point, it had been the *Länder* that dominated electrification in Austria, and Grengg—a manager in the Styrian provincial utility—saw this position as justified. In the following paragraphs, I will analyze aspects of the "battle of the systems" debate that show how already during the First Republic, Austrian engineers developed conceptions of the Tauern energy that they would safeguard through to realization.

While Grengg agreed that the future of "our waterpower" pointed towards "Reichsdeutschland," he argued that such fantastic plans did a disservice to hydropower development in Austria and prevented objective discussion of Austria's energy supply problems. Grengg sought to prove that AEG's projected energy harvest—which by his calculations was not much lower than the entire available hydropower potential in Austria—was an impossibility. Using the Grossglockner map of the German-Austrian

Alpine Association, he argued that it would be impossible to transfer so much water to the Kaprun valley without substantial use of pumps. This would, in turn, diminish the energy bounty. Grengg curtly dismissed the idea of transferring water from the south slope of the Tauern to the Kaprun valley as "utopic."[20]

A short time later, Grengg felt compelled to expand his criticism in another issue of *Wasserwirtschaft*. By this point, additional details of the AEG project had become available, allowing the Styrian to zero in on the plan's faults. He focused now on the slope canals, the innovation that would allow the capture of more Tauern water than previously thought possible. "If it is already from the outset improbable that the entire previous construction technique, developed in Switzerland and common today through the Alps, has been mistaken . . . a closer investigation proves the entire system to be unworkable." "Nobody familiar with high-altitude mountains," Grengg contended, could take it seriously. His comments emphasized the belief that there was a right way to build dams in the high-Alps, and that Austrians knew it better than a company in Berlin.[21]

"Too much in the great plan runs not just contrary to nature, but also against the economic and legal order." In this manner, Grengg characterized perhaps the most absurd fault of the project for him: its ignorance of the sanctity of inner-Austrian borders. By taking water from across the Tauern range and diverting it to Kaprun, the AEG plan entailed a gigantic economic bonus for Salzburg, while disadvantaging Tyrol and Carinthia. "It will escape the Tyroleans," Grengg explained, why the precipitation in the Tyrolean Defereggengebirge should not be used in a Tyrolean power plant near Lienz but sent via tunnel through the main ridge of the Alps to Kaprun. The Carinthians, for their part, "in the correct understanding of the needs of their land," would reject sending water destined for the Drau to the Salzach in Salzburg.[22] For Grengg, it was common sense that one day Kaprun would be home to a large dam. The rest, however, was "a geographic fantasy."[23]

After all this criticism, Grengg closed by presenting what he saw as the fundamental problem. While the AEG idea likely made for great copy in their advertisements by promising impossible amounts of energy at impossibly low prices, it would cast a shadow over the past and future of Austrian hydropower development. Previous achievements and future projects would pale in comparison.

> To stand up against this, to counter the assertion that Austrian engineering on our waterpower has been inexpedient, to prevent further confusion within the decisive lay circles—this service to the

> continuation of our hydropower development should not be left to one person.[24]

Grengg had now staked out the Austrian stance towards utilizing the potential of the Hohe Tauern. In a nutshell, his outlook welcomed the idea of utilizing Austria's highest mountain range to generate electricity on a large scale. However, it needed to be done in a way that did not deviate too far from previous Austrian methods, and it needed to conform to Austrian political realities. In the meantime, the Upper Austrian provincial utility (ÖKA) presented a competing project, one that conformed better to these strictures by calling for several dams in the Hohe Tauern in addition to Kaprun. But an Upper Austrian utility getting the nod to carry out such an endeavor in Salzburg was not a high probability.

In the wake of Grengg's campaign, experts from across Austria and Germany also weighed in. This literature is too vast to analyze in its entirety.[25] Nevertheless, a few examples are included here to illustrate the crystallization of an Austrian position on the matter. An engineer from Villach confirmed Grengg's assertions about the willingness of Carinthians to donate their water to Salzburg:

> Our land certainly has a rich treasure of natural beauty and valuable waterpower, otherwise it is poor, and the proponents, who, with their long grasping tentacles, seek to haul the white coal out of the land, should not be surprised if we defend our possession and only want to sacrifice to the federal government, that which is absolutely necessary in the interest of the national economy.[26]

Similarly, two engineering associations asked for a statement about the projects by the provincial government in Tyrol spurned the planned diversion of water from Eastern Tyrol to Salzburg. Instead, they argued, the province should build its own dams in Eastern Tyrol to utilize the Tauern water.[27]

In framing the Tauern issues as an "Austrian problem," Oskar Vas contributed a couple of important ideas to the debate. First, he argued that Austria's highest duty was not to utilize the Tauern to generate the greatest number of kilowatt-hours but to exploit the mountains for water storage. Taking advantage of the Tauern valleys to serve as reservoirs, in his opinion, was more important than producing the maximum number of kilowatt-hours. Only storage, Vas insisted, could compensate for the general drop in waterpower availability that happened during the winter in Austria. Second, Vas seized upon the term that from this point forward would be used to describe the essence of the AEG plan: "concentration." Going forward, the Austrian position was for maximum storage and against maximum concentration. "Decentralization," instead, became the motto.[28]

Austrian objections notwithstanding, the influential group behind the AEG scheme moved to explore its viability in the form of preliminary groundwork. This included digging a test canal in the Mooserboden in the summer of 1929. It was supposed to demonstrate the feasibility of the slope canal system by capturing glacial outflow (Willingerkees) and several other rivulets. In all, the considerable sum of three million schillings was spent assessing various aspects of the proposal. These efforts were overtaken by the broader economic context, however. By 1930, the worsening world depression diminished interest in the expensive project. Simultaneously, the ascent of National Socialism in Germany, hampered political relations with Austria and made AEG activity there a non-starter. However, as with most engineering projects, the plans for tapping the power of Hohe Tauern did not simply disappear. Instead, they sat in a filing cabinet, awaiting a political and economic constellation more conducive to their realization.

Setting the Austrian Dam in Stone

With the Anschluss in 1938, the political stars aligned once again. One of the primary economic reasons behind the Anschluss was the desire to access Austrian hydropower resources. Hermann Göring himself underscored this in a landmark speech in Vienna's Northwest Station a mere two weeks after Nazi Germany's annexation of Austria. The head of the German economy listed the construction of a power plant in the Hohe Tauern as the first priority of hydropower development. To finance and execute the exploitation of Austrian waterpower, the Reich established a state-owned corporation, the Alpen-Elektrowerke AG (AEW).[29] For reasons that are not entirely clear, AEW named Hermann Grengg technical director in charge of the Tauern project. Certainly, Grengg's long history with the Austrian Nazi Party helped. Regardless of how he came to be in this position, however, his presence there ensured that he would play a vital role in determining what got built. He had the opportunity to literally set some aspects of the power plants in stone, and he overcame considerable resistance to implement a version that conformed to what he saw as Austria's interests.

Throughout late 1938 the Styrian composed his plan for Tauern energy. Its outlines reflected the decentralized variants preferred by Austrian engineers and rejected the concentration favored by AEG. In supporting decentralization, Grengg had now adopted the viewpoint earlier expressed by his colleague, Oskar Vas, that the special purpose of any Tauern project should be to store as much water as possible. He argued that only by building dams throughout the various valleys of the Tauern could AEW achieve the greatest amount of "super storage" (*Großspeicherung*) possible. For Grengg super storage represented nothing less than the "special function of the Tauern waterpower in the big picture." Super storage, he explained, consisted of adapting the release of water for power generating purposes to the annual rhythms of energy demand. Essentially, Grengg wanted to create a series of "winter works" in the Tauern. These were large dams built to store as much summer meltwater as possible in order to utilize the bulk of this energy during the winter months. Precisely during the cold months, when many of Austria's rivers would be running low, the Tauern dams could make up for hydroelectric shortfalls. The first and most important winter work would be constructed in Kaprun. Later reservoirs would be established in other parts of the range as the demand for electricity grew. Utilizing the Hohe Tauern in this manner was necessary because the range represented one of the few places on German soil where it remained possible. Far western Austria's reservoirs in Vorarlberg had already fallen into the Ruhr industry's sphere of influence.[30]

Furthermore, Grengg had another parochial reason for his pursuit of storage. Like many hydraulic engineers throughout the Alps, he had come to believe that the uplands should be exploited to the fullest for their unique storage capabilities, in order to fulfill a critical role in the regional electricity supply. High-Alpine reservoirs, he believed, had to serve as the "regulators" for the regional electricity grids in the Alps. Reservoirs, he argued, eased the difficulties that arose from trying to coordinate the pooling of current from several different sources within an electricity grid; they offered "steadiness." Moreover, in contrast to brown coal—which otherwise functioned as excellent supplementary energy to inconstant waterpower—Alpine reservoirs lay nearby. Accessing their power did not require expensive—and vulnerable—transport infrastructure. In his arguments in favor of super storage, Grengg acknowledged that the concept likely seemed foreign to the water management concerns prevalent in the other German lands but maintained it was necessary in the high-Alps.[31] Here again, the Styrian suggested that only Austrians truly understood the exigencies of mountain dam-building. Nevertheless, by this time, Grengg had adopted one of the major features of the AEG plan that he had previously rejected out of hand. The notion he borrowed involved damming the outflow of the Pasterze glacier and diverting this water through a tunnel across the main ridge of the Alps and into the reservoirs of the Kaprun valley.

Beyond these considerations, Grengg believed a decentralized project to be more expedient. As he later wrote of the AEG plan, "It had not required the mathematical demonstration of the inferiority of this plan vis-à-vis a development in separate groups to help the latter to victory." In his analysis neither the possibility nor the need existed for the superlative facility. The centralized plan was impossible in Grengg's estimation due to the very limited economic resources of labor and materials that were being spread throughout all sectors of the Austrian economy following the *Anschluss*. The resources for the realization of regular hydropower projects scarcely existed, to say nothing of the materials required for a supersized facility. Moreover, the centralized plan called for the Tauern waterpower to play a role in an interconnected, Reich-spanning electricity grid that did not yet exist: "It seemed to me a mistake to want to even consider developing the power of the entire Tauern range with exceedingly expensive storage works for use in a German electrical grid (*zentralisierte deutsche Verbundwirtschaft*) that had not even been conceptualized, rejecting a 'natural' development of the Tauern waterpower for a 'once-and-for-all' in the Kaprun valley."[32]

Construction on this decentralized, Austria-oriented variant was to proceed in four phases, with the erection of the *Tauernkraftwerk* Kaprun-Glockner coming first. This first phase would consist of an upper and a main power stage in the Kaprun valley, each replete with its own high-altitude reservoir. First, the main stage would be completed. Grengg reckoned that by 1941, the main stage would be able to operate as a run-of-river plant; after five years, the completion of the main stage dam would enable the plant to function as a storage work. The schedule for the upper stage reservoir was left for the future. Initially, the Kaprun-Glockner dams were to serve the electricity supply of eastern Austria, the location of the country's greatest industrial and urban concentration. By the mid-1940s, as development of Austria's other white coal expanded enough to cover Austrian energy demands, the Tauern power would be connected to the high-voltage line heading north from Austria into East Germany to send any excess current to the industry of the lignite fields there.

Completing the main stage became the first order of business, and to ensure that it could begin delivering at least some power within three years, Grengg had to fix certain dimensions of the project. To a degree, these actions set the future of the project in stone. Tunnels, for example, had to be measured and drilled in accordance with the amount of water the powerhouses would process. Enlarging them later would incur additional costs.

Foundation work for the dams also largely dictated the future height of the reservoirs. In early January 1939, AEW reported to Field Marshal Göring that the drilling of the principal tunnel had begun. It was these sorts of path dependencies that made Grengg's decision an "ultimate" one. Even if his actions did not go unquestioned, they "determined up until this day and in the future the development of the Tauern waterpower."[33]

Challenges to Grengg's decisions emerged in the spring of 1939. Almost simultaneously, two high-level Nazi functionaries raised doubts about his conclusions. Josef Bürckel, the Commissar for the Reunification of Austria with the German Reich, realized that Grengg aimed for an Austrian regional facility. In the margins of his copy of the first AEW annual business report, Bürckel made notes apparently criticizing the organization's project. He noted that what AEW was currently building was a "completely different and more limited project." When the report explained that the Tauern project would act as reserve power for the dams on the "climatically different" Drau and Danube rivers—and therefore as a "new, reliable foundation for the electricity supply of the Ostmark," Bürckel scribbled: "that means the Tauernwerk is destined only for the el. supply [sic] of the Ostmark!"[34] Bürckel engaged two Reich-German engineers to review the entire history of Kaprun and make a recommendation. Independently, the Reich's newly appointed energy czar (Plenipotentiary for the German Energy Supply) Just Dillgardt also contacted Bürckel with questions about the Kaprun project. In April 1939, Dillgardt traveled to Vienna to discuss these issues with Bürckel.[35] Afterward, Dillgardt forwarded the completed review to Grengg at AEW and demanded a swift response.[36]

This arrived in the form of a lengthy written statement. In its rhetorical strategy, it sought to undermine the centralized idea with three main arguments. First, it cast doubt on the viability of the technology. As he had objected from the earliest days, Grengg once again declared that the vaunted high-altitude slope canals could not deliver the promised water. Second, it maintained that even if by some miracle diverting all Tauern water to Kaprun was technically possible, it would result in unacceptable consequences for agriculture, thus threatening the food supply of the German racial community. Finally, Grengg conceded that even if these two concerns were dismissed, altering plans would only negate all progress that had been made and result in catastrophic delays.[37] In May 1939, energy czar Dillgardt ultimately decided to continue Grengg's project. Dillgardt approved the decentral solution in part because he agreed that it would be better for Austrian agriculture. However, he also offered a justification that had not yet occurred to the hydraulic experts: national defense. Military considerations, according to Dillgardt, spoke against concentrating all of the energy of the Tauern range in a single work.[38]

Conclusion

Grengg had fought hard for Austrian interests, but he would not see the project through to completion. Immediately after the Nazi invasion of Poland, progress slowed considerably. Though the dams remained a priority among energy projects, procuring both materials and labor became difficult. AEW increasingly used forced labor to overcome the latter shortage. The initial timeline had called for the plant to produce limited power by 1941 and the main stage to be completed by 1943. It quickly became apparent that there was no chance of meeting either of these deadlines, and completion would not be possible under wartime conditions. Only the intense use of forced labor allowed for the generation of some power by late 1944. Less than a year after the generators in Kaprun first started feeding electricity into the Third Reich's grid, Allied forces captured the facility. In the summer of 1946, the US transferred the Kaprun construction site and its shares of AEW to the Austrian government. It would not be until 1947 that the necessary political, legal, and financial circumstances permitted the resumption of construction. Only with the help of Marshall Plan aid could construction on Kaprun resume. It is an indication of Grengg's satisfactory decision-making that the project he had begun in 1938 was not only continued during the Second Republic but vigorously defended against American objections. American authorities could not understand the Austrian insistence on completing the relatively expensive Kaprun dams, when cheaper possibilities existed. The Austrians ultimately succeeded in convincing US authorities of the necessity of Kaprun, though one functionary would later claim it was only because he had been sick at the time of the final decision.[39]

Grengg was not included in the postwar construction team, however. In the course of denazification, he lost his position at AEW and was held in custody for nine months in the American camp at Glasenbach. Though he quickly re-established his career—he worked clandestinely at the Styrian electric utility and became a professor at the Technische Hochschule in Graz in 1948 and rector in 1954—he clearly never forgave the Americans for what he saw as his unjust internment. In contrast to the positive words he had for Russian forced laborers—he called them his "elite troops"—he referred to the Americans in his autobiography variously as "the uniformed hordes," the "American winner vermin" (*Sieger-Gesindel*), the "crusaders," and the “do-gooders” (*Weltverbesserer*). Grengg’s actions had nevertheless decisively influenced the final project, and, therefore, the foundation of Austria’s postwar electricity supply. Belatedly Grengg’s contributions have been recognized. In 1994, exactly fifty years after Tauern water began to turn the first generator there, a bust of Grengg was dedicated in the Kaprun power house.[40]

Endnotes

1. Biographical information on Grengg in Stefan Karner, *Im Strom der Zeit: 100 Jahre Energie der Steiermark* (Graz: Styria Media Design, 2021), 227–28.

2. Georg Rigele, "Das Tauernkraftwerk Glockner-Kaprun—Neue Forschsungsergebnisse und offene Fragen," *Blätter für Technikgeschichte 59* (1997): 59.

3. Hermann Grengg, *Das Großspeicherwerk Glockner-Kaprun* (Vienna: Springer, 1952), 1–3.

4. Oskar Vas, foreword to *Das Großspeicherwerk Glockner-Kaprun*, by Hermann Grengg (Vienna: Springer, 1952), iv.

5. Kaprun received 1,428,000,000 Austrian Schillings of a total investment in the electricity supply of 2,961,000,000. Marshall funds covered around 70% of total electric investment. Oliver Rathkolb, "NS-Erbe, Wiederaufbau, Marshallplan und das 'Weiße Gold' in den europäischen Netzwerken," in Oliver Rathkolb et al., ed. *Wasserkraft: Elektrizität. Gesellschaft. Kraftwerksprojekte ab 1880 im Spannungfeld* (Vienna: K&S, 2012), 197, 200.

6. On Kaprun's function as a stamp Christian Rohr, "The Austrian Environment *en miniature*: 'Official' Perceptions of the Austrian Landscape Reflected Through Postal Stamps since 1945," in *Austrian Environmental History*, ed. Marc Landry and Patrick Kupper, Contemporary Austrian Studies 27 (New Orleans: University of New Orleans Press, 2018), 175–76.

7. One of the first efforts came from a journalist, Clemens M. Hutter, *Geschichte eines Erfolgs* (Salzburg: Residenz, 1994); Rigele, "Das Tauernkraftwerk Glockner-Kaprun." A good summary of Kaprun can be found in Ernst Hanisch, *Landschaft und Identität: Versuch einer österreichischen Erfahrungsgeschichte* (Vienna: Böhlau, 2019), 180–86.

8. Oliver Rathkolb and Florian Freund, eds., *NS-Zwangsarbeit in der Elektrizitätswirtschaft der "Ostmark" 1938–1945* (Vienna: Böhlau, 2002).

9. Georg Rigele, "The Marshall Plan and Austria's Hydroelectric Industry: Kaprun" in The Marshall Plan in Austria, ed. Günter Bischof, Anton Pelinka, and Dieter Stiefel, Contemporary Austrian Studies 8, (New Brunswick, NJ: Transaction, 2000): 323–56; Georg Rigele, "Das Tauernkraftwerk Glockner-Kaprun—Neue Forschsungsergebnisse und offene Fragen," *Blätter für Technikgeschichte 59* (1997): 55–94; Georg Rigele, "Der Marshall-Plan und Österreichs Alpenwasser-Kräfte: Kaprun," Günter Bischof and Dieter Stiefel, eds., *"80 Dollar": 50 Jahre ERP-Fonds und Marshall-Plan in Österreich: 1948-1998.* (Vienna: Ueberreuter, 1999): 183–216.

10. Martin Schmid and Ortrun Veichtlbauer, *Vom Naturschutz zur Ökologiebewegung: Umweltgeschichte Österreichs in der Zweiten Republik* (Vienna: Studienverlag, 2006), 28–35.

11. Rolf-Peter Sieferle, *The Subterranean Forest: Energy Systems and the Industrial Revolution* (Cambridge: White Horse, 2001), ix.

12. Sara B. Pritchard, *Confluence: The Nature of Technology and the Remaking of the Rhone* (Cambridge, MA: Harvard University Press, 2011).

13. Hanisch, *Landschaft und Identität*, 180.

14. A similar point is made in David P. Billington and Donald C. Jackson, *Dams of the New Deal Era* (Norman: University of Oklahoma Press, 2006). All of the iconic dams of the 1930s were based on much older plans.

15. Cf. Ernst Bruckmüller, ed., *Wiederaufbau in Österreich 1945-1955: Rekonstruktion oder Neubeginn?* (Vienna: 1995).

16. My current book manuscript (which looks at Kaprun in a broader context) traces this history: *Europe's Battery: The Alps, Water, and Power in the Fossil Fuel Age*.

17. "Tauernwerke-Projekt der Württ. Elektrizitäts-AG Stuttgart," *Deutsche Wasserwirtschaft: Zentralblatt für Wasserbau und Wasserwirtschaft* 24, no. 6 (20 June 1929): 81–88.

18. "Tauernwerke-Projekt der Württ. Elektrizitäts-AG Stuttgart," *Deutsche Wasserwirtschaft: Zentralblatt für Wasserbau und Wasserwirtschaft* 24, no. 6 (20 June 1929): 81-88.

19. Franz Rehrl, "Bericht der Landesregierung über das Projekt einer Verwertung der Wasserkräfte im Bereiche der Tauernkette" (29 January 1929), RehrlTW 1929/0001, Salzburger Landesarchiv, Salzburg (hereafter SLA).

20. Hermann Grengg, "Das Tauernprojekt," *Die Wasserwirtschaft* 22, no. 7 (1929): 1.

21. Hermann Grengg, "Das Tauernkraftwerk," *Die Wasserwirtschaft* 22, no. 12 (1929): 17.

22. Hermann Grengg, "Das Tauernkraftwerk," *Die Wasserwirtschaft* 22, no. 12 (1929): 18.

23. Hermann Grengg, "Das Tauernkraftwerk," *Die Wasserwirtschaft* 22, no. 12 (1929): 18.

24. Hermann Grengg, "Das Tauernkraftwerk," *Die Wasserwirtschaft* 22, no. 12 (1929): 18.

25. Cf. *Die Wasserwirtschaft* 22, no. 18 (1929): 341–42; *Die Wasserwirtschaft* 22, no. 22 (1929): 408; *Die Wasserwirtschaft* 22, no. 23 (1929): 420; *Die Wasserwirtschaft* 22, no. 28 (1929): 496; *Die Wasserwirtschaft* 22, no. 30 (1929): 515–18; *Die Wasserwirtschaft* 22, no. 35 (1929): 636; *Die Wasserwirtschaft* 23, no. 1 (1930): 10–12, 15; *Die Wasserwirtschaft* 23, no. 5 (1930): 87; *Die Wasserwirtschaft* 23, no. 11 (1930): 187; *Die Wasserwirtschaft* 23, no. 31 (1930): 663; *Die Wasserwirtschaft* 24, no. 8 (1931): 109–17; *Die Wasserwirtschaft* 24, no. 11 (1931): 157–162; *Die Wasserwirtschaft* 24, no. 12 (1931): 169–75; *Die Wasserwirtschaft* 24, no. 13–14 (1931): 181–231; *Die Wasserwirtschaft* 24, no. 17–18 (1931): 289–95; *Die Wasserwirtschaft* 24, no. 21 (1931): 358; *Die Wasserwirtschaft* 24, no. 30 (1931): 507–13; *Die Wasserwirtschaft* 25, no. 15 (1932): 213–15.

26. Richard Moro, "Betrachtungen über das Tauernkraftwerks-projekt der AEG," *Die Wasserwirtschaft* 24, no. 8 (1931): 109.

27. "Stellungnahme der Ingenieurkammer für Tirol und Vorarlberg und des Vereines der Ingenieure in Tirol und Vorarlberg zu den Projekten der Allgemeinen Elektrizitäts-Gesellschaft Berlin (AEG) und der österreichischen Kraftwerke A.-G. (Oeka) für das Tauernkraftwerk," *Die Wasserwirtschaft* 24, no. 11 (1931): 158–62.

28. Oskar Vas, "Die Ausnutzung der Tauernwasserkräfte als österreichisches Problem," *Die Wasserwirtschaft* 24, no. 13–14 (1931): 191–201.

29. AEW was a subsidiary of the Reich owned industrial giant *Vereinigte-Industrieunternehmungen AG* (VIAG). On the history of the AEW, see Maria Magdalena Koller "Elektrizitätswirtschaft in Österreich, 1938–1947: von den Alpenelektrowerken zur Verbundgesellschaft," (PhD diss., Karl-Franzens-University of Graz, 1985).

30. "Die Eigenart und die besondere Aufgabe der Tauern-Wasserkraft im Rahmen der deutschen Elektrizitätswirtschaft (zweite Auflage Jänner 1939)," 5–9, RStH V/3 171, SLA.

31. "Die Eigenart," 5–9, SLA.

32. Grengg, *Großspeicherwerk Glockner-Kaprun*, 4.

33. Grengg, *Großspeicherwerk Glockner-Kaprun*, 5.

34. Marginalia in *Alpen-Elektrowerke Aktiengesellschaft Wien,* "Geschäftsbericht über das erste Geschäftsjahr 1938," 5–6, AdR, 04, "Bürckel Materien" Kt. 88, 2155/O Bd. II-E-Wirtschaft in d. Ostmark Allgemein.

35. AT-OeStA/ AdR, 04, "Bürckel-Materien" 2155/2: Letter Dillgardt to Bürckel (9 March 1939).

36. Hermann Grengg, "Stellungnahme der Alpen-Elektrowerke A.G. Wien (AEW) zum Gutachten Thürnau-Schmidt vom 11.IV.1939," RStH V/3 171, SLA.

37. Grengg, "Stellungnahme," RStH V/3 171, SLA.

38. Summary of meeting on 24 May 1939, RStH V/3 171, SLA. Just Dillgardt and Arno Fischer attended in the office of Josef Bürckel.

39. Rigele, "Der Marshall-Plan und Österreichs Alpen-Wasserkräfte," 201–10.

40. The biographical information on Grengg comes from Rigele, "Das Tauernrkraftwerk," 66–67, as well as footnote 17.

ROUNDTABLE:
The Pioneers of Austrian Holocaust Studies

Introduction

Günter Bischof

This roundtable came about as a result of Joseph Moser giving a paper on his father in the Austrian Studies Association (ASA) meeting in Bowling Green, Ohio, in April 2019. This gave me an idea to organize a panel on "Early Austrian Holocaust Historians." During the 2018 ASA-meeting at the University of Vermont in Burlington, I worked with the Raul Hilberg Papers in the Special Collections Library. Hilberg was a Jewish Anschluss-refugee from Austria who spent most of his distinguished career as the founding father of Holocaust history in the Political Science Department of the University of Vermont. We organized a panel on "The Role of Austrians in the Origins of Holocaust Studies (Pioneering Austrian Holocaust Scholars)" for the annual meeting of the German Studies Association (GSA) in Indianapolis in October 2020 (thanks to Gerald Steinacher for submitting the panel). Due to the Covid pandemic this meeting was postponed; the panel took place online a year later during the GSA meeting in Indianapolis and is now being published in vol. 31 of *Contemporary Austrian Studies*. Unfortunately, the paper delivered by Olaf Bortz on Raul Hilberg in the GSA panel was not submitted for this roundtable. So, an important part of the original vision of Austrian Holocaust pioneers is missing and we will try to make up for it in this introduction.

The papers published here are the ones delivered on Simon Wiesenthal (Gerald J. Steinacher), Jonny Moser (Joseph W. Moser), and Hermann Langbein (Winfried R. Garscha). Two of these early pioneers of Holocaust studies, Wiesenthal and Moser, were Austrian Jews who survived the Holocaust and Nazi genocide, and were determined to actively remember, tell their stories, and keep the tragedy of the Holocaust alive. All three of these pioneers of Holocaust education personally experienced Nazi concentration/extermination camps: Wiesenthal endured multiple camps, ending up in Mauthausen (the only concentration camp in the *Ostmark/ Donau und Alpen Gaue* (with an extensive and infamous subcamp system); the Communist Langbein was incarcerated soon after the "Anschluss" and spent the war in Dachau and then Auschwitz; Moser and his family were lucky to escape [deportation to] Auschwitz, [and then obtained] Schutzpässe from the Swedish diplomat Raoul Wallenberg during their

Hungarian exile in the war; after a period of being underground refugees, he and his family ended up in a labor camp in Eastern Hungary.

Remarkably, these three survivors recognized the Nazis' genocidal action as being an extraordinary historical criminal event and wrote about it during and soon after the war ended. Langbein had smuggled, out of the camps to Vienna, a firsthand 4-page type-written document about the extermination process going on in Auschwitz (the gassings and the "normal daily work" in the crematoria) as early as the spring of 1944, before the Hungarian Jews arrived there in May. In April 1945 he wrote a single-spaced 26-page typed report on events that he had witnessed in Auschwitz, known as the 'Hanover report.' Langbein became known for his 2-volume documentation of the Auschwitz trial in Frankfurt (1965) and for his detailed report, *Menschen in Auschwitz* (1980). Jonny Moser kept a detailed journal during his time in Budapest and wrote a dissertation about Austrian anti-semitism at the University of Vienna, which he completed in 1961. Moser was the first Austrian historian to write a history of the persecution of the Jews in Austria in 1966, long before professional historians began to pay attention to the Holocaust in the 1990s. They were "one man shows," lone wolves who tried to keep the memory of the Shoah alive vis-à-vis the silences they experienced all around them. Like Jonny Moser, these survivors collected documents and preserved their Vienna homes as early Holocaust archives.

While in Linz, Simon Wiesenthal began to collect evidence from Displaced Persons (DP's) on Austrian and German perpetrators after his liberation from Mauthausen, working with American intelligence and authorities to bring Nazi perpetrators to justice.[1] Thus, he provided witnesses for the Mauthausen trial and trials at Austrian people's courts (*Volksgerichte*) in the prosecution of perpetrators. As early as 1947, he institutionalized his efforts by founding the Center for Jewish Historical Documentation (*Zentrum für Jüdische Historische Dokumentation*), which moved to Vienna in 1961. There, he opened the Documentation Center of the Association of Jewish Victims (*Dokumentationszentrum des Bundes jüdischer Verfolgter des Naziregimes*). Wiesenthals importance in documenting Nazi war crimes comes with the collection of documents and witness reports in his two centers, going well beyond the capture of Adolf Eichmann in 1961, which gave him the title of "Nazi hunter." He also was instrumental in making Austrian authorities aware of the fact that Austrians harbored many Nazi perpetrators in their midst. As early as July 1952 he wrote a memorandum to Chancellor Leopold Figl, reminding him that restitution should be paid to slave laborers who had worked in Austrian industries during the war (this would only happen in the early 2000s, fifty years after his memorandum).

In October 1966, Wiesenthal wrote a lengthy memorandum to Chancellor Josef Klaus, reminding him of the prominent roles Austrian perpetrators played in the Holocaust and proposing a reform of the Austrian judicial system to efficiently prosecute Austrian war criminals. Austrian historians are now coming to recognize this as a crucial document in early Austrian Holocaust research.

All of this early documentation of Austrian perpetrators in the Holocaust preceded Raul Hilberg's dissertation at Columbia University, which was eventually published into his classic work: *The Destruction of the European Jews*, 3 vols. (1961).

Raul Hilberg was the first scholar to engage in critical Holocaust research. Neither academia nor publishers were ready for such a topic. It took Hilberg years to find a publisher for his foundational 3-volume study. Hilberg considered himself lucky to find a professional home in the Political Science Department of the University of Vermont, where he spent his entire academic career.[2] As a younger cohort of scholars, such as Christopher Browning, began to study the Holocaust in the 1970s, Hilberg became their mentor and supporter.[3] Holocaust scholarship became a thriving academic field in the 1990s, a generation after Austrian Holocaust survivors invented the field by bearing witness.

Wiesenthal, Moser and Hilberg also wrote autobiographies: Wiesenthal's *Justice not Vengeance* (1989), Moser's *Wallenberg's Laufbursche* (2006), and Hilberg's *The Politics of Memory: Journey of a Holocaust Historian* (1996). These autobiographies documented their difficult lives during World War II and allowed historians to trace early Holocaust research.

What is most surprising about these early Austrian contributions to Holocaust research is that it comes at a time when Austria officially proffered its infamous "victim theory," based on the 1943 Moscow Declaration, claiming that Austria was the "first victim of Nazi Germany." Holocaust survivors struggled to keep both the focus on Austrian perpetrators as well as exposing the victim myth, which allowed Austrian perpetrators to hide their crimes from prosecution and/or being acquitted by Austrian courts. It would be interesting to see what survivors thought about the longevity of Austria's victim theory, which survived legislation until the election of Kurt Waldheim in 1986. The journals of Günther Anders, who survived the war in the United States and returned to Vienna in 1950 with his Austrian wife, Elisabeth Fröhlich, give us an idea of what Jewish refugees thought about Austrians' failure to confront their World War II past. Anders spoke to many Viennese about their wartime experience and wrote down what was said and, most importantly, unsaid (for example, he never heard Hitler's name spoken) in his journals. The Viennese liked to talk about their victimhood in the bombing war and their "very real privation as a means of total exoneration." Anders encountered widespread, grim antisemitism in postwar Vienna, especially on the issue of Jewish survivors returning to reclaim their "aryan-ized" homes and businesses. He confided to his first wife Hannah Arendt in a letter: "the Jew-lessness of the world here is hardly bearable."[4] Jason Dawsey's "critical ethnography" of Anders' philosophical observations of everyday life and thought in postwar Vienna gave us a good idea of how Wiesenthal, Langbein, and Moser must have felt about their neighbors' failures to come to terms with their past.

Endnotes

1 On Mauthausen, see Bertrand Perz, *Die KZ-Gedenkstätte Mauthausen: 1945 bis zur Gegenwart* (Innsbruck: StudienVerlag, 2006).

2 As told in Raul Hilberg, *The Politics of Memory: The Journey of a Holocaust Historian* (Chicago: Ivan R. Dee, 1996).

3 See Christopher Browning's autobiographical essay "Vietnam, Watergate, and the Emergence of Holocaust Studies," published as part of the essay series on "Learning the Scholar's Craft" on H-Diplo, accessed January 16, 2022 https://networks.h-net.org/node/28443/discussions/8706955/h-diplo-essay-380-christopher-r-browning-learning-scholars-craft; Browning wrote his dissertation on the German Foreign Office under Nazism at the University of Wisconsin-Madison in 1973/74 and published it in 1978: Christopher Browning, *The Final Solution and the German Foreign Office* (New York: Holmes & Meier, 1978).

4 Jason Dawsey, "Where Hitler's Name Is Never Spoken: Günther Anders in 1950s Vienna," in *Austrian Lives*, Contemporary Austrian Studies 21, ed. Günter Bischof, Fritz Plasser, Eva Maltschnig (New Orleans: University of New Orleans Press; Innsbruck: *i*nnsbruck university press, 2012), 212–39 (here 231, 232).

The Nazi Hunter: Simon Wiesenthal and the *Täterforschung* [1]

Gerald J. Steinacher

Remember. Do not forget

זכור. אל תשכח

Apart from Mozart, Simon Wiesenthal is arguably one of the most well-known Austrians worldwide. A powerful moral voice and famous "Nazi hunter," he helped capture Adolf Eichmann and many other Holocaust perpetrators. Wiesenthal became the conscience of the Holocaust despite Austria's reluctance to confront its part in it. "One of the officials of the Wiesenthal Center in Los Angeles observed that if he had not existed, Wiesenthal would have to be invented, because people all over the world, both Jews and gentiles, needed him as an emblem and a source of hope," his biographer wrote.[2] In addition to his heroics, he paved the way as an early pioneer of Holocaust scholarship, and for that reason was featured prominently in the 2021 Vienna "House of Austria's History" exhibition about early pioneers on Holocaust research.[3] While much could be said about Wiesenthal, this article will focus on his early research on Holocaust perpetrators, the *Täterforschung*. Three areas of his work warrant special attention:

- Documenting crimes and criminals
- Austrians as perpetrators
- The postwar lives of Nazi criminals

His Early Life

Simon Wiesenthal was born in 1908 in Butschatsch (Polish: Buczacz, Ukrainian: Бучач), a town in the Ukraine today, but at the time part of the Austrian-Hungarian Empire. The Wiesenthals were members of a large Jewish community in the Austrian province of Galicia, where 870,000 Jews constituted around 20% of the total population. Young Wiesenthal spoke mostly German at home with his mother, but the day-to-day language of the Eastern European Jews was Yiddish. Polish, Ukrainian, and Russian too were languages of his childhood environment. He did not grow up in a very religious household, but his family followed some Jewish traditions primarily during high holidays. His father, a sugar merchant, died in 1915 while serving in the Austrian army on the Russian front. Thereafter the family fled the frontlines of WWI to the capital Vienna during the dying years of the Habsburg monarchy.[4] Eventually his mother with her two sons went back to Galicia and settled in Lemberg (Polish: Lwów, Ukrainian: Львів), which would later become part of Poland. In Lemberg they found pogroms, hunger, and moving borders. Despite this instability Wiesenthal was unbowed: He studied architecture in Prague and showed some interest for the Zionist movement. In 1936 he married his childhood sweetheart Cyla Müller and worked as an architect in Lemberg. In 1939 Hitler and Stalin split Poland in two, and Soviet troops occupied Lemberg. On June 22, 1941, Nazi Germany invaded Soviet Poland and took over Lemberg. At this point between 160,000 and 170,000 Jews remained in the city. When the Soviets returned in 1944 only 3,400 Jews were left alive.[5] During the Nazi occupation Wiesenthal was arrested and survived imprisonment in different ghettos and camps. On May 5, 1945, US forces liberated him from the Mauthausen concentration camp in Austria.[6]

Documenting Crimes and Perpetrators

Just a few weeks after liberation, Wiesenthal handed the War Crimes Office in Mauthausen a list of ninety-one Nazi perpetrators whose names he had memorized. Dated 25 May 1945, one of the earliest documents of his postwar life, this list demonstrates both Wiesenthal's good memory and his commitment. Driven by the murder of his entire family (he learned only later that Cyla had survived), he made his eagerness to help identify and arrest Nazi war criminals clear to the US military authorities: "Although I am a Polish citizen and would like to return to my homestead, I feel that the crimes of these men are of such magnitude, that no effort can be spared to apprehend them."[7] But his time in Mauthausen after liberation was short lived. The area in which the Mauthausen concentration camp stood was eventually assigned to the Soviet zone of occupied Austria. The Americans moved their offices farther west to the city of Linz and Wiesenthal followed them. There, Wiesenthal worked with the US wartime secret service OSS (Office of Strategic Services) until the fall of 1945 and then with the Counter Intelligence Corps (CIC). The OSS and CIC arrested wanted

Nazis, documenting crimes and identifying looted goods. They also aimed to gather information about the Nazi regime, its inner workings, and plans, including potential plans for postwar activity and resistance. With US forces Wiesenthal helped the many survivors of the Holocaust who like himself were stranded in Austria and lived camp life as so-called "displaced persons" (DPs).[8] Together with local authorities and Jewish organizations he established his own modest displaced persons information center, Goethestraße 63 in Linz. Austria was a perfect way station for Zionist underground organizations to smuggle survivors illegally over the Austrian mountains into Italy, and from there through the British blockade by ship to Palestine/Israel.[9] Wiesenthal became active in Jewish organizations that organized with the Brihah, the escape organization, routing an estimated 200,000 Jews illegally through the British blockade from Austria to the Mandate of Palestine in the immediate postwar years.[10]

Wiesenthal saw an opportunity once he realized that these survivors could provide firsthand accounts of crimes and perpetrators. But time was limited. Most DPs were eager to leave Europe and emigrate to the US, Palestine, or elsewhere to start anew. While the survivors were all there "in the Austrian waiting room,"[11] he wanted to make the best of their collective situation. He spent "… mornings in the War Criminal Prosecution Office and the afternoons with the [refugee] Committee."[12] His documentation work was initially a bit improvised, as he told one of his biographers: "I went to the camps, or wrote to them, and in every camp I selected one or two people. I gave them questionnaires, and they sat day and night, taking down the oral histories of the survivors, where they had been, whom and what they had witnessed. And six months later I collected the questionnaires, and we had a list of a thousand places where crimes had been committed for which we had witnesses."[13] Wiesenthal believed that as the victims, Jews had the moral right to do this kind of work in search of justice. He shared all collected information with the Americans at the Mauthausen trial. This trial provided a space for approximately one hundred Nazi victims to tell their stories and contribute to the search for, arrest, and prosecution of Nazi perpetrators.[14] Wiesenthal and hundreds of witnesses also assisted the Austrian People's courts and other similar institutions in Austria, Germany, and beyond, thereby giving victims a voice.[15]

In those years Wiesenthal's life bustled with activity. In addition to working with American and Austrian authorities to help prosecute Nazis, as well as supporting Jewish refugees, he created the Center for "Jüdische Historische Documentation" (JHD) in 1947. Its purpose was to search for Nazi criminals, fight antisemitism and collect information about perpetrators hiding among victims in the survivor and displaced persons camps.[16] This (first) documentation center would change his life. Wiesenthal's center was run with modest means. Jewish organizations like Adolf Silberschein's Jewish aid organization (Relico) in Geneva supported Wiesenthal with $50 monthly stipend to cover the telephone and postage bills.[17] Instead of "limiting itself to purely historical work," Wiesenthal believed that the JHD in Linz should also "be fighting for the atonement for the crimes of the war years [and] using compelling facts to force the authorities to prosecute and punish war criminals."[18] The active role of survivors in the search for and arrest of Nazi criminals was not uncommon in the first years after the war. For example, in 1949 survivors of the ghetto in Vilnius (Lithuania) accused Martin Weiß of murdering Jews. Since the end of the war he had been living under an assumed name as a janitor in a German hospital. Working with the Central Committee for Liberated Jews in Germany, survivors provided Munich's public prosecutor with additional details and witnesses. Additionally, they accused August Hering of murder in Vilnius. Indeed, Weiß and Hering had been members of a Nazi killing squad and were put on trial in 1950 for the murder of Jews in Vilnius.[19]

In the immediate postwar years, the Allies and Austrian authorities exerted great effort to hold Nazi criminals responsible. But by the summer of 1947, as the Cold War was heating up, priorities shifted: Fighting Communism became a top priority, while prosecuting Nazis lost traction. The Truman Doctrine had been released earlier that year, the Communists took over the government in Prague in February 1948, and the Berlin blockade followed swiftly in June 1948. At this point in the Cold War, US authorities (and leaders of other nations) were interested in German know-how and expertise and were willing to turn a blind eye to one's wartime past if the benefits were promising. The US and its allies needed West Germany and the Germans to fight the Soviet enemy. Thus many former Nazis were "recycled" in the cause. Wernher von Braun and his team of Nazi rocket scientists are arguably one of the best-known examples of this.[20] Christian churches spearheaded the "forgive and forget" mentality, and perpetrator societies eagerly embraced the reprieve. With the change in political tides, the perpetrators were quickly forgiven and the victims subsequently forgotten.[21]

It seems that Simon Wiesenthal was well aware of this development. Writing in November 1947: "Anyone who hears about this topic will have the thought of whether one can do anything at all, in the time of a petrified conscience of mankind, in the time when the powerful of this world propagate silence and throw a cloak of oblivion over the issue. We are faced with the fact that the world wants to pay the bill for millions of victims with the punishment of a few hundred." There it was, "the political change of course" [...] "Ukrainians, Russian Vlasov gangs and other auxiliary killers became a 'noli me tangere,' a taboo. Only then did the time [of protection] come for German and Austrian war criminals."[22] Wiesenthal summarized what happened in the early Cold War years: The West protected many Eastern European Nazi collaborators from Stalin's rage because they were anticommunist. Shortly thereafter German and Austrian Nazis hardly had to fear any prosecution.

The outbreak of the war in Korea in 1950 propelled this shift in international political priorities. Former *Wehrmacht* officers told Chancellor Konrad Adenauer that there could be no (West) German military contribution to the Cold War fight as long as German generals were still on trial or imprisoned as war criminals. The message was clearly received. In 1951 the Supreme Allied Commander in Europe, Dwight D. Eisenhower, stated: "For my part, I do not believe that the German soldier as such has lost his honor.'"[23] By 1955 West Germany had built a new army and had joined NATO. The last war criminals in Germany left their prison cells in 1958.[24] Wiesenthal became a lone voice, his demand for justice yet unserved. As seen in the quote above, Wiesenthal was dismayed that many perpetrators went without punishment and could continue their lives and start new careers. Undeterred, he continued to look for Nazi criminals and kept asking questions about crime and punishment. But the world was moving on. In 1954 Wiesenthal closed his center and in 1956 transferred large parts of his Linz archives to the State of Israel, where it is now conserved at Yad Vashem.[25]

Austrians as Perpetrators

When Wiesenthal was liberated from the Mauthausen camp, Austria as a country found itself in a strange hybrid situation: It was simultaneously liberated from the Nazis and occupied by the Allies. In many ways Austria's Allied occupation was similar to Germany's, but by October 1945, unlike its northern neighbor, Austria had a provisional national government recognized by all four Allies. In late November the Austrians held their first postwar elections under Allied supervision. The country's dual status reflects the Allies' wartime decisions. The Allies agreed in late 1943 to return Austria as an independent country and declared the "Anschluss" (its annexation by Germany in 1938) null and void. In this "Moscow Declaration" the Allies stated that Austria was the first victim of Nazi aggression, but also reminded Austrians of their own responsibility in the crimes of the Hitler regime.

This declaration was meant to encourage resistance against the Nazis, a yardstick of justice against which the Allies planned to measure Austria's fate after the war. In the end, discontent and opposition did exist among Austrians, but armed resistance against the Nazis was almost non-existent.[26]

Wiesenthal cared deeply for Austria, and later in life called himself an "Austrian patriot."[27] The lack of resistance or opposition to the Nazis combined with the widespread collaboration by many Austrians worried him. Wiesenthal saw the need for a reckoning, and according to biographer Tom Segev, "Wiesenthal wanted to purge Austria of its racism."[28] From the very beginning, Wiesenthal knew that many Austrians were among the Nazi perpetrators. In his 1947 memorandum on the founding of his center, he pointed to the "The example of Austria" ("Das Beispiel Österreich") and the need to bring to justice the "German and Austrian war criminals."[29]

In 1952 he wrote another memorandum, this time to Austrian chancellor Leopold Figl about the unresolved question of payments to former non-Austrian slave laborers in Austria. The issue had nothing to do with reparations, Wiesenthal argued, because Austria did not exist as a country between 1938 and 1945. Therefore, the Viennese government was not responsible and therefore could not be legally held responsible for "reparations." However, he also stated that "many Austrians participated in deportations and exterminations as part of the German murder machinery." Austrian companies and factories had profited immensely from exploiting concentration camp slave labor. He therefore suggested: "A compensation fund should be set up and the industries and companies that employed concentration camp inmates should make payments to this fund." Wiesenthal showed himself to be impatient, explaining how even Austrian victims were still waiting to be compensated ("entschädigt"). Bear in mind: This was 1952. Yet it took over four more decades before such a fund was created by the Republic of Austria.[30] Wiesenthal attached to his letter a detailed memorandum on this issue to the chancellor.[31] The attachment stated that slave labor built most of the buildings, factories, and other infrastructure—mainly bridges—between 1940 and 1945. For Wiesenthal this was no small issue since so many slave laborers were involved. The Allies liberated 27,000 Jews from concentration camps in Austria in May 1945, and many of them had worked as slaves. The limited results of Wiesenthal's efforts were summarized well by the Viennese historian René Bienert: "In their response letters, the companies - such as the Steyr Daimler Puch Aktiengesellschaft or the former Göring-Werke (today VOEST) - cynically pointed out that the daily rates applicable to the prisoners were paid to the concentration camp administration at the time, and the claim would now constitute a double payment.

Presumably for this reason, former prisoners gave Wiesenthal the power of attorney in June 1947 to represent them against the former Göring-Werke before the labor court in Linz, but the efforts were unsuccessful. Forced labor was not known to receive compensation until more than 50 years later, if at all."[32] For their part, Austrian officials emphasized the country's victim status and hid behind legal formalities in order to reject claims. Even still Wiesenthal considered Austrians the true perpetrators, not Austria.

The 1960 capture of Adolf Eichmann, one of the chief organizers of the Holocaust, followed by the former SS officer's trial in Jerusalem, became a turning point in Wiesenthal's life. He became famous rather quickly at the press conference at Yad Vashem where, in 1961, he presented his first major book, *Ich jagte Eichmann* (*I Hunted Eichmann*). The book revealed Wiesenthal's obsession with Eichmann and at the same time laid the foundation for his fame as a "Nazi hunter."[33] While the book and press coverage on his Eichmann hunt made him famous, he made clear that many of the *Eichmänner* (others like Eichmann) had an Austrian background, too. Although born in Germany and a German citizen, Eichmann spent his childhood and early adult life in the Austrian city of Linz. Linz was also the city that Ernst Kaltenbrunner called home. And of course, Austrian-born Hitler, even in the last months of his life, discussed with Albert Speer how to rebuild his beloved Linz after the final victory.

In November 1961, Wiesenthal opened the Documentation Center of the Association of Jewish Victims of the Nazi Regime ("Dokumentationszentrum des Bundes jüdischer Verfolgter des Naziregimes") in Vienna, which would become the center of his work for the next five decades. His biographer Segev wrote: "Buoyed by this climate, Wiesenthal left Linz and set up a new documentation center in Vienna. At the same time, he secretly worked for the [Israeli intelligence service] Mossad. The ten years that followed were the most important and the most exciting of his life."[34] According to Segev, Wiesenthal provided Israeli intelligence early on about war criminals and neo-Nazis.[35] Wiesenthal made no progress with Austrian government officials when he reminded them that many Nazi perpetrators had ties to Austria and stressed the government's need to respond. Not many Austrians wanted to challenge the mostly positive image of Austria as the *Sound of Music* country, as depicted in the hit 1965 US musical: Singing, peaceful, god-loving people in beautiful nature, and (many of them) anti-Nazis. Wiesenthal's pivotal 1966 memorandum completely contradicted this (Austrian) view of the recent past.

In a 1966 memorandum, Wiesenthal systematically approached the topic of Austrian perpetrators stressing again the high percentage of

Austrian Nazis among the Holocaust perpetrators. He rejected the false and widespread idea that all Nazi perpetrators were German. The percentage of Austrian perpetrators was far above the 8.5 percent of the "Ostmark" population inside the Third Reich, and thus, he concluded that Austrian Holocaust perpetrators were just as guilty of the murder of millions of Jews as German perpetrators. Wiesenthal also made clear that organized physical violence started on Austrian soil, referring to the "Anschluss" of March 1938 which preceded the November pogroms of that year. His 1966 memorandum, which reads like a clearly structured research paper, detailed the history of Austrian national socialism and the leading roles of many Austrian perpetrators like *SS Gruppenführer* Gustav Otto Wächter, "Governor of Galicia," Franz Stangl, commander of Treblinka extermination camp, and Franz Murer ("Butcher of Vilnius"). In short, Wiesenthal gave a compact history lesson in just thirty pages.[36] It should come as no surprise that he apparently referred to earlier drafts of the memorandum as "a scientific dissertation on the SS" ("*eine Dissertation in SS-Wissenschaften*").[37]

Wiesenthal sent a cover letter to his memorandum titled "Guilt and Responsibility" to the Austrian chancellor Josef Klaus in which he stated that Austrian government ministers were not well informed about the prominent roles of Austrian perpetrators in the Holocaust, nor were the Austrian justice authorities acting according to these facts. He proposed a judicial reform to truly enable the Austrian courts to deal with the many cases of suspected Nazi criminals. Competent authorities experienced chronic understaffing, and many judges and policemen had Nazi pasts, he stated. Near the end of the cover letter to the chancellor, Wiesenthal wrote almost prophetic words: "But if this problem remains unresolved, Austria is guilty of a failure before history and burdens its reputation for all time."[38] A few weeks after mailing it, Wiesenthal also presented the memorandum in a press conference on November 2, 1966, in Vienna. And for good measure, he published it in his documentation center's journal, *Ausweg: Jüdische Zeitschrift fur Aufklärung und Abwehr*.[39] The press conference received widespread coverage in and outside of Austria, but the memorandum was quickly forgotten.[40]

As Wiesenthal was not a trained historian, the Austrian academic establishment generally belittled or ignored his achievements.[41] In a 1998 talk, Austrian historian Gerhard Botz called for the overdue recognition of Wiesenthal as an important historian "who made or could have made an outstanding contribution to a new conception of the history of Austrian National Socialism […]"[42] Botz put Wiesenthal's 1966 memorandum at the center of his argument. In his talk, he revealed that he found an earlier version of the memorandum in Wiesenthal's archive from the 1950s. Botz stressed that this revelation proved the Viennese Nazi hunter was an even greater pioneer in Holocaust studies.[43] For perspective, the ground-breaking dissertation by the Austrian-born Holocaust scholar Raul Hilberg (1926-2007), "The Destruction of the European Jews," was completed in 1955 (first published in 1961).[44] Jonny Moser (1925-2011) was another Austrian historian, who studied the Holocaust as early as the 1960s, collecting primary documents at a time when very few scholars were interested in this topic. His first book, *Die Judenverfolgung in Österreich* (1966), was the primary reference for decades regarding the Holocaust in Austria.[45] Other works addressing Austrian perpetrators were published decades later, like the important work *Hitler and the Forgotten Nazis* by Bruce F. Pauley in 1987.[46] Only in the late 1980s and early 1990s did the general silence on Austrian perpetrators change for good: After the Waldheim controversy, the end of the Cold War, and change in generational leaders, the role of Austrians in the Holocaust became a widely discussed topic both nationally and internationally, also becoming a research topic for historians.[47] Not until 1991, almost three decades after Wiesenthal's memorandum, did an Austrian chancellor, Franz Vranitzky, publicly admit that "Many Austrians greeted the Anschluss, supported the [Nazi] regime and upheld many levels of the hierarchy. Many Austrians took part in the repressive measures and persecution of the Third Reich, some of them in prominent positions."[48]

The Postwar Lives of Nazi Criminals

Simon Wiesenthal, too, conducted pioneering research on the subject of postwar biographies of Nazi perpetrators. Arguably Wiesenthal's longest lasting, most impactful yet controversial contribution in this context was connected to the so-called "ODESSA" (Organization of former SS members). Wiesenthal depicted Odessa as a worldwide, active, powerful, and secret society of former SS members who enabled Nazis to escape justice (if necessary by fleeing overseas) or to start new careers in business and public service in Germany. Wiesenthal is sometimes called the father of Odessa, and for good reason. In the immediate postwar years, Wiesenthal likely came across this organization in CIC reports about Nazi networks. But these official reports about Odessa were vague and lacked concrete information. Odessa was just one of many rumors about secret Nazi organizations and networks in the immediate postwar years. The Allies expected widespread underground Nazi resistance to the occupation, but, their fears had little foundation.[49] The actual "Odessa" was at best a small group of former Nazis helping each other, smuggling out mail from an internment camp or getting extra food in. But Wiesenthal encouraged—and possibly believed in—rumors about an active, powerful, and worldwide secret Nazi organization that was pulling strings in postwar Germany and Austria and, in his telling, even smuggling wanted Nazis overseas.

While Wiesenthal did not invent the Odessa group, he invented the myth of Odessa that captured the world's attention. With the Odessa myth, he created a vehicle easily comprehended by and fascinating to the public for generations. Odessa showed that Wiesenthal had an undeniable talent as communicator, media professional, and publicist, giving him a powerful platform for his agenda. And with the help of the Odessa narrative, he kept the topic of unatoned crimes and loose Nazi perpetrators alive for decades. This is not a minor achievement, given that the early Cold War decades showed little interest in facing the Nazi legacies and the "*Schlamm drüber*" (let the past rest and don't stir the pot)[50] mentality that was widely shared. Inspired by Wiesenthal's 1967 book, *The Murderers Among Us*, British bestselling author Frederick Forsyth worked closely with Wiesenthal when he wrote his semi-fictional novel *The Odessa File*. One of Wiesenthal's biographers wrote: "The initial one-hour interview turned into three days of intensive talk. Between researching the book in Germany and Israel, Forsyth came back to Wiesenthal twice more."[51] The main character of Forsyth's novel was Eduard Roschmann, an Austrian Holocaust perpetrator, who had been hiding under a false name in Argentina since 1948. As the book and subsequent film saw great success in the early 1970s, Odessa became a reality for many.[52] And Wiesenthal got what he wanted: the real Roschmann was forced out of hiding.

Wiesenthal's efforts brought many perpetrators hiding in Europe or overseas into the bright light of public attention from journalists, legal authorities, and also eventually historians. However, historians have accused the Viennese Nazi hunter of mixing facts with fiction in his telling of the Odessa narrative. Former German diplomat Heinz Schneppen had very little good to say about Wiesenthal, and rebuked the Holocaust survivor rather harshly for alleging the existence of the SS underground movement.[53] For Wiesenthal, Odessa was the "greatest escape organization in world history."[54] Segev makes this point: "Wiesenthal did not invent the name, but he did a great deal to disseminate it. Almost certainly, he believed in its existence."[55] When one of his biographers interviewed him in 1996, Wiesenthal defended the story of Odessa as factual organization behind the Nazi escape.[56]

Research on Nazi postwar biographies has seen great progress since the end of the Cold War.[57] In the now booming field of postwar research on Nazi perpetrators, Wiesenthal was an early pioneer. In his own works he went far beyond the overly simplistic and mostly fictitious Odessa explanation, and by the time the myth was circulating, he had already identified the main elements of the escape structures. And he achieved this despite many obstacles—chiefly, exceptionally limited access to postwar records and a hostile political climate. While there was no almighty Odessa, Wiesenthal was right that networks existed, where Nazis helped each other with new careers in Europe or overseas.[58] Wiesenthal not only named Italy as the main escape route out of Europe, but also detailed the routes, stopovers, and practical logistics. Wiesenthal knew that for people stranded in central Europe Italy was the easiest way out. Holocaust victims and perpetrators alike wanted to reach nearby Italian seaports like Genoa. In reconstructing the escape structures Wiesenthal could rely on personal experience as his biographer noted: "Reconstructing the escape routes of the Nazis from Germany to Italy, [through Austria] he found that they used the same mountain paths that the Briha [Jewish escape organization] used, and the same roadside inns. On occasion the two groups found themselves in the same lodgings at the same time, the Nazis in the cellar, the Jews on the floor above them, both groups keeping utterly silent, lest they be discovered."[59] He repeatedly identified key players in the so-called "Italian Ratline," such as Vatican institutions and Catholic dignitaries. Among them was Austrian bishop Alois Hudal and other Catholic churchmen who helped Nazis flee to the Middle East and the Americas.[60] He noted the role of the International Committee of the Red Cross and its travel papers in Italy, which enabled many Nazis on the run to get away.[61] Wiesenthal showed that in addition to perpetrating the crimes against humanity in the Holocaust, after 1945 many Austrians, not only Hudal or Roschmann, were involved in helping Nazis escape justice.[62] As we have already seen, Wiesenthal was also aware of the crucial Cold War background, which made escape from prosecution in the postwar years relatively easy.

Conclusion

Wiesenthal came to fame as a "Nazi hunter," a role which earned him many foes as well as support for his championing of "justice, not vengeance." Additionally, Wiesenthal greatly contributed to Holocaust scholarship, especially to research on Holocaust perpetrators. These contributions, however, were often overlooked or downplayed by academic scholars. In recent years, these aspects of his very active life are being re-visited and re-evaluated. This short paper focused on three aspects of his work: First, he led early documentation of Holocaust crimes and criminals. Thanks to his efforts we now have rich documentation about Nazi perpetrators, including two hundred *Laufmeter* (running meters) of materials in the Vienna Wiesenthal Institute for Holocaust Studies. These sources provide much material for future researchers and research of a younger generation. Second, Wiesenthal illuminated the issue of Austrians' guilt and responsibility in the Holocaust. Working as a source for the Israeli secret services[63], there can be little doubt that Wiesenthal understood the sometimes-cynical cost-benefit calculations of intelligence services and governments in the Cold War. Maneuvering those dynamics, Wiesenthal smartly kept pressure on the Austrian government and the Nazi perpetrators themselves. His 1952 memorandum on slave labor in Austria and his 1966 memorandum on Austrian Holocaust perpetrators represent important milestones in this effort. Third, at a time when the topic was largely ignored by academics, Wiesenthal sustained attention on the postwar fates of Nazi perpetrators still on the loose. By using the Odessa paradigm, he swiftly navigated tricky political waters and kept the blame for obstructing justice on the perpetrators. Simultaneously he went beyond the Odessa myth, detailing the complex structures, routes, and organizations which made escape and new postwar careers possible for Nazis.

Wiesenthal's ultimate goal was to bring perpetrators to justice and "to make the remaining free Nazi criminals feel that they would never be safe from ultimate retribution" as one historian stated.[64] As a result, the three elements in Wiesenthal's program, as laid out in his 1947 memorandum, of combatting antisemitism, prosecuting perpetrators, and documenting history served all one greater goal: To remember the victims of the Holocaust and, therefore, to sanctify life.[65]

Endnotes

1 I was very honored to be named the 2021 Senior Fellow at the Vienna Wiesenthal Institute for Holocaust Research (VWI). Simon Wiesenthal was not a trained academic historian, but I always considered him the moral conscience of Austria, a lonely voice calling for justice, a groundbreaker, and a role model. I will work hard to do him justice when working on my new book about the Vatican and the Nuremberg Trials. Special thanks to the staff of the VWI archives and library especially René Bienert, Jan Kiepe, and Barbara Grzelak. Special thanks also to Dr. Elizabeth Anthony, Prof. Günter Bischof, Anne Johnson, Steven Wees, and Timothy Turnquist for feedback.

2 Tom Segev, *Simon Wiesenthal: The Life and Legends* (New York: Schocken, 2010), 7.

3 The special exhibition "Verfolgen und Aufklären" was shown until April 26, 2021 in the "Haus der Geschichte Österreich." Next to Wiesenthal, other pioneers such as Nachman Blumental, Raphael Lemkin, and Eva Reichmann were remembered.

4 Hella Pick, *Simon Wiesenthal: A Life in Search of Justice* (Boston: Northeastern University Press, 1996), 34 ff.

5 Segev, *Simon Wiesenthal*, 43.

6 Pick, *Simon Wiesenthal*, 73.

7 Simon Wiesenthal to Col. Richard R. Seibel, May 25, 1945, VWI-SWA, II.1, A-I.6.1. Seibel was the U.S. Camp Commander of the liberated Mauthausen concentration camp.

8 Simon Wiesenthal, *Ich jagte Eichmann* (Gütersloh: Sigbert Mohn, 1961), 19 ff.

9 Thomas Albrich, ed., *Flucht nach Eretz Israel: Die Bricha und der jüdische Exodus durch Österreich nach 1945* (Innsbruck: Studienverlag, 2018).

10 Pick, *Simon Wiesenthal*, 105.

11 Wiesenthal, "Die Rolle der Jüdischen Historischen Documentation bei der Verfolgung und Bestrafung der Kriegsverbrecher (Das Beispiel Österreich)," JHD memorandum, Nov. 25, 1947, p. 2, VWI-SWA, I.1.

12 Simon Wiesenthal, "Doch die Mörder leben," *Der Spiegel*, 33, Jun. 8, 1967, 52–65 (here 55).

13 Pick, *Simon Wiesenthal,* 100.

14 Tomaz Jardim, *The Mauthausen Trial: American Military Justice in Germany* (Harvard University Press, 2012). Winfried Garscha, "Simon Wiesenthals Beitrag zur gerichtlichen Verfolgung der NS-Täter in Österreich," (paper at conference "Österreichs Umgang mit der NS-Täterschaft," Vienna, December 2–3, 1998), 1–15, 8, accessed May 25, 2021, https://www.doew.at/cms/download/6kqis/garscha_wiesenthal.pdf

15 See René Bienert, "'Eine Institution, geschaffen unter den jüdischen DPs': Simon Wiesenthals frühe Suche nach NS-Verbrecherinnen und -Verbrechern

als Überlebendeninitiative," in *Displaced Persons: Forschung in Deutschland und Österreich. Eine Bestandsaufnahme zu Beginn des 21.* Jahrhunderts, ed. Nikolaus Hagen et. al. (Marburg: Frank & Timme, 2022), 271–92.

16 See Pick, *Simon Wiesenthal,* 95 ff.

17 Segev, *Simon Wiesenthal*, 102.

18 Wiesenthal, "Die Rolle der Jüdischen Historischen Documentation bei der Verfolgung und Bestrafung der Kriegsverbrecher," 2.

19 Hans-Christian Jasch and Wolf Kaiser, *Der Holocaust vor deutschen Gerichten: Amnestieren, Verdrängen, Bestrafen* (Stuttgart: Reclam, 2017), 65.

20 Brian E. Crim, *Our Germans: Project Paperclip and the National Security State* (Baltimore: Johns Hopkins University Press, 2018).

21 Gerald J. Steinacher, "Forgive and Forget: The Vatican and the Escape of Nazi War Criminals from Justice," *S:I.M.O.N. – Shoah: Intervention. Methods. Documentation* 9 (2022), 1, 4-28.

22 Wiesenthal: "Die Rolle der Jüdischen Historischen Documentation bei der Verfolgung und Bestrafung von Kriegsverbrecher," 1.

23 Quoted in Kim Christian Priemel, *The Betrayal: The Nuremberg Trials and German Divergence* (Oxford: Oxford University Press, 2016), 352.

24 There were very few exceptions such as Rudolf Hess and others in Spandau prison, who were under the jurisdiction of the four Allied powers.

25 This large documentation is currently organized and catalogued in the Vienna Simon Wiesenthal Archive (SWA) in cooperation with Yad Vashem under the project title: "Early Wiesenthal – The Linz Papers, 1945–1961," which is co-financed by the Claims Conference in New York.

26 Günter Bischof, "Die Instrumentalisierung der Moskauer Erklärung nach dem 2. Weltkrieg," *Zeitgeschichte* 20 (Nov.–Dec. 1993), 345–66.

27 Segev, *Simon Wiesenthal,* 85.

28 Segev, *Simon Wiesenthal,* 85.

29 Wiesenthal, "Die Rolle der Jüdischen Historischen Documentation bei der Verfolgung und Bestrafung der Kriegsverbrecher," 1.

30 Wiesenthal to the Bundeskanzler Dr. Leopold Figl, July 22, 1952, VWI-SWA, I.1, Wiedergutmachung Österreich.

31 Memorandum, VWA-SWA I.1, Wiedergutmachung Österreich.

32 Bienert, "'Eine Institution, geschaffen unter den jüdischen DPs.'"

33 Fredrik Lindström, "Out of the Past: Simon Wiesenthal's Hunt for Nazis as a Form of Collective Testimony," *S:I.M.O.N. – Shoah: Intervention. Methods. Documentation* 6 (2019), 2, 4–20. The US journalist Andrew Nagorski and author of popular history books prominently features Wiesenthal together with Fritz Bauer, Tuvia Friedman, Beate and Serge Klarsfeld, Efraim Zuroff and a few others in his 2016 book *The Nazi Hunters* (New York: Simon & Schuster, 2016), 5.

34 Segev, *Simon Wiesenthal,* 157.

35 Segev, *Simon Wiesenthal,* 24, 26, 156–57, 248, 346.

36 Wiesenthal memorandum to the Bundeskanzler Dr. Josef Klaus, "Die Beteiligung von Österreichern an Nazi-Verbrechen und deren strafrechtliche Verfolgung," Oct.12, 1966, VWI-SWA, I.1, Österreich 2. See complete memorandum, accessed June 22, 2021, https://www.doew.at/cms/download/bvfro/bb_memorandum.pdf.

37 Wiesenthal, *Ich jagte Eichmann*, 232; Lindström, "Out of the Past," 7.

38 Wiesenthal to Dr. Josef Klaus, "Schuld und Sühne der NS-Täter aus Österreich," Oct. 12, 1966, VWI-SWA, I.1, Österreich 2, Anschreiben Klaus. German original: "Wenn aber dieses Problem ungelöst bleibt, macht sich Österreich eines Versäumnisses vor der Geschichte schuldig und belastet sein Ansehen für alle Zeit."

39 Simon Wiesenthal, "Schuld und Sühne der NS-Täter aus Österreich," *Der Ausweg: Jüdische Zeitschrift für Aufklärung und Abwehr* 4 (1966), 5, 1–8. For an excellent study of the reception of Wiesenthal and his memorandum, see Fredrik Lindström, "Out of the Past: Simon Wiesenthal's Hunt for Nazis as a Form of Collective Testimony," *S:I.M.O.N. – Shoah: Intervention. Methods. Documentation* 6 (2019), 2, 4–20.

40 For international and national reactions to the memorandum, see Pick, *Simon Wiesenthal*, 164–65. See also Philipp Rohrbach: "Das Memorandum 1966: Druck auf Politik und Öffentlichkeit," presented at one of the talks organized by the Vienna Wiesenthal Institute on Sept. 22 2020 in memoriam (Jorzajt far Shimon) of Simon Wiesenthal, accessed Aug. 10, 2021, https://www.youtube.com/watch?v=CsiYNtkASqA.

41 On Wiesenthal's achievements for historical research on Austria's Nazi past, see Gerhard Botz, "Simon Wiesenthals Beitrag zur Aufarbeitung der Geschichte des österreichischen Nationalsozialismus. Sein (fast) vergessenes 'Memorandum' zur 'Beteiligung von Österreichern an Nazi-Verbrechen' und die 'österreichische Täter-These,'" in *Forschungen zum Nationalsozialismus und dessen Nachwirkungen in Österreich: Festschrift für Brigitte Bailer,* ed. Wolfgang Neugebauer and Christine Schindler (Vienna: Dokumentationsarchiv des Österreichischen Widerstandes, 2012), 169–99, https://www.doew.at/cms/download/0067/bb_botz.pdf. The talk was given in 1998 but only published in 2012. Historian Fredrik Lindström points out: "The fact that this article was only published 14 years after the conference took place in 1998 has arguably delayed its effect on Austrian historiography. I believe the line of thought pursued by Botz here merits renewed consideration." Lindström, "Out of the Past," 7.

42 Botz, "Simon Wiesenthals Beitrag," 170.

43 Botz, "Simon Wiesenthals Beitrag," 172–73. On this point see also Fredrik Lindström, "Out of the Past," 2, 4–20 (here 7).

44 Raul Hilberg, *The Destruction of the European Jews* (Chicago: Quadrangle Books, 1961); Botz, "Simon Wiesenthals Beitrag," 173. See also Olof Bortz, "Early Reactions to Raul Hilberg's History of the Holocaust, 1961–7," *Journal of Contemporary History* 56, vol. 3 (2021), 1–21. See also the works by the Jewish-

French historian Léon Poliakov with the first analytical work on the Holocaust: *Bréviaire de la Haine - Le IIIeme Reich et les Juifs* (Paris: Calmann-Levy, 1951).

45 Jonny Moser, *Die Judenverfolgung in Österreich 1938-1945* (Vienna: Europa-Verl. 1966).

46 Bruce F. Pauley, *Hitler and the Forgotten Nazis: A History of Austrian National Socialism* (University of North Carolina Press: Chapel Hill, 1981).

47 For a good summary on these issues see: Günter Bischof, Fritz Plasser, and Barbara Stelzl-Marx, eds., *New Perspectives on Austrians and World War II*, Contemporary Austrian Studies 27 (New Brunswick: Transaction 2009); Heidemarie Uhl, "Vom Opfermythos zur Mitverantwortungsthese: NS-Herrschaft, Krieg und Holocaust im 'österreichischen Gedächtnis,'" in *Transformationen gesellschaftlicher Erinnerung: Studien zur österreichischen Gedächtnisgeschichte*, kultur. wissenschaften 9, ed. Christian Gerbel et al. (Vienna: Turia + Kant, 2005), 86–130. See also Gerald Steinacher, "The Limits of Integration: Nazi officials and their new political careers after 1945 in West-Germany and Austria," in "After Nazism: Relaunching Careers in Germany and Austria," ed. Susanna Schrafstetter and Jürgen Zarusky, *German Yearbook of Contemporary History* 5 (2021), 196–214.

48 Michael Z. Wise, "Austria Admits Role in Holocaust," *Washington Post*, July 9, 1991, accessed Jul. 9. 2021, https://www.washingtonpost.com/archive/politics/1991/07/09/austria-admits-role-in-holocaust/a7485c1c-3a82-4558-852e-b222983a386a/.

49 Segev, *Simon Wiesenthal*, 106 ff.

50 I prefer *Schlamm* over *Schwamm* in this context.

51 Pick, *Simon Wiesenthal*, 219.

52 The film *The Odessa File* came out in 1974 with Austrian-born actor Maximilian Schell playing Roschmann and with the film music composed by British composer Andrew Lloyd Weber.

53 Heinz Schneppen, *Odessa und das Vierte Reich: Mythen der Zeitgeschichte* (Berlin: Metropol, 2007), especially 214 ff.

54 Simon Wiesenthal, *Justice, Not Vengeance* (New York: Grove Weidenfeld, 1989), 54.

55 Segev, *Simon Wiesenthal*, 106.

56 Pick, *Simon Wiesenthal*, 125. On these issues, see also Daniel Stahl, "*Odessa* und das 'Nazigold' in Südamerika: Mythen und ihre Bedeutungen," *Jahrbuch für Geschichte Lateinamerikas* 48 (2011), 333–60, https://www.vr-elibrary.de/doi/pdf/10.7767/jbla.2011.48.1.333

57 Ernst Klee, *Persilscheine und falsche Pässe: Wie die Kirchen den Nazis halfen* (Frankfurt: S. Fischer, 1991); Holger Meding, *Flucht* vor *Nürnberg? Deutsche und österreichische Einwanderung nach Argentinien* (Vienna: Böhlau, 1992); Uki *Goñi, The Real Odessa: How Perón Brought the Nazi Criminals to Argentina (London: Granta Books, 2002);* Bettina Stangneth, *Eichmann before Jerusalem: The Unexamined Life of a Mass Murderer* (New York: Vintage Books, 2014); Gerald Steinacher, *Nazis*

on the Run: How Hitler's Henchmen Fled Justice (Oxford: Oxford University Press, 2011); Peter Hammerschmidt, *Die unglaubliche Nachkriegskarriere von Klaus Barbie* (Frankfurt: S. Fischer, 2014); Guy Walters, *Hunting Evil: The Nazi War Criminals Who Escaped and the Quest to Bring Them to Justice* (New York: Broadway Books, 2010); Daniel Stahl, *Hunt for Nazis: South America's Dictatorships and the Prosecution of Nazis Crimes* (Amsterdam: Amsterdam University Press, 2018).

58 Felix Bohr, *Kriegsverbrecherlobby* (Berlin: Suhrkamp, 2018).

59 Segev, *Simon Wiesenthal*, 107.

60 On Hudal, see Gerald Steinacher, *Nazis on the Run* and Johannes Sachslehner, *Hitlers Mann im Vatikan: Bischof Alois Hudal: Ein dunkles Kapitel in der Geschichte der Kirche (Vienna: Molden, 2019).* Wiesenthal to the editor, "Fleeing Nazis' Friend in Postwar Rome," *New York Times*, Mar. 13, 1984, A 26.

61 In Pick's biography on Wiesenthal, she dedicated a whole chapter to the Red Cross and the Holocaust including its role in Nazi escape. This is unusual, because that aspect of the postwar years (with very few exceptions) was not addressed until the early 2000s. An early pioneer was Heiner Lichtenstein, *Angepaßt und treu ergeben: Das Rote Kreuz im Dritten Reich* (Köln: Bund Verlag, 1988); see also Gerald J. Steinacher, *Humanitarians at War: The Red Cross in the Shadow of the Holocaust* (Oxford: Oxford University Press, 2017); Steinacher, *Nazis on the Run*.

62 See e.g., Gerald Steinacher, "Österreich und die Flucht von NS-Tätern," *Jahrbuch Mauthausen* (2016), NS-Täterinnen und -Täter in der Nachkriegszeit, 35–50; *Edith Blaschitz*, "*Austrian* National Socialists in Argentina after 1945," in *Revisiting the National Socialist Legacy: Coming to Terms with Forced Labor, Expropriation, Compensation and Restitution*, ed. Oliver Rathkolb (Innsbruck: Studienverlag, 2002), 226–40.

63 According to biographer Segev, Wiesenthal was secretly working for the Israeli Intelligence Service Mossad. See Segev, *Simon Wiesenthal,* 157, 207. See also Jan Kiepe, "Agent Simon? Wiesenthal und die Geheimdienste: Legende und Wirklichkeit," Vortrag im Rahmen der Gedenkveranstaltung Jorzajt far Shimon (September 2020).

64 Lindström, "Out of the Past," 14.

65 Segev, *Simon Wiesenthal*, 10.

Documentation, Analysis and Political Action: Hermann Langbein on Auschwitz

Winfried R. Garscha

In April 1944, Austrian communist Hermann Langbein, political prisoner and clerk to the SS-physician Eduard Wirths from 1942, smuggled his first description of the extermination process in Auschwitz out of the camp. One year later he transmitted a report on Auschwitz to a British officer in Hanover. In both papers,[1] he documented and analyzed the specificity of the mass crimes committed in Auschwitz-Birkenau. The papers show insights into the genocidal nature of the persecution of Jews and Roma. This rates them in a row with other reports of Auschwitz prisoners like the early Witold's report[2] (written by Witold Pilecki in 1943) and the Vrba-Wetzler report[3] of 1944.

Langbein's insistence on the special character of the extermination process, in comparison with other Nazi crimes, led to conflicts with other surviving political prisoners. Eventually, he lost his leading position in the International Auschwitz Committee, which he had co-founded, and was expelled from the Communist Party.

In the years to come Langbein was instrumental in organizing the survivors, bringing perpetrators before the courts, and disseminating knowledge about Auschwitz as a camp of racist mass extermination.[4] Immediately after the Auschwitz trial in Frankfurt, he published a detailed documentary report about the trial in two volumes.[5]

Hermann Langbein's decisive role in achieving judicial prosecution of some of the Nazi perpetrators has been recognized by many scholars and was thematized in *Labyrinth of Lies* (2014)[6] and *The People vs. Fritz Bauer* (2015),[7] two films depicting the fate of Frankfurt trial prosecutor, Fritz Bauer. Whereas *The People vs. Fritz Bauer* focuses on the role of Fritz Bauer in bringing Adolf Eichmann to justice, *Labyrinth of Lies* was promoted as a "story that exposes the conspiracy of prominent German institutions and government branches to cover up the crimes of Nazis during World War II."[8] One of the topics of *Labyrinth of Lies* is how Hermann Langbein, the then secretary general of the International Concentration Camps Committee, successfully convinced survivors to testify against the defendants. The majority among them originally had refused to cooperate with German prosecutors.

Who was Hermann Langbein? Until his deportation to the Auschwitz concentration camp, his vita resembled, in many aspects, that of other Austrian communists.[9] In 1933, he joined the Communist Party at the age of nineteen and was engaged in clandestine networks which opposed the Austro-fascist regime from 1934 until 1938. After the *Anschluss* of 1938, he joined the International Brigades in the Spanish Civil war, fled to France, and was extradited by the fascist Vichy collaboration regime to Germany in 1941. From the Dachau concentration camp, where he had served as a clerk to the camp doctor, he was deported to Auschwitz in August 1942. As a non-Jewish political prisoner, he was assigned as clerk to the infirmary, which was led by the so-called *Standortarzt*. This was, as already mentioned, SS-physician Eduard Wirths, who supervised all other SS-physicians in the Auschwitz concentration camp and its subcamps. In his position, Langbein had first-hand knowledge of the torture and killings of prisoners as well as the medical mistreatment and experiments. German historian Katharina Stengel states, "only few SS men understood the administrative procedures[10]

However, even this privileged position did not protect him from being persecuted by the camp Gestapo (the "political department") for suspected political actions. In autumn 1943 he spent more than nine weeks in the so-called "*Bunker*," the special prison of the political department.

Langbein documented the atrocities in a clandestine manner. Furthermore, he made contacts with the underground resistance movement in the camp. He became a leading member of the "Kampfgruppe Auschwitz" ("Grupa Bojowa Oświęcim"), an international resistance group led by Polish socialists and Austrian communists with close contacts to Polish nationalists of the Home Army ("Armia Krajowa," AK). The Auschwitz branch of the AK had been guided by the aforementioned Polish officer Witold Pilecki. After the liberation, Pilecki, one of the best-known heroes of Polish anti-Nazi resistance, started organizing clandestine networks in order to gather intelligence about communist rule in Poland for the exile government in London. He was arrested in 1947 and, despite pardon pleas from Auschwitz survivors, executed in 1948.

In mid-May 1944 Special Operation Hungary began. Organized by Adolf Eichmann, German Nazis and their Hungarian accomplices deported more than 400,000 Jews from Hungary to Auschwitz. The vast majority among them were gassed upon arrival. It is an amazing fact that Hermann Langbein's first description of the extermination process in Auschwitz was written several weeks *before* the arrival of the Hungarian Jews. Because he worked in Wirths' office, he managed it to typewrite his report. He was able to smuggle it out of the camp with the help of Maria Stromberger, an Austrian nurse working in the SS hospital at Auschwitz. Stromberger used her hairbrush to bring the report to Langbein's brother in Vienna who used the informative report to make covert leaflets which he produced for Austrian communist resistance groups. Stromberger's hairbrush is displayed in one of the exhibits in the new Austrian exposition in Block 17 of the Auschwitz memorial site which opened in October 2021.

The transcript of Langbein's secret message in the Austrian State Archive[11] consists of four pages. In the first paragraph, the author differentiated between the camp (*Stammlager*), its subcamps, and of "Auschwitz II" (Birkenau, a "complex of four camps" for men, women, gypsies and Jewish families). The "main thing" in Auschwitz II is "the crematoria with its gas chambers," he stated.[12] Two paragraphs of the paper are dedicated to gassing and cremation. Langbein distinguishes between the 40,000 prisoners poisoned by gas because they were ill or weak and therefore regarded as useless by the SS and those who were sent to the gas chambers directly from the deportation transports without receiving a prisoner number. He estimated the total number of people gassed at arrival at one and a half million.[13] (In the introduction paragraph he wrote that it could be possible that already "several millions" Jews had been murdered in Auschwitz.)

Langbein characterized "normal daily work" in the five new crematoria in Birkenau as the "gassing and incineration of the—almost exclusively Jewish—transports from all over Europe who are being sent to the gas."[14]

Langbein's knowledge of what was going on in the infirmary enabled him to give an extensive description of different methods of killing sick prisoners. Gassing became the preferred method of "treating" the typhus epidemic, but for sick prisoners they also used other methods of killing, such as injection with phenol. He also described the gassing of weak prisoners from the *Häftlingskrankenbau* (the sick prisoners' barracks). The "justification" for these murderous deeds were utilitarian considerations. Although Langbein did not explicitly address the racist rationale, he makes clear that the SS denied the right to life to those prisoners who were deemed "useless." The Jews of the transports, however, were denied this right because they were Jews.

Langbein also points out the genocidal character of the mass murder of not only Jews and Roma, but also of Poles—by using the word *ausrotten* (exterminate). After describing the discretionary executions of political opponents, he continued: "Especially former Polish officers or intellectuals were exterminated in that manner."[15]

In his book *People in Auschwitz*, Langbein gave reasons as to why he, and other prisoners, took the risk to document the procedures in Auschwitz:

"Besides the saving of human lives, another task in the extermination camp forced itself on those who could think beyond themselves and the barbed wire: not to let the truth about the extermination methods of Nazism perish together with the victims."[16]

Langbein's second paper on Auschwitz is much longer. It consists of twenty-six single-spaced typed pages, written in Hanover between 22 and 25 April 1945. He made a carbon copy for himself, which is stored in the Austrian State Archive,[17] together with a handwritten sheet of paper "Korrekturen Hannover." Some of Langbein's handwritten remarks, supposedly drafted a few years before his death in 1995,[18] contain additional information and substantive corrections. For example, he rectified the following paragraph: "There were transports, which were completely exterminated without any previous selection. The majority of them were transports of Jews from countries Hitler had power over, but among them were also transports of Poles and Soviet POWs."[19] His rectification ran as follows: "Nur Judentransp., keine P oder R" ("Only transports of Jews, no Poles or Russians").

Langbein gave an overview over the Nazi system of concentration camps in the first nine pages. On page ten, he succinctly described Auschwitz as: "Auschwitz is an extermination camp."[20]

A considerable part of the paper dealt with the hygienic conditions in Auschwitz II (Birkenau), especially in camps for women and gypsy-families. Langbein chose a graphic language to depict mud, dirt, and improper sanitary installations.

Another topic of the Hanover paper was the description of the nationalist antagonisms among the prisoners, fostered by the SS, and resulting in a hierarchy between different groups of prisoners. Katharina Stengel calls this section of the paper an "almost sociological [description of] the different groups and classes of the inmate community, for instance . . . the Polish 'camp aristocracy' consisting of the few survivors of the first transports of Poles."[21]

Peculiarly, Langbein combined unemotional description and analysis in the Hanover paper with few personal recollections, which he seemed to judge appropriate to help people to comprehend what had happened in Auschwitz. So, he reported with particular compassion about his harrowing experience in early December 1942, when he was cured from typhus in the *Häftlingskrankenbau*. A group of sick Jewish prisoners, who were too weak to work, were beaten and forced by SS-men to undress outside, before they were allowed to enter the building. Inside the hospital they had to wait naked for hours in the cold hallway before being treated. When Langbein left the building in the evening, he had to walk over the dead bodies and dying prisoners. Contrary to him, a privileged prisoner functionary, no other treatment than gassing was foreseen for sick Jews.[22]

It seems evident that one of the aims of the paper was to induce political action. Langbein concluded the Hanover paper: "Now, the task is not only to bring rank and file SS men to justice, but to eradicate the Nazi mind as such, to track down its sources and to dry them up. This we owe to the millions, who had to die at the sign of the swastika in the concentration camps."[23]

It took German judiciary two decades before deciding to initiate proceedings in the Frankfurt Auschwitz trial (1963-1965); six defendants were sentenced to life imprisonment. The proceedings lasted even longer to bring four Austrian perpetrators before a Viennese court (1972). All four of them were acquitted by the jury.

Endnotes

1 Both texts are analyzed and, at some length, quoted by Katharina Stengel, *Hermann Langbein: Ein Auschwitz-Überlebender in den erinnerungspolitischen Konflikten der Nachkriegszeit* (Frankfurt am Main: Campus, 2012), 48–51 and 51–60.

2 Full text, including supplements of 1944: Rotmistrz Witold Pilecki—Witold's report (Report by Captain Witold Pilecki, translated from Polish by Jacek Kucharski), https://www.rodaknet.com/rp_czytelnia_pilecki_raport_eng.htm, accessed Dec. 10, 2021.

3 Miroslav Kárný, "The Vrba and Wetzler report," in *Anatomy of the Auschwitz Death Camp*, ed. Michael Berenbaum and Yisrael Gutman (Bloomington: Indiana University Press, 1994); a facsimile of the English translation of the Slovak original, written in Zurich in July 1944, can be accessed at: https://www.jewishvirtuallibrary.org/jsource/Holocaust/auschprotocol.pdf, accessed Dec. 10, 2021.

4 Langbein's most influential book was *Menschen in Auschwitz*, first published in 1972, available also in English: Hermann Langbein, *People in Auschwitz* (Chapel Hill: University of North Carolina Press, 2003).

5 Hermann Langbein, *Der Auschwitz-Prozess: Eine Dokumentation* (Vienna: Europa Verlag, 1965).

6 German original title: *Im Labyrinth des Schweigens*, directed by Giulio Ricciarelli, released at the Toronto International Film Festival on 6 September 2014, with Lukas Miko as Hermann Langbein and Gert Voss as Fritz Bauer.

7 German original title: Der Staat gegen Fritz Bauer, directed by Lars Kraume, released at the Locarno Film Festival on 7 August 2015.

8 *Im Labyrinth des Schweigens* (2014), plot summaries, accessed Dec. 10, 2021, https://www.imdb.com/title/tt3825638/

9 For biographical information compare the abovementioned work of Katharina Stengel, and Brigitte Halbmayr, *Zeitlebens consequent: Hermann Langbein 1912–1995. Eine politische Biografie* (Vienna: Braumüller, 2012).

10 Stengel, *Hermann Langbein,* 48.

11 Österreichisches Staatsarchiv, Allgemeines Verwaltungsarchiv, Nachlässe, Neue Zivile Nachlässe, Nl HL, E/1797 (hereinafter: ÖStA, Nachlass Langbein), 286/1.

12 ÖStA, Nachlass Langbein, 286/1, 1.

13 ÖStA, Nachlass Langbein, 286/1, 2.

14 ÖStA, Nachlass Langbein, 286/1, 2.

15 ÖStA, Nachlass Langbein, 286/1, 3.

16 Langbein, *People in Auschwitz,* 254.

17 ÖStA, Nachlass Langbein, 269/8.

18 The sheet is from a writing pad of the Bund Verlag with Langbein's name on each sheet. Because Langbein published two books in this publishing house in 1985 and 1991, it can be reasonably assumed that he wrote these remarks in the late 1980s or early 1990s.

19 ÖStA, Nachlass Langbein, 269/8, 11.

20 ÖStA, Nachlass Langbein, 269/8, 10. (In his corrections he added: "Not from the very beginning.")

21 Stengel, *Hermann Langbein,* 56.

22 ÖStA, Nachlass Langbein, 269/8, 12.

23 ÖStA, Nachlass Langbein, 269/8, 26.

Jonny Moser (1925–2011): An Early Historian of the Holocaust in Austria

Joseph W. Moser

My father, Jonny Moser, was a pioneer historian of the Holocaust who collected primary documents in the 1960s: a time when very few scholars were interested in this topic. His first book *Die Judenverfolgung in Österreich* (1966) was, for decades, the primary reference on the Holocaust in Austria. In 1977, he co-edited *Der gelbe Stern in Österreich*, which accompanied one of the first exhibitions on the Holocaust in Austria and ran in Eisenstadt. He wrote many articles and published the important demographic study, *Demographie der jüdischen Bevölkerung Österreichs 1938–1945* (1999), which was based on primary sources that he collected in his personal archive. In 2006, he published his autobiography, *Wallenbergs Laufbursche* (2006), which chronicled his and his family's survival in the Holocaust in Hungary. There, he worked for Raoul Wallenberg as an errand boy, making Jonny Moser an eyewitness and reference person for scholars studying Wallenberg. In his final year, he completed *Nisko: Die ersten Judendeportationen*, which was published posthumously in 2012. This book was based on deportation lists and other primary documents that he collected on the first deportations of Jews from Vienna.

Jonny Moser experienced the so-called *Anschluss* to Nazi Germany at the age of twelve. His and his family's incredible survival story inspired him to understand and document the history he lived through. Jonny Moser spent the rest of his life documenting his past, unlike many Holocaust survivors who tried to forget about the atrocities they experienced or were unable to confront their trauma. The Holocaust was a daily topic in my father's life. Growing up in Vienna in the 1970s and 1980s, I essentially lived in a Holocaust archive. Many historians from all over the world visited my father in our apartment in Vienna, Raul Hilberg among them. I became aware of Hilberg's visit a few years ago when I saw an interview with him in Claude Lanzmann's documentary film, *Shoah*, and I suddenly remembered having poked Hilberg in his face as a four-year-old boy while he was talking with my father. My father was always recounting the events that led to his survival, though I was not able to put all of his narratives into a chronological context until he published his autobiography, *Wallenbergs Laufbursche*, which deals with a nearly forgotten aspect of Austrian-Jewish history: the expulsion of Burgenland's Jews in the first months following the Nazis' takeover of Austria in March 1938. The surprisingly quick looting of his parents' general store in Parndorf by local Nazis, as well as the attempted deportation of Parndorf Jews across the open border with Hungary during Passover, were formative events for twelve-year-old Moser. Jonny Moser's father, who had converted to Judaism in 1921, was issued an *Ariernachweis*, which identified his religion as being Jewish, a curiosity of the time. But, it allowed him to sue the mayor of Parndorf as well as the Eisenstadt Gestapo chief Otto Koch for looting into their own pockets. In order to remove his father as a potential witness in the upcoming trial, the Gestapo sent him to Hungary, and Jonny Moser, along with his mother and sister, was illegally smuggled by the Gestapo into Hungary in October 1940. In Budapest, they lived as illegal immigrants until they had to come out in late 1941, hoping for a Hungarian exit permit to use their visa to the U.S. However, this exit plan became impossible days later with the bombing of Pearl Harbor, after which Hungary declared war on the U.S. The family was sent to a labor camp for foreign Jews in Ricse, Eastern Hungary. After being released from the labor camp in spring 1944 and the German invasion of Hungary, the family just barely managed to remove themselves from being deported to Auschwitz from the deportation site, a brick factory in Békásmegyer (a suburb of Budapest). Meeting the Swedish diplomat Raoul Wallenberg, who issued them Swedish *Schutzpässe* in early August 1944, which helped them survive the final year of the war in Budapest. At eighteen-years-old, Jonny Moser got to know Wallenberg and he was an important witness of Wallenberg's rescue efforts in Budapest until the end of his life. Together with his parents and his sister, Moser returned from their exile in Hungary to Vienna in June 1945; though, one must understand this as a new beginning because the family never returned to live in their former hometown in Burgenland.

In contrast to many Holocaust survivors, Jonny Moser spent his whole life dealing with the history of the Holocaust, which in his notes from 1944/45 he already termed as the "Judenverfolgung" (persecution of the Jews) in an essay with the title "Die Budapester Judenverfolgung." In this multipage text, he confronts the time from October 15, 1944, to January 15, 1945, during which the Nyilas (Arrow Cross Guards—Hungarian Nazis) murdered Jews in the streets of Budapest. This notebook gave Moser an opportunity to deal with the reality in Budapest which he recorded with great detail. He had two notebooks: a red notebook that details events from 1944 to 1945, and a black one he purchased in Vienna in June 1945 for RM 1.50 (the receipt is still in the book) and it describes the three return trips from Budapest to Vienna, until they could take up permanent residence there again. As a coping mechanism, Jonny Moser actively wanted to remember his experience, not repressing anything. In his red notebook, there was also a chronology of the years 1945 to 1938 going backwards, and there are corrections for the years 1942 to 1938, where he updated events to their correct dates. He had a calendar-like memory and collected calendars throughout his life. This chronology helped him decades later to write his autobiography with an eye for precise dates. Even though about fifty years passed between his notes from 1945 and his work on his autobiography in the years 1997–2006, the events from the time of the Holocaust were always at the center of his life.

Before my father passed away in 2011, I was only allowed to touch his notebook once, after the publication of his autobiography. I had asked him for it for a few hours, so I could read it and ask him questions. His notes are written in a legible script and, besides the chronology, there are also literary writings and short essays about the present in Budapest, some of which are even in Hungarian. Detailed drawings of the places at which he stayed or was detained during the Holocaust are particularly interesting. For example, there is a drawing of the brick factory in Békásmegyer, on the regional rail line (HÉV) to Szentendre, from where Budapest Jews were deported to Auschwitz from July 2 to July 8, 1944. Moser's family narrowly escaped being sent on the last train to Auschwitz because my father told one of Eichmann's henchmen, Franz Novak, that they were not Jewish at the deportation site. Novak liked Moser's Burgenland dialect, so he allowed the family to return to Budapest and check their identity at the *Toloncház* (police jail for illegal foreigners) at Mosonyi utca 9. This was possible because Regent Horthy had allowed for some Hungarian Jews to be exempted on the final day of the deportations, before the deportations were stopped all together. So, Novak allowed the Mosers to join the group of those newly exempted Jews. When they returned to Békásmegyer, the brick factory was deserted the following day, and they had escaped the last transport from there to Auschwitz. Jonny Moser described the brick factory in Békásmegyer the day after the deportations looking as if nothing had ever happened there.

My father had no records from the time preceding summer 1944 because the Nazis took away his posessions before being moved to the brick factory in Békásmegyer. From May 15 to July 1, 1944, the Hungarian authorities had locked the Mosers up in the Tsuk factory on Csepel, a Danube island just south of Budapest. This was the time of the first heavy Allied air raids and some Hungarians believed that buildings that were inhabited by Jews would not be bombed. During these weeks, they were locked up in an industrial area above ground with a large group of Jews. They would not have survived a direct hit. They were lucky that the Tsuk factory was hit in the nights of July 1 to 2, when they were already aboard a Danube ship upstream through the eerie blacked out city of Budapest on the way to Békásmegyer. Some Hungarian anti-Semites saw themselves confirmed that the Allies only bombed buildings that had no Jews in them. Following the incarceration in the Tsuk factory, my father was afraid all his life of being locked up. Our apartment in Vienna was never locked at night, as the fear of break-ins was less significant than the fear of not being able to evacuate quickly in the case of an emergency. Although he had lost all papers from before summer 1944, he made drawings of the places, in which he had spent time before. For example, he made a drawing of the Hungarian concentration camp for foreign Jews in Ricse, Eastern Hungary. He also made a concise drawing of the Zsidókorház (Jewish hospital) in Budapest's Szábolcs utca 39, in which he had spent time recovering from pleuritis.

A key turning point in Jonny Moser's life was meeting Raoul Wallenberg at the residence of the Molnars in the Minerva utca 1a, which was next door to the Swedish embassy. On August 12, 1944, my father and his sister, Herma, visited the Molnars, a well-off family that was Jewish according to the Nazi racial law, and who did charity work and had helped them before. Mici Molnar was a member of the Zwack family and housed all her relatives in her basement at the time. The Zwacks are well known for the herbal liqueur Unicum. The Molnars were happy to see my father and my aunt because it was surprising to see these two impoverished foreign Jews who had managed to avoid being deported. They asked them to stay for the day and wait for Wallenberg, who lived upstairs, to return, as it was conveniently located to the Swedish embassy and provided the Molnars with some security. When Wallenberg arrived around 10 pm that day, he asked them if they had any personal connections to Sweden. My father did not see any, but Herma was quite alert and made up the story that they had once received some toys made in Sweden. That was good enough a reason for Wallenberg to issue *Schutzpässe* to them and their parents. It was one of the first passes that Wallenberg issued five days after meeting my aunt and father on August 17. My aunt Herma's *Schutzpass* is number 148, and my father's pass is number 151, both of which are preserved to this day. What is remarkable about their *Schutzpässe* is that they were some of the few that received a German transit visa stamped on the back on November 21, 1944, as well as the Hungarian exit permit, in order to travel to Sweden. They decided not to travel to Sweden due to the chaotic final months of the war.

However, they belonged to a small group of *Schutzpass* holders who were issued these official travel permits by the Nazis. The Swastika stamps on the German transit visa impressed the Hungarian Nazis who usually did not respect the Swedish *Schutzpässe*.

The Mosers experienced the liberation by the Red Army on the Pest side of the city, which was liberated two months before Buda. My father made a drawing of the cellars that had been connected during the war to provide escape routes during air raids. In the front of the drawing, one can see the Kalvin tér, which my father erroneously spelled with a C. The Üllöi utca is a broad arterial road that leads from downtown Pest out of the city towards the southeast. They were exposed to significant fighting in this strategically important area, and needed to seek shelter, as the Soviets advanced block by block. My father described in detail in his notes as well as in his autobiography how the front advanced through these cellars. The front part of the block was completely destroyed in the war and was not rebuilt until the late 1990s.

His autobiography ends on July 28,1945, when the family had permanently relocated to Vienna. "Wir waren wieder zurück in Österreich, konnten neu beginnen" ("we were back in Austria again, could start anew") (360), reads the last sentence of his book. Only the epilogue by Eleonore Lappin and Albert Lichtblau give any indication of Jonny Moser's post-war life, which was quite interesting, but for Moser it was overshadowed by his difficult survival in the days of the Holocaust.

After the failed Communist coup attempt in Austria in October 1950, after which it was clear that Austria would not become a People's Republic, Jonny Moser and his parents decided to remain in Austria and not take advantage of the U.S. immigrant visas, which they had been issued. It was certainly an unusual decision for a Holocaust survivor to remain in Austria. His mother had taken cover a Trafik in the Novaragasse, in Vienna's second district in 1946, which had formerly been Jewish owned and then "aryanized" (taken over by Nazis). Jonny Moser would run this Trafik until his retirement in 1997. He became active in the Social-Democratic party in 1951, though remaining strictly anti-Communist, and served as a *SPÖ Bezirksrat* for Vienna's first district for over 32 years (1964-1996). In the early 1950s, he began studying for his chemistry degree, which was interrupted by his father's death in 1952 and his mother's in 1953. He studied history at the University of Vienna where he completed his dissertation in 1961 on the history of Antisemitism in Austria.

His sister Herma married Wilhelm Krell (1902–1973) in 1947, who would become the Amtsdirektor of the Israelitische Kultusgemeinde in

Vienna. Through his brother-in-law, Jonny Moser gained access to documents and personal contacts in the IKG. He became acquainted with Emil Maurer and Ernst Feldsberg, the presidents of the IKG in the 1950s and 1960s, who gave him documents related to the Holocaust, which the IKG did not want to hold on to in the 1960s. This may be difficult to understand today, but in those days almost nobody was interested in this painful history. The IKG were custodians of a tiny Jewish community that paled in comparison to the pre-Holocaust era and their future seemed uncertain. Non-Jews especially, but also some Jews in Austria, often wanted to forget. While Jonny Moser's understanding of the Holocaust grew through the insights from these documents and the many conversations and correspondences with eyewitnesses of the history, he lacked the support of an academic institutional affiliation. Of course, it was inconceivable for a Holocaust historian to be employed at an Austrian university in the 1960s or even 1970s. He made do without such an affiliation, and he was a founding member of the DÖW (Dokumentationsarchiv des österreichischen Widerstands) in 1963 and remained on the board for the rest of his life. One of his proud achievements involved curating the 1978 exhibit on the Holocaust in Burgenland at the Jewish Museum in Eisenstadt, where he is still fondly remembered as a survivor of the Holocaust and where he was featured in a 2018 joint exhibition at the Landesmuseum and Jewish Museum commemorating the so-called *Anschluss*. He gave talks on the Holocaust in Austria and abroad, including in the US in 2000, and continued this work until he passed away in 2011.

One of the highlights of remembering Jonny Moser in recent years was the 2018 dedication of the Jonny-Moser-Park near Vienna's Schottenring U-Bahnstation, close to where he lived for the last 40 years of his life. This was a nice tribute to remembering one of the first Holocaust historians in Austria.

Select Bibliography

Moser, Jonny. *Demographie der jüdischen Bevölkerung Österreichs 1938–1945*. Vienna: DÖW, 1999.

———. *Die Judenverfolgung in Österreich*. Vienna: Europa Verlag, 1966.

———. "Die Katastrophe der Juden in Österreich 1938–1945—ihre Voraussetzungen und ihre Überwindung." In *Der gelbe Stern in Österreich*, edited by Jonny Moser and Kurt Schubert, 67–137. Eisenstadt: Edition Roetzer, 1977.

———. *Nisko: Die ersten Judendeportationen*. Edited by Joseph W. Moser and James R. Moser. Vienna: Steinbauer, 2012.

———. *Wallenbergs Laufbursche: Jugenderinnerungen 1938–1945*. Vienna: Picus, 2006.

REVIEW ESSAYS

"Rethinking Red Vienna at a Moment of Transition"
Rob McFarland, Georg Spitaler, and Ingo Zechner, eds., *The Red Vienna Sourcebook* (Rochester: Camden House, 2020).

Jason Dawsey

Obscured by the frightening reemergence of right-wing populist, neo-fascist, and neo-Nazi organizations in Europe and North America, renewed attention to the legacy of Karl Marx and Marxism is one of the more remarkable and promising developments of the early twenty-first century. Contrary to popular wisdom, though, this phenomenon predates the onset of the worldwide economic downturn in 2007–2008. As Peter Hudis observed, the acceleration of "globalization" certainly reinvigorated interest in Marx's writings, as did the "emergence of a global-justice movement over the past two decades" focused on "the economic inequality, social instability and environmental destruction that have accompanied the global expansion of capitalism."[1] Still, the scale, duration, and socio-political implications of the Great Recession, unmastered after a decade, have certainly accounted for much of the greater attentiveness to Marxist thinking.

While not downplaying the vibrancy of Marxist currents in other areas of the world, the "Marx revival" and the "returns of Marxism" have been primarily Anglophone phenomena.[2] Publishers like Verso (an outgrowth of *New Left Review* and New Left Books) and the UK journal, *Historical Materialism,* along with their American counterparts, Haymarket Books and *Jacobin*, spearheaded the reestablishment of a socialist public sphere in the English-speaking world with ample room for Marxist ideas.[3] An array of young radicals have called for rigorous investigation of the intertwined histories of socialism, Marxism, modern revolution, and labor's confrontations with capital through a "return to the sources" and a critical, non-dogmatic spirit of inquiry. Beyond the expected forays into Marxology, this research, unbound from the confines of academic respectability, has excavated debates and journals, polemics and pamphlets, congresses and resolutions long forgotten—and done so for the explicit purpose of informing a reconstituted socialist workers' movement in the twenty-first century. Although this renascence of Marxism has thus far produced meager results organizationally, it has demonstrated 1) that the so-called "demise" of Marx and Marxism pronounced so frequently around 1990 proved extremely short-lived and 2) that Marxist critique still resonates forcefully with masses of human beings, particularly youth, who refuse to identify with or submit to a global capitalist order marked by massive inequality, ecological devastation, recurrent crises, systematic theft of time and precarity of livelihood, and increasing authoritarianism.

Austrian socialism's incredibly fecund history has not stood outside this moment of renewal and rediscovery. This is not, though, the first English-language "rediscovery" of the Left in Austria as a "third way" between communism and social democracy; a wave of research in the immediate aftermath of the New Left and Eurocommunism led to a modest but quite valuable series of texts and translations.[4] After a few decades of neoliberal onslaught and Cold War triumphalism, a resurgence of general interest in this tradition came about. Due to the diligence of scholars like William Smaldone, Mark Blum, and Gabriel Kuhn, we now can access a much broader range of English translations of the exemplars of what, by the mid-1920s, had already attained general recognition as "Austro-Marxism," with Julius Deutsch complementing the better-known cases of Otto Bauer, Karl Renner, Friedrich Adler, Max Adler, and Rudolf Hilferding.[5] There seems to be no signs this is slowing down. The appearance in 2021 of Eric Canepa and Walter Baier's Haymarket Books edition of Bauer's *The Austrian Revolution* (1923), a classic of Marxist history-writing comparable to Leon Trotsky's outstanding *History of the Russian Revolution*, is a real event in the study of European socialism and deserves detailed treatment.[6] Austro-Marxism, as a coherent body of social, political, and philosophical critique, can now be readily reexamined, discussed, and utilized.

With the publication by Camden House of *The Red Vienna Sourcebook*, the same scrutiny may also be applied to that bold and systematic implementation of Marxist ideas in the Austrian capital during the interwar period.[7] Joining a vast literature on the subject, this work will enlighten and inspire those unfamiliar with this "experiment" in "municipal socialism."[8] And why should it not? That a socialist government in Vienna, proudly adhering to Marxist thought, democratically and repeatedly elected, and enjoying deep working-class support, embarked over 15 years (1919–1934) on the transformation of a modern city with some 2 million inhabitants into "Red Vienna" will understandably captivate left-wing intellectuals and activists.

After the well-received 2019–2020 exhibition *Das Rote Wien 1919–1934* at Wien Museum MUSA, the release of this sourcebook should be greeted as a continuation, retrospective, and critical response to the already decades-long engagement with the history of Red Vienna.[9] In their introduction, Rob McFarland, Georg Spitaler, and Ingo Zechner, the editors of *The Red Vienna Sourcebook*, endorse and proceed from Austrian Social Democracy's self-understanding as navigating a path independent from non- (or anti-)Marxist social democracy, as became predominant in Weimar Germany, and Soviet-style communism. Looking back on the exhaustion of both, they voice great hopes about the impact of the documents they present: "The texts of Red Vienna—coping as they do with refugees, poverty, wealth inequality, the threats of a globalizing economy, and craven populist strongmen—form an alternative history that speaks to the present moment. They should not only not be regarded as failed ideas from a distant time, but as possibly viable ideas that did not have a chance to be fully implemented" (11). For contemporary leftists focused on the city as a site of radical change, McFarland, Spitaler, and Zechner contend that "Red Vienna can function as a critical point of orientation for cutting-edge emancipatory municipal policies, especially considering the possibilities of communal action as it runs up against questions of housing policies, international austerity politics, the 'right to the city' and strategies against right-wing populist movements" (8).

In addition, the editors, in what is a most refreshing moment of reflexivity, attempt to justify the choice of a sourcebook as a genre. "Having the documents collected and annotated in a sourcebook allows readers to see," they maintain, drawing on Walter Benjamin, "what was possible but did not happen. It also allows readers to see that even though the emerging threats were recognized by farsighted observers, they still could not be stopped" (11). This amalgam of high expectations for the future and sobering reminders of past failures runs throughout the book. If we are, now into the twenty-first century's third decade, amidst a moment of transition—as the editors seem to indicate—then a painstaking retrospective of Red Vienna may spur just the kind of linkage of theory and practice that can ensure that what succeeds the neoliberal era is not only not worse but genuinely liberating.

The Red Vienna Sourcebook grew out of a truly collective effort of scholarship forged by the Austrian Labor History Society, the International Research Network (connecting researchers in Vienna, Harvard University, Tübingen, and Berkeley), and the Ludwig Boltzmann Institute for Digital History. The list of 22 contributors, several of them members of the curatorial group for *Das Rote Wien 1919–1934*, is impressive but does not include all the translators involved. If any work exemplifies the drive to "go to the sources" among the recent spate of publications on European socialism, it is this text.

Overall, the volume contains twelve robust parts with thirty-six chapters and a total of 273 primary sources spread out over some 700 pages. Each superbly illustrated chapter is introduced by one or more of the team of 22, and the 6–11 selections per chapter, though usually excerpts, are not excessively brief. The translations are of high quality and designed for non-specialists. An excellent timeline tracking Vienna from the November Revolution of 1918 to the February 1934 uprising and a bibliography accompany the materials. *The Weimar Republic Sourcebook* and *The Third Reich Sourcebook*, two essential collections for German history, 1919–1945, likely will and should become its companion texts.[10] Researchers will have to dig strenuously to locate topics not already covered in this book.

"Totality" may best specify what McFarland, Spitaler (who supported, too, Baier and Canepa's work on *The Austrian Revolution*), and Zechner have achieved here. By "totality," I mean something twofold: that the collection strives for comprehensiveness, and that the subject of most of those documents was, itself, a totalizing project—political, socio-economic, cultural, and theoretical. The aim was to bring about *neue Menschen*, Max Adler's conception smartly rendered here as "New Humans," or "New Human." This causes special problems for the reviewer, however. Given the scope and number of documents in *The Red Vienna Sourcebook*, I will confine my remarks here to identifying its contribution to a critical history of the Austrian, if not also European, Left, as well as singling out some specific texts which warrant closer inspection.

As a source collection, the book offers plenty of content beyond the Austro-Marxists and the progenitors of the various programs of municipal socialism. Virtually all of the luminaries in philosophy, political theory, theater, literature, psychology, sociology, music, the fine arts, cinema and filmmaking, photography, and architecture from the interwar period are represented. Although Weimar Germany dethroned Vienna as Central Europe's center for intellectual and cultural innovation and experimentation, the inclusion of Sigmund Freud, Alfred Adler, Wilhelm Reich, Karl Kraus, Hans Kelsen, Adolf Loos, Béla Balázs, Anton Webern, Theodor W. Adorno (from his tenure as editor of *Anbruch*, a journal of the New Music), Georg Lukács, Otto Neurath (excerpted six times), Ludwig Wittgenstein, Stefan Zweig (protesting against "The Monotonization of the World"), Joseph Roth, and Hermann Broch should hinder any hasty denigration of the capital of the First Republic. Indeed, the editors contend the Vienna of 1919–1934 was the "epoch of the second Wiener Moderne," a body of "new ideas, methods, and works," "all part of a new intellectual, political, and aesthetic laboratory that was created and safeguarded by the politics of Red Vienna."(5)

To begin to assess this very strong but certainly not unwarranted claim, the chapter on "Jewish Life and Culture" is an outstanding resource. Each of the selections speaks to the sense of perpetual crisis confronting Vienna's Jewish community after 1918. What to do about escalating antisemitism (hardly new in Vienna before the founding of the First Republic) and how to respond to the influx of Eastern European Jewish refugees? These questions become real again in the readings as do debates among Viennese Jews about assimilation and renewal or Zionism and Marxism. For this chapter, the editors initiate some striking comparisons with the educational and cultural programs of Red Vienna by utilizing a work from Josef Löwenherz, Vice-President of the Jewish Community Vienna (usually remembered for his post-*Anschluss* dealings with Adolf Eichmann), where Löwenherz demands, "*We as the Jewish Community must therefore consider it our most sacred duty to carefully draw each Jew into the circle of our community right from the tenderest of ages*" (208, italics in the original). While the Social Democrats were the most progressive political force, they certainly, as the Löwenherz reading indicates, did not hold a monopoly on striving for a total transformation of individuals.

Part IX, with chapters on "Antisemitism," "Black Vienna," and "Brown Vienna," is immensely suggestive. Careful study of these sections will aid historical understanding of the growth, ferocity, and coalescence of the Austrian Right in the 1920s and '30s. The sourcebook does so without falling into a teleology of inevitable rightist triumph. Furthermore, the placement of Othmar Spann, the theorist of corporatism, and advocates of conservative political Catholicism such as Joseph Eberle and Alfred Missong in a chapter separate from the even more vile Walter Riehl, for many years the top propagandist of the Austrian Nazis, hinders facile conflation of these distinct currents on the right. There was much overlap and convergence between "Black Vienna" and "Brown Vienna" (the titles of two of the book's chapters), but these should not be overstated.[11] That something like a quasi-united Right existed at all in interwar Austria owed so much to the arch-reactionary Ignaz Seipel, the Catholic priest, two-time Christian Social chancellor, and bitter enemy of Otto Bauer. Seipel's statements, extracted from his 1926 essay "The Great Trajectory of Spiritual Development in Our Time," about the "search for a new, truer, and better democracy," a "democracy that allows few people—who are, nevertheless, completely accountable to everyone—to operate controls" to replace "democracy steered by the ballot alone," were chilling forebears of a coming authoritarian state.(633) As Azadeh Yamini-Hamedani and Wolfgang Fichna point out, "Seipel turned Red Vienna into a bogeyman and created a counterpart that meant to unite all of the political shades to the right of the Social Democrats, even uniting those groups whose ideologies contradicted one another" (627). The reprint of the 1927 "Rallying Cry of Vienna's Intellectuals" lays out just how seriously many of Vienna's leading lights took the threat posed by Seipel's Unity List and how they threw their support behind the Social Democrats that fateful year.

Ultimately, though, this sourcebook orbits the programs, people, and political vision of "Red Vienna" as a project of working-class emancipation. By broadening the unofficial canon of Austro-Marxist texts and, at the same time, reinforcing the well-known portrait of the SDAP as a mass socialist party of the Austrian working class (with significant support from intellectuals and artists), the collection contributes enormously to our historical understanding of how the Social Democrats dominated politics and culture in Vienna (itself made a province in 1922) for so long. In contrast to other revolutions such as the Paris Commune (72 days) or the case of the neighboring Hungarian Soviet Republic (133 days), to name just two, the "experiment" that was Red Vienna endured for a decade-and-a-half.[12]

If the chapter of *The Red Vienna Sourcebook* dedicated to Austro-Marxism offers the traditional names of leaders of the right wing of the SDAP (Karl Renner), the party's left (Otto Bauer), the University of Vienna philosopher and sociologist Max Adler, as well as the all-important revolutionary Linz Program of 1926, the work as a whole presents a much more diverse array of Marxist voices. We get texts by Robert Danneberg, city councilor and jurist, from Karl Seitz, mayor (after Jakob Reumann) of Vienna, Hugo Breitner, the city councilor for finance responsible for the taxation policy directed at the wealthy, Friedrich Austerlitz, editor of the SDAP daily, *Arbeiter-Zeitung*, Julius Braunthal, manager, from 1920, of the party's impressive election campaigns (later a historian of the Internationals) and member of its executive committee, and Otto Glöckel, the planner behind Red Vienna's rightly lauded panoply of changes to the educational system. In point of fact, Glöckel's push to break clerical influence over instruction, create general standards for schools, and make schooling more egalitarian—for both girls and boys of working-class origin—within a larger struggle "*for a free school system* [with free tuition and textbooks], *for the abolition of educational privilege, for a free people*" is one of the more inspiring moments detailed in this publication.(325, italics in the original) Also chosen for inclusion are Julius Deutsch, a key player in the Austrian Revolution, in the party-organized paramilitary *Republikanischer Schutzbund*, and in Social Democratic sports activity, and Joseph Buttinger, after 1934 crucial to the clandestine Revolutionary Socialists of Austria.

Resuming and building upon Helmut Gruber's expanded notion of Austro-Marxism, the editors do not restrict their definition only to theoreticians but encompass significant members of the party apparatus who exerted influence over Vienna's working masses beyond the printed and spoken word.[13] In so doing, Spitaler, Zechner, and McFarland raise anew, whether it is their intention or not, the question: what kind of Marxism was this?

No answer to that question can evade the centrality of Otto Bauer to Austro-Marxism and Red Vienna. Along with Neurath, he is the most frequently cited author in the book. While he is still mainly familiar to Americans, if at all, for his 1907 interpretation of nationality—and Joseph Stalin's rebuttal, no single person embodied the hopes and aspirations, the intellectual vitality, as well as, it must be said, the hyper-hesitancy of "Austro-Marxism" (a concept he defined) in the 1920s and 1930s than Bauer.[14] He served as the First Republic's first Minister of Foreign Affairs, and chaired, in 1919, Austria's State Commission of Socialization, penned the 1926 Linz Program, and championed the working class against the depredations of the Christian Socials and the other factions of the Austrian extreme right as the latter waxed stronger after the July 1927 massacre of workers in Vienna. In retrospect, the degree of influence and inspiration he exercised within the Austrian workers' movement right up to the desperate February 1934 Uprising is extraordinary. So, the few pages from Chapter 12 ("The State and the Working Class") of Bauer's *The Austrian Revolution*, selected and translated for the sourcebook by Rob McFarland, are crucial; this monograph advanced *the* Marxist exegesis of revolution and counter-revolution from 1918 to 1921 in "German-Austria" for socialists in Austria, and for many outside it.

These excerpts yield so much insight about Bauer's politics. A central aspect of the text is the initial dynamic he depicts between external constraint (elaborated in the larger book as dependence on food from outside the country, loss of vital raw materials like coal to newly independent countries, the threat of Entente invasion, and the blocking of *Anschluss* with Germany) and proletarian restraint. Bauer's explains this dilemma as the "twofold inner contradiction of the German-Austrian revolution," "the contradiction between the strong political power of the working class and their horrible economic misery; the contradiction between the inward freedom of the working class and its crushing dependence upon foreign capitalist entities" (119–20). In response—and this was fundamental to Bauer's Marxism—the proletariat had "to restrain itself of its own volition and realization," with the SDAP at hand "to guide them [Austrian workers] in a way that they realize on their own not to overstep the boundaries brought upon them by the economic plight and the economic and military impotence of their new revolutionary country." (120) Internally, the socialist workers' movement soon lost a position of strength against conservative forces in Austria, giving way to what Bauer terms an "equilibrium of class forces," which, in turn, was succeeded by a full-blown bourgeois "restoration" outside of Vienna by 1921. "The working class still commands the capital city, which contains nearly three-tenths of Austria's people," he asserts, defiantly, late in the book.[15] There, the working-class could still successfully pose "functional democracy," i.e. a type of democracy grounded in "societal or economic function" to the "political democracy," an inheritance of bourgeois predominance, rooted in abstract conceptions of the citizen (120–21). Counterrevolutionary forces did not yet possess enough power in Parliament, in the armed forces, in the workplace, and in the communication and transportation sectors to finish the "Restoration."

Bauer's history, then, reflects back on the Austrian Revolution and creation of the First Republic and how the Revolution's enemies had wrested from the Left or, better, been ceded the initiative. In this precarious situation of power-sharing with the Right, the tutelage of the party had instilled a "sense of responsibility" in the workers' movement and "empowered them to bridle their own passions, to bear scarcity and sacrifice without violence, for the sake of the preservation and security of the republic," argues Bauer. These comments, in their honesty, bluntness, and distrust of proletarian militancy, spell out the socio-political conditions for Red Vienna, for what can be labeled "socialism in one city," taking place within a national context of defeat and containment.

The path of avoidance of confrontation and civil war Bauer charted as a politician certainly found allies. On this point, the inclusion of Karl Kautsky in this sourcebook is significant, if easy to miss. In the deeply combative mass socialist politics of the pre-World War I period, Kautsky exercised prodigious political and theoretical influence over Marxists, not least among the most recognizably revolutionary of them: Rosa Luxemburg, Vladimir Lenin, Leon Trotsky, and Anton Pannekoek. Kautsky did this through the dozens of books and hundreds of articles he produced during his 34-year editorship (1883–1917) of *Die Neue Zeit*, the flagship journal of historical materialism worldwide. Austrian Social Democrats were no exception. A longtime friend of party leader Victor Adler, Kautsky reviewed and revised Adler's draft of the SDAP's 1889 Hainfeld Program, two years before he co-authored the SPD's famed Erfurt Program.[16] He resided in Vienna in 1882–1883 and again in 1888–89, before settling there in 1924 with his Viennese Jewish wife, Luise Ronsperger, to be closer to their three sons. Otto Bauer reviewed Kautsky's seminal 1909 book *The Road to Power* in *Der Kampf*, the theoretical journal of the SDAP, while Karl Renner devoted a work to Kautsky, the German working-class's *Lehrmeister* (Master Teacher), on the occasion of the latter's 75th birthday.[17]

The Kautsky we encounter here is the Marxist of 1920 who staunchly opposed the Bolsheviks from the standpoint of "democracy," which meant by this point bourgeois, parliamentary democracy. If he once upheld the Paris Commune as the epitome of a "democratic and social republic" and asserted that only social revolution would topple capitalist rule, this far more moderate Kautsky emphasized that socialists "strive for democracy not because it appears idyllic to us but because it provides the best foundation for resolving the class antagonism between capital and the proletariat" and that "in a democracy, class struggle takes place within the framework of the constitution" (21). Calling for, in the most muddled terms, "full democracy," Kautsky in 1920, condemned now by Vladimir Lenin who once revered him, as a "renegade," could readily shift to the SDAP which, unlike the devastating fratricide of German Social Democracy, had largely retained its unity and avoided civil war.(21) A photograph from October 1931, inserted among the illustrations in *The Austrian Revolution*, with Kautsky to the right of Bauer and Friedrich Adler in Vienna, perfectly captures his future political course.

Neither Austro-Marxism, at least during the First Republic, nor Red Vienna were exclusively men's affairs though. Women, as the editorial team demonstrates quite forcefully, asserted themselves in every aspect of the SDAP's field of action, even when faced with overt sexism or indifference to their issues. According to Veronika Duma and Marie-Noëlle Yazdanpanah, "after the first election in February 1919, 8 women representatives entered the Austrian Parliament, 7 Social Democrats [one of them the venerated and longtime feminist- socialist Therese Schlesinger] and 1 Christian Social. Between 1920 and 1923, 12 women served as representatives, a number not to be reached again in Austria until 1978" (233). Of the 165 members of the Vienna Municipal Council in the first four years of the Republic, 19 were women. The Social Democrats devoted two separate periodicals to feminist issues and concerns: 1) the (from 1921) monthly *Arbeiterinnen-Zeitung: Sozialdemokratisches Organ für Frauen und Mädchen* (renamed in 1924 *Die Frau*) and 2) *Die Unzufriedene: Eine Unabhängige Wochenschrift* für alle Frauen, founded in 1923. These periodicals discussed pay equity, chances to pursue education and meaningful work outside the home, decriminalization of abortion, and fairer division of domestic labor and the obligations of childrearing. Socialist debates about the ideal of the

New Woman, a major feature in social life in Europe and North America throughout the 1920s and early 1930s, stressed health and athleticism and rejection of alcohol and cigarettes for female party members.

Among the prominent women in the SDAP, Käthe Leichter, whose later incarceration in Ravensbrück and death in one of the Nazi T-4 killing centers can overshadow her astonishing life as a woman of the Left, easily warrants an entire essay devoted just to her. Her study of 1300 working women, *This is How We Live*, is a brilliant indictment of insufficient progress (with recommendations for household technologies, kindergartens, and daycare centers) coupled with the insistence that "the *demands* and *struggles* of *working women* will help burst the bounds" of the capitalist system.(251) Leichter would go on to strongly and incisively criticize the passivity of the SDAP's leadership and the "*faith in the automatic*, inevitable nature of economic and historical processes" when Dollfuss dissolved Parliament in 1933; selections from this work appear in the sourcebook and should be mandatory for any class or study group investigating the rise of fascism.(129, italics in the original) To bring in another legendary figure from Austrian Social Democracy's women's movement, Adelheid Popp, a tireless opponent of anti-abortion laws, moved toward a notion of intersectionality in her 1922 essay "The Double Burden of Women." This era of feminist socialism in Austria is particularly relevant when one recalls how the Great Depression impacted the ability of Social Democrats in office to fund programs for women, before Christian Social and Nazi regimes attacked notions of empowerment for girls and women.

Of the many striking images reproduced in *The Red Vienna Sourcebook*, the one opening the chapter on "Global Resonances" is especially vivid. Taken from an April 1932 issue of the Social Democratic periodical *Der Kuckuck*, it says "The Red Metropolis is the hope and the ennoblement (*Erhebung*) of the working people of all capitalist countries in the world. Therefore, may Vienna forever remain red!" (586). It was not only Austro-Marxist ideas which, seizing the masses, helped keep the Austrian capital red but, primarily, the magnificent nexus of programs devised to directly better the lives of workers—women, men, and children. Here, the sourcebook is particularly effective in conveying the experience of Social Democracy as an alternative and oppositional society and polity. In 1927 Robert Danneberg claimed that more than 468,000 men and 201,000 women belonged to the SDAP. This certainly qualified it as one of the largest socialist parties per capita in the world.

With its fervent affirmation of party (e.g. "We have a goal of transforming the capital-serving republic into a social republic, a community, a united country. We the party!"), Danneberg's text collides with the deep suspicion many of the Left harbor today toward organizations deemed too vertical in structure (679). Party-membership, party-expansion, and party-advocacy define the lives of comrades; says Danneberg, "who have become the visible tool of history, builders of a state, refuge for the desperate and perplexed, hope for the discouraged pioneers of a great future" (679). Danneberg also exudes a confidence that probably will alienate some contemporary activists, likewise those of us who know "how this story ends." "The day is coming when the red flag will be hoisted victoriously. Then, thanks to the efforts of the party, the celebration of the republic will become a celebration of socialism," he predicts (679).

Confidence of this sort flowed from the astounding organizational presence attained by the SDAP in working-class life. As is well-known, the party's network of programs, augmented by activities undertaken by the trade unions, touched everything workers did. The document selections in *The Red Vienna Sourcebook* truly clasp this. An eight-hour workday promulgated by Parliament in 1918–1919 allowed workers, as Julius Braunthal expresses it, "the necessary free time not only to recover their exhausted energy but also to enjoy an intellectually and socially active life" (336). For those drawn to the history of socialism, this aspect of the sourcebook—how the participation in and enjoyment of "an intellectually and socially active life was integral to the Austro-Marxist hope for the emergence of "New Humans" based on freedom, equality, solidarity, non-alienated work, and socialization of the means of production—is particularly trenchant.

We encounter in the collection the Female Labor Unit of the Chamber of Labor (headed by Käthe Leichter), the Central Office for Workers' Education, the Vienna Workers' Libraries, and the Workers' Bank. Thanks to efforts by the Vienna Municipal Council, "almost sixty-four thousand apartments in nearly four hundred municipal housing complexes, about two thousand business premises, over five thousand lots for settler homes, as well as a large number of community buildings—kindergartens, schools, public baths, sport facilities, health clinics, libraries, artist studios, and so on—were designed, built, and opened for public use" (405). There were the vigorous efforts by David Josef Bach and the Social Democratic Arts Council to make art, music, and literature more accessible and to guarantee workers received the same exposure to the tradition of German-language humanism (i.e. literature and theater) as bourgeois individuals. While still wedded to print media, the Social Democrats by no means stayed away from new forms of mass culture and sports (though the latter clearly engendered controversy within its ranks). For example, in 1924 the national radio station, Radio Verkehrs AG (RAVAG), was created. Love of athletics could be channeled into the Austrian Workers Association for Sports and Physical Culture, which owed so much to the dedication of Julius Deutsch.

Chapter Nineteen, a series of readings of "Nature," is especially intriguing, showing the Social Democrats' connections to the older tradition of Alpine Clubs and *Lebensreform* and how, despite Robert Winter's radical assertion that "nature is the oldest socialist," love for the natural world did not belong exclusively to the Left (372). The editors remind us that the SDAP planned "green spaces and buildings that let in plenty of natural light," encouraged "allotment gardens so people could grow their own food for a healthy diet," and pushed for a substantive "appreciation of nature" among Vienna's working class (370). Calling this an ecological perspective would go too far for a number of reasons. Yet the emphasis on working-class people securing exposure to sunshine, blue skies, fresh air, trees, and mountains denotes much greater balance between humans and nature and the necessity of valuing and preserving non-human nature. Karl Renner describes rather lyrically the Friends of Nature, an organization of which he was a founding member. The Friends of Nature answer, Renner says, proletarians' lack of access to "field, meadow, wood, or pasture, or of urban land," due to the demands of work, the poorly lit squalor of their residences, and the pull of the tavern, with "nature propaganda" and "a love of nature and the joy of exploring the world of nature," bespeaking a "green" socialism of sorts decades before the appearance of the modern environmental movement (380, 381). Yet at the same time talk of the need to "reconquer" nature and the fixation on healthiness will certainly jar readers attracted to contemporary ecosocialism and reveals a tension within the socialist politics underpinning Red Vienna (381).

Despite this incredible project binding individual and social transformation within a setting where right-wing elements always menaced socialist politics, the editors do not shy away from criticizing Austrian Social Democracy. Undoubtedly, the striving for and maintenance of healthy minds and bodies was essential to the implementation of the "New Human." Pointing to the salience of Julius Tandler, an anatomist and Social Democratic Councilor of Welfare and Public Health, Birgit Nemec identifies how "on the one hand, emancipative and class-militant ideas, as in the case [Otto] Neurath [director of the Vienna Social and Economic Museum and heavily involved in educating young people about public health] , and on the other hand, the paternalistic and utilitarian notions of health politics, meaning the attempt to achieve the greatest benefit to the majority of the population by means of extensive governance" pulled in opposite political directions (274). At times, these policies crossed over into downright interventionism in the lives of working-class families when it came to rearing children. One might legitimately ask what was socialist about the outlook of a Tandler? The editors also ensure we do not forget that Social Democrats deported Jewish refugees from Vienna under the Sever Decree of 1919. Moreover, Austrian socialists, some of them of Jewish descent themselves, turned to antisemitic stereotypes of "Jewish capitalists" to strike back at right-wing accusations that Marxist socialism was a "Jewish" theory and practice.

Perhaps one of the most startling works in *The Red Vienna Sourcebook* is an anonymous, one-page document contained in the chapter on "Demography." Published in the Communist Party's newspaper, *Die Rote Fahne* in early 1932, the text lambasts Vienna Mayor Karl Seitz for the police's hounding of Roma (called "Gypsies" in the text) in the capital. It could have easily appeared in any number of newspapers about anti-immigrant and anti-refugee policing in the early 2020s. The author accuses Seitz of permitting the deportation from the city of dozens of Romani families, falsely designated "wealthy merchants from Romania and Hungary" by the authorities (189). According to the article, children were separated from their parents and the lack of proper documentation used as a pretext for removal. Defending this "eternally persecuted people," the Communist writer waxes indignant at the "true hunt for people in 'red' Vienna" (189). The discovery of this text and the outrages by a socialist government it exposes should prompt further explorations into the history of antiziganism on the Left and how to confront in Marxist theory and politics the specificities of enmity against Roma, as distinct from other forms of extreme prejudice like antisemitism or antiblack racism.

It is Leon Trotsky's 1930 attack that is the fiercest and most effective criticism of Bauer and the Austrian Social Democrats launched from the Left. Having spent several years there before the First World War, Trotsky was well acquainted with Victor and Friedrich Adler, Otto Bauer, and Karl Renner. If he admired Victor Adler and made overtures to Friedrich during the Russian Civil War, overall, he rarely missed an opportunity after 1917 to assail Austro-Marxism (Kautsky was another target). The 1930 piece in *The Red Vienna Sourcebook*, written the year after Joseph Stalin expelled him from the Soviet Union, exhibits Trotsky at his most polemical and insightful. With Chancellor Johann Schober proposing the rollback of the power of parliament, Trotsky queries just what the Social Democrats would do (it was Schober, who, as President of Police, oversaw the massacre of 85 protesters at the Palace of Justice in Vienna in July 1927). He acknowledges the SDAP's electoral strength, and the "net of political, union, municipal, cultural, and sports institutions" which "enmeshed the working class" (127). Nonetheless, the Austrian Social Democrats never deviate from a "conservative-conciliatory policy" utilizing "reformist-pacifist methods" and relying too heavily on propaganda against sworn enemies of bourgeois democracy (126, 127).

Getting to the heart of the matter, Trotsky distills Austro-Marxism's "central idea" as "'In Vienna we are strong, but in the country we are still weak. Besides, we have a master over us. We must retain our positions within the democracy and—wait'" (127). He also singles out Bauer for having force-fed Austrian workers a ceaseless and pernicious barrage of "arguments on the impermissibility of violence except for the defense of the existing democracy" with fascists on the move (127). Such a position eventuated, Trotsky grasped, in the proletariat in Austria always deferring insurrection and stressing the overwhelming strength of the class enemy. He thought the opportunity for revolutionary action had passed. Presciently, Trotsky envisages, "Austrian 'democracy' is doomed," and "its future is foreordained" (128). A similarly withering critique of the German Left would soon issue from his pen. For this reviewer, Trotsky comprehended the fundamental weakness of Austro-Marxism and the entire project of Red Vienna.

The severity of Trotsky's broadside/prediction must be linked to Otto Bauer's "The Rebellion of the Austrian Workers: Its Causes and Its Effects" (1934). Although Hans Kelsen is the final author selected, it is Bauer's tormented retrospective, termed accurately by Ingo Zechner a "lament about a lost opportunity, an admission that the [February 1934] rebellion of the Austrian workers came too late," that truly concludes the sourcebook (718). Despite the decades that separate the reader from Bauer's work, "The Rebellion of the Austrian Workers" preserves its capacity to horrify. In blunt, razor-sharp sentences, Bauer relates the outlawing of the SDAP and the occupation of its headquarters, the banning of the massive party press, the dissolution of the trade unions, and Social Democratic associations. "The blood of workers is flowing like water. Workers are dying on the battle lines, in the bullet-ridden houses, in the infirmaries, on the gallows. Fascism is rejoicing! Fascism is winning!" (718). As bitter as those lines are to take, he hammers home the essential point in the first part of the excerpt: "Everything that hundreds of thousands of Austrian workers have built for forty-five years has been destroyed" (718). Then in exile in Czechoslovakia, Bauer tries to explain what had made this catastrophe possible.

In accounting for mistakes, Bauer turns back to March 1933, to the procedural issue involving Karl Renner that allowed Christian Social Chancellor Engelbert Dollfuss to dissolve Parliament. He confesses that Austrian workers spoiled for fight at that decisive moment. Instead, he and the party leadership trusted Dollfuss's promise to restart negotiations. "We might have been able to prevail at that time, but we shied away from a fight. We still believed that we could come to a peaceful solution through negotiations . . . We dodged the fight because we wanted to spare our country the disaster of a bloody civil war" (721–22). Yet adherence to strict legality and constitutionalism and a unilateral renunciation of violence meant nothing to the Austrian extreme Right. A bloody civil war did ensue—on Dollfuss's terms—which resulted in the extirpation of Red Vienna and the suppression of the mighty Social Democratic workers' movement. Sociologist Hans Zeisel, the socialist scholar most remembered for his contribution (along with Marie Jahoda and Paul Lazarsfeld) to the 1933 *The Unemployed of Marienthal*, recollects how Bauer "was horrified by violence" and "his entire policy was directed toward preventing it at any price," except for his own party's suppression.[18]

Zeisel's comment on Bauer's reluctance to employ revolutionary proletarian force looks all the more prescient when juxtaposed with the statements about the proletariat's "sense of responsibility" and "restraint" in *The Austrian Revolution* and Bauer's 1934 elegy for Austrian socialism. Twenty years later, Joseph Buttinger, once a key figure on the radical left wing of the SDAP, remembered, too, "March 15, 1933—the black day when the party had refused armed resistance against the elimination of parliament."[19] Trotsky's critique, however, argues for placing the date of refusal earlier than Bauer or Buttinger, to 1930. Should we not ask, though, whether the "missed opportunity" was not 1918–19, the time of the revolution itself? Did Bauer and other leaders of the left-wing of Austrian Social Democracy, like Friedrich Adler, through their hesitancy, preclude a radical social revolution in "German-Austria" that might have forestalled the "equilibrium of class forces," much less the "Restoration" of bourgeois might in the First Republic, which ensued? This question will haunt any political evaluation of the Austrian Left between the world wars. With this sourcebook and the new edition of Bauer's *The Austrian Revolution*, activists of all ages and left-wing tendencies can more adequately approach this vital time in the history of European socialism.

It is this reviewer's hope that anyone with a serious interest in this history will track down *The Red Vienna Sourcebook*. The "transformative ideas" and yearnings for a radical shift from a "vertical hierarchical order," to a post-capitalist "horizontal egalitarian order" deserve a wide, thoughtful, passionate, and active audience (5). More ruthless questioning of the Marxism of the

Second International, out of which Austrian Social Democracy emerged, is already underway and promises to yield considerable historical and political insights.[20] Leftists have much to consider in this moment of transition about Marx's idea of a "democratic and social republic" and that idea's ramifications for contemporary bourgeois democracy—and the Red Vienna "experiment" will gainfully inform such considerations.

To quote the Hainfeld Program of the SDAP, the aim of liberating "the entire people, regardless of nationality, race, or gender, from the chains of economic dependence, to end its political powerlessness, and to reverse its stunted intellectual growth" lives on. These forms of oppression and exploitation cannot be separated from the "decisive fact that the means of production are monopolized in the hands of individual property owners" and the "political and economic domination" of the "capitalist class," "whose political and economic domination finds its expression in the modern state."[21] A steadfast grounding in critical history, epitomized by this collection, will only push us closer to the realization of that goal.

Endnotes

1 Peter Hudis, *Marx's Concept of the Alternative to Capitalism* (Chicago: Haymarket Books, 2013), 1.

2 Marcello Musto, ed., *The Marx Revival: Key Concepts and New Interpretations* (Cambridge: Cambridge University Press, 2020); Sara R. Farris, ed., *Returns of Marxism: Marxist Theory in a Time of Crisis* (Chicago: Haymarket Books, 2016). See also Robert X. Ware, *Marx on Emancipation and Socialist Goals: Retrieving Marx for the Future* (Cham: Springer International, 2018); David Fasenfest, ed., *Marx Matters* (Leiden: Brill, 2022).

3 At the time of writing, a new wave of Marxist journals has appeared, including *Spectre* (USA), *Prometheus* (UK), and *Cosmonaut* (USA), with the latter also publishing pamphlets.

4 For examples of this English-language "rediscovery," see Tom Bottomore and Patrick Goode, eds., *Austro-Marxism* (Oxford: Clarendon Press, 1978); Raimund Loew, "The Politics of Austro-Marxism," *New Left Review* 1, no. 118 (November/December 1979): 15–51; Melanie A. Sully, *Continuity and Change in Austrian Socialism: The Eternal Quest for the Third Way*, East European Monographs 114 (Boulder: East European Monographs, 1982); Mark E. Blum, *The Austro-Marxists: 1890–1918: A Psychobiographical Study* (Lexington: University Press of Kentucky, 1985). The renewed interest in Austro-Marxism among Austrian intellectuals, spurred by Social Democratic Chancellor Bruno Kreisky, was far greater and more sustained.

5 For works in English, see Ernst Hanisch, "Otto Bauer (1881–1938): Politician and Public Intellectual," in *Austrian Lives*, Contemporary Austrian Studies 21, eds. Günter Bischof, Fritz Plasser, and Eva Maltschnig (New Orleans: University of New Orleans Press; Innsbruck: Innsbruck University Press, 2012); Gareth Dale, "Karl Polanyi in Vienna: Guild Socialism, Austro-Marxism and Duczynska's Alternative," *Historical Materialism* 22, no. 1 (2014): 34–66; Ewa Czerwinska-Schupp, *Otto Bauer (1881–1938): Thinker and Politician*, trans. Maciej Zurowski (Chicago: Haymarket Books, 2016); Julius Deutsch, *Antifascism, Sports, Sobriety: Forging a Militant Working-Class Culture*, ed. and trans. Gabriel Kuhn (Oakland: PM Press, 2017); Mark E. Blum and William Smaldone, eds., *Austro-Marxism: The Ideology of Unity*, vol. 1, *Austro-Marxist Theory and Strategy* (Chicago: Haymarket Books, 2015); Mark E. Blum and William Smaldone, eds., *Austro-Marxism: The Ideology of Unity*, vol. 2, *Changing the World: The Politics of Austro-Marxism* (Chicago: Haymarket Books, 2018); William T. Smaldone, "Between Reform and Revolution: The Politics of Austro Marxism," *Jacobin*, March 23, 2018 (online edition); Walter Baier, "Luxemburg, Lenin, Bauer—The Left and the National," in *The Radical Left in Europe—Rediscovering Hope, Transform! Yearbook 2019*, eds. Walter Baier, Eric Canepa, and Haris Golemis (London: Merlin Press, 2019); Charles H. Clavey, "Resiliency or Resignation: Paul F. Lazarsfeld, Austro-Marxism, and the Psychology of Unemployment, 1919–1933," *Modern Intellectual History* 18, no. 1 (March 2021): 146–170.

6 Otto Bauer, *The Austrian Revolution*, eds. Eric Canepa and Walter Baier, trans. Eric Canepa (Chicago: Haymarket Books, 2021).

7 There is also a German edition of the sourcebook, *Das Rote Wien: Schlüsseltexte der zweiten Moderne 1919–1934* (Berlin: De Gruyter, 2020).

8 Anson Rabinbach, *The Crisis of Austrian Socialism: From Red Vienna to Civil War, 1927–1934* (Chicago: University of Chicago Press, 1983); Anson Rabinbach, ed., *The Austrian Socialist Experiment: Social Democracy and Austromarxism, 1918–1934* (Boulder: Westview Press, 1985); Helmut Gruber, *Red Vienna: Experiment in Working-Class Culture, 1919–1934* (Oxford: Oxford University Press, 1991); Sheldon Gardner and Gwendolyn Stevens, *Red Vienna and the Golden Age of Psychology: 1918–1938* (New York: Praeger, 1992); Eve Blau, *The Architecture of Red Vienna, 1919–1934* (Cambridge, Mass.: MIT Press, 1999); Judith Beniston and Robert Vilain, eds., "Culture and Politics in Red Vienna," special issue of *Austrian Studies* 14 (2006); Matthew Paul Berg, "Reinventing 'Red Vienna' after 1945: Habitus, Patronage, and the Foundations of Municipal Social Democratic Dominance," *Journal of Modern History* 86, no. 3 (2014): 603–32; Rob McFarland, *Red Vienna, White Socialism, and the Blues: Ann Tizia Leitich's America* (Rochester: Camden House, 2015).

9 Werner Michael Schwarz, Georg Spitaler, and Elke Wikidal, eds., *Das Rote Wien 1919–1934: Ideen, Debatten, Praxis* (Basel: Birkhäuser, 2019). For some other representative works from the literature in German, see Michael Krätke, "Austromarxismus und politische Ökonomie: Die Austromarxisten in ihrer Epoche," *Austriaca* 40, no. 80 (June 2015): 31–52; Veronika Duma and Hanna Lichtenberger, "Das Rote Wien: Sozialistische Stadt im konservativen Staat," *Luxemburg: Gesellschaftsanalyse und linke Praxis* no. 2 (2016): 122–130; Andreas Fisahn, Thilo Scholle, and Ridvan Ciftci, eds., *Marxismus als Sozialwissenschaft: Rechts- und Staatsverständnisse im Austromarxismus* (Baden-Baden: Nomos, 2018); Bernhard Hachleitner, Matthias Marschik, and Georg Spitaler, eds., *Sportfunktionäre und Jüdische Differenz: Zwischen Anerkennung und Antisemitismus: Wien 1918 bis 1938* (Berlin: DeGruyter, 2018); Veronika Duma, *Rosa Jochmann: Politische Akteurin und Zeitzeugin* (Vienna: Verlag des Österreichischen Gewerkschaftsbundes, 2019), 67–167; Helmut Weihsmann, *Das Rote Wien: Sozialdemokratische Architektur und Kommunalpolitik 1919–1934*, 3rd ed. (Vienna: Promedia, 2019).

10 Anton Kaes, Martin Jay, and Edward Dimendberg, eds., *The Weimar Republic Sourcebook* (Berkeley: University of California Press, 1994); Anson Rabinbach and Sander Gilman, eds., *The Third Reich Sourcebook* (Berkeley: University of California Press, 2013).

11 These chapters acknowledge the importance of Janek Wasserman's *Black Vienna: The Radical Right in the Red City, 1918–1938* (Ithaca: Cornell University Press, 2014).

12 It would be useful to think how Red Vienna fits and complicates the framework for approaching the history of revolution developed by Enzo Traverso in his book *Revolution: An Intellectual History* (London: Verso, 2021).

13 See Gruber, *Red Vienna*, 30–38.

14 For a recent example, see Ronald Grigor Suny, *Stalin: Passage to Revolution* (Princeton: Princeton University Press, 2020), Ch. 23. For the English translation of Bauer's book, see *The Question of Nationalities and Social Democracy*, ed. Ephraim Nimni, trans. Joseph O'Donnell (Minneapolis: University of Minnesota Press, 2000). Among extensive secondary literature, the most important recent study of Bauer is Ernst Hanisch, *Der grosse Illusionist: Otto Bauer, 1881–1938* (Vienna: Böhlau, 2011).

15 This is an all-too-brief overview of Parts III–V of *The Austrian Revolution*. The quotation is from page 388 of the latter.

16 The friendship between Adler and Kautsky can be followed through the pages of Victor Adler, *Briefwechsel mit August Bebel und Karl Kautsky*, ed. Friedrich Adler and the Parteivorstand der Sozialistischen Partei Österreichs (Vienna: Verlag der Wiener Volksbuchhandlung, 1954).

17 For Bauer's review, see *Austro-Marxism: The Ideology of Unity*, Vol. 2, 26–37; Karl Renner, *Skizze zur Geschichte der geistigen und politischen Entwicklung der deutschen Arbeiterklasse, ihrem Lehrmeister Kautsky zum fünfundsiebzigsten Geburtstag* (Berlin: J.H.W. Dietz, 1929).

18 Hans Zeisel, "The Austromarxists in 'Red' Vienna: Reflections and Recollections," in *The Austrian Socialist Experiment*, 126.

19 Joseph Buttinger, *In the Twilight of Socialism: A History of the Revolutionary Socialists of Austria* (New York: Frederick Praeger, 1953), 6–7.

20 A catalyst for this rethinking is Eric Blanc, *Revolutionary Social Democracy: Working-Class Politics across the Russian Empire (1882–1917)* (Chicago: Haymarket Books, 2022). Students of Second International Marxism owe an enormous debt to the labors of Richard Day, Daniel Gaido, Ben Lewis, and Mike Taber. See Richard Day and Daniel Gaido, eds. and trans., *Witnesses to Permanent Revolution: The Documentary Record* (Chicago: Haymarket Books, 2011); Richard Day and Daniel Gaido, eds. and trans., *Discovering Imperialism: Social Democracy to World War I* (Chicago: Haymarket, 2012); Karl Kautsky, *Karl Kautsky on Democracy and Republicanism*, ed. and trans. Ben Lewis (Chicago: Haymarket, 2020); Mike Taber, ed., *Under the Socialist Banner: Resolutions of the Second International, 1889–1912* (Chicago: Haymarket, 2021).

21 These extracts from the Hainfeld Program appear in *Austro-Marxism*, vol. 2, *The Ideology of Unity*, 18.

The Second Republic: New Literature

Günter Bischof

Lothar Höbelt, *Die Zweite Republik und Ihre Besonderheiten*, Schriftenreihe des Forschungsinstitutes für politisch-historische Studien der Dr.-Wilfried-Haslauer-Bibliothek, Salzburg, Vienna: Böhlau, 2020.

Manfried Rauschensteiner, *Unter Beobachtung: Osterreich Seit 1918*, 2. akualisierte und erweiterte Auflage, Vienna: Böhlau, 2021.

Ernst Bruckmüller, *Geschichte Kompakt: Österreich*, Vienna: Böhlau 2021.

Gerald Stourzh and Wolfgang Mueller, eds., *Der Kampf um den Staatsvertrag, 1945–1955: Ost-West-Besetzung, Staatsvertrag, und Neutralität Österreichs*, Vienna: Böhlau, 2020.

Franz Cede and Christian Prosl, eds., *Diplomaten im Dialog: Zeitzeugnis einer Generation*, Vienna: Jan Sramek, 2021.

This is not the first time *Contemporary Austrian Studies* has presented a review essay on the Second Republic.[1] However, it is the first time *CAS* has dedicated a volume to the Second Republic, and therefore an update of select recent literature is in place. The volumes under review are all from elite Austrian historians, all affiliated with the University of Vienna, past, and present. Among the books under review, only Lothar Höbelt's volume is dedicated solely to the Second Republic. Manfried Rauchensteiner's book is a history of the two Austrian Republics since the collapse of the Habsburg Monarchy, as well as the difficult times of Austria under National Socialist rule. More than half, namely 313 of the 570 pages of the volume, are devoted to the Second Republic (surpassing Höbelt's 281-page volume). Ernst Bruckmüller's book is a short history of Austria, beginning with the Romans in Austria, and the final 46 of the volume's 276 pages are dedicated to the Second Republic.

Höbelt's account is lively and opinionated. His primary focus is on domestic politics, which is his strong suit as he makes clear that he knew many of the actors that he is writing about personally, not only from the

FPÖ (Willfried Gredler, Friedrich Peter, Alexander Götz, and Jörg Haider) but also from the ÖVP (Karl Gruber, Hans Igler, Alois Mock, and Kurt Waldheim), and SPÖ (Franz Olah and Leopold Gratz). As no other historian probably was friends with so many political elites after the war, Höbelt is sure-footed in dealing with the role of these politicians in the Second Republic. The strength of Höbelt's book is his thorough documentary base, having studiously read the minutes of the various People's Party (ÖVP) internal meetings, as well as the cabinet minutes (*Ministerratsprotokolle*) published since the late 1940s. These sources give his writing authority and depth. Höbelt considers Julius Raab "the central figure of the Second Republic" (p. 203) instead of the "sun king" Bruno Kreisky, the only political figure he dedicates an entire—the longest—chapter to (pp. 231–70). After the crucial Moscow Council of Foreign Ministers in March/April 1947, when no progress was made in Austrian State Treaty negotiations, Höbelt quotes Raab from an ÖVP-Club meeting: "Moscow was a great disappointment for us all [...] it is not necessary to keep begging for the love of the Allies" (my translation, p. 60). Moreover, a day before Parliament passed the law on Austria's "permanent neutrality" on October 26, 1955, Raab noted in the same party council that "neutrality must not water down our disposition (*Gesinnung*)" (p. 33).

To show Raab's prominence in Austrian postwar domestic politics, Höbelt does not only talk about the well-known "Raab-Kamitz Course" (the "stability program," amounting to liberal market economic policies initiated by the finance minister in the early 1950s) (p. 147), but also the hitherto unknown "Raab-Bischoff Course" (the friendly policies Raab initiated vis-à-vis the Soviet Union with Austria's long-term ambassador in Moscow, leading to the conclusion of the State Treaty and Austrian neutrality in 1955) (pp. 27—33), as well as "the Raab-Böhm Course" (the chancellor and the head of the Austrian Union Council defining wage-price controls in the "social partnership" during its best years of economic prosperity) (pp. 183–91), and the "Raab-Olah Course" (Raab, no longer chancellor, still springing a deal on the "social partnership" with the leader of the Socialist Party on his successor government) (p. 185).

Höbelt's book concentrates on the "specific characteristics" (*Besonderheiten*) of the Second Republic: the high concentration of voters in the traditional political camps (Christian Conservatives, Social Democrats, German Nationals), the "grand coalition governments" (ÖVP/SPÖ) defining the first twenty years of the Second Republic, the dense network of the "social partnership," the high concentration of state-owned industries (*Verstaatlichte*) inherited from the Third Reich. When these characteristics began to vanish after Waldheim was elected in 1986 and Austria joined the European Union in 1995, Höbelt sees the Second Republic coming to an end. What emerged was the "Second-and-A-Half Republic," not the "Third Republic" since FPÖ *enfant terrible* Jörg Haider had given that designation a bad name in the 1990s (pp. 281, 272). Höbelt argues that Austrian neutrality eroded with the end of the Cold War and was "only embraced as a local fad" (*nur noch als lokale Marotte gepflegt*). With EU membership, "Austria continued to be seemingly neutral, but was no longer fully sovereign" (p. 272). In 1986 the "two-and-a-half party system" became a different animal with the rise of Haider's populist FPÖ (overtaking the ÖVP in the number of votes in the October 1999 election) and the Green Party entering parliament for the first time (pp. 273–75). The economic crisis of the mid-1970s hit the state-owned sector particularly hard. While Kreisky tried to save the vast number of jobs in state-owned industries with deficit spending ("Austro-Keynesianism") (pp. 248–56), his socialist successors privatized this sector (p. 276).

Höbelt is critical of gender historians and those who criticize the "victims doctrine" and advocate for "mastering the past" (he makes fun of the *Vergangenheitsbewältiger*, p. 269). He impugns gender historians for not addressing the topic of 400,000 Austrian women being raped by Soviet soldiers at the end of World War II (pp. 14–15). Höbelt also speaks of the *leyenda negra* of Austrian women (*Trümmerfrauen*) being forced to clean up the rubble at the end of the war, when in fact, all Viennese citizens were forced to clear the rubble (p. 139). He argues that everybody agreed with the *Opferthese* because "everybody profited from it in one form or another" (p. 18). For Höbelt, the term "collective memory of a society" is a "construction of self-important intellectuals" (*geltungssüchtiger Intellektueller*) (p. 48). With Höbelt's deep empathy for the wartime generation, he dismisses the terms *Verdrängung* and *Pflichterfüllung* (p. 48). If the wartime generation wanted to talk about anything when they got together, it was the war, and they did not want to be incriminated like Waldheim for just "having done their duty" (p. 48). Höbelt devotes an entire chapter to "denazification" (pp. 45–78). He does not think much of the process since it was an impossible job to do as too many Austrians were members of the Nazi Party (every family had to deal with the Nazis [*Ehemalige*] in their midst, p. 54). He blames denazification mainly on the pressure of the occupation powers on the Austrian government (p. 58). He cites Raab realizing that unless the Austrian government became more determined with denazification, "we won't ever get rid of the occupation powers" (p. 59). He gleefully cites Education Minister Heinich Drimmel (ÖVP), Kreisky (SPÖ) and Gredler

(FPÖ) making fun of the term *Vergangenheitsbewältigung* (p. 49), as if the parties agreed on denazification policies.

While Höbelt only analyzes domestic politics, Rauchensteiner covers both domestic and foreign policy. Furthermore, while Höbelt has made prodigious use of archives in Austria, Rauchensteiner has also looked at foreign archives in the US, Great Britain, and Germany. His main point is that Austria was constantly "under observation" by the outside world—the cover image is a picture of Otto Dix's 1922 painting with a stern-looking man and woman, eying the world intently (with suspicion?). The great powers and Austria's neighbors watched the country not considered "viable" intensively after World War I, the "stern men" of the occupation powers after World War II (pp. 283ff), the European Union after 1995, and a close watch was kept on the "Schüssel Government" after 2000 (pp. 489ff). Rauchensteiner notes how the occupation zones developed at different economic paces during the occupation, and in 1955 (mainly due to Marshall Plan aid), the Western zones ("golden West") were ahead of the Eastern zone (pp. 306, 333). While the partition of the country was often feared and was seemingly happening during the decade of occupation, it did not come to pass (pp. 295, 310).

Rauchensteiner thinks the year 1956 marked the end of the occupation. Chancellor Raab made his first trip to the Federal Republic to improve relations with Konrad Adenauer and the Germans. Austria joined the Council of Europe, and Foreign Minister Figl traveled to Strasbourg and gave a speech affirming Austria's Europeanness. Austria also mastered the Hungarian crisis. Rauchensteiner argues that Austria was more than a mediator between East and West; it became "the hub (*Drehscheibe*) of Europe" (p. 344–45). Rauchensteiner started out as a military historian, so he is sure-footed on Austrian defense and security policy.[2] He covers topics such as the "secret rearmament" of Austria after the 1950 "October strike" (pp. 311–12, 315) and is very critical of Chancellor Kreisky's lack of reforms of the Austrian Army in the early 1970s (pp. 400–401). He speaks of a "broken defense system" (*Scherbenhaufen der Landesverteidgung*) (p. 417), and an "almost complete military vacuum" (*militärisches (Fast-) Vakuum*) in Austria in the 1970s (p. 418). Rauchensteiner's book covers the history of Austria all the way up to 2019/20—the Ibiza affair, the fall of the first Kurz government, and the beginnings of the Corona pandemic in Austria. He covers the rise of the Green movement and Haider's populist FPÖ (pp. 446ff) but does not engage in speculations about the end of the Second Republic or the beginnings of a Third Republic.

Unlike Höbelt, who is very astute on economic policies (pp. 142–48), Rauchensteiner does not devote much space to the importance of the

Marshall Plan for Austria's economic recovery after the war. Austria indeed received the most ERP aid in per capita terms after Iceland and Norway (Great Britain, Italy, and France received more aid overall, but not in per capita terms) (p. 306). The Marshall Plan ended in Austria in 1952, after the Americans refused to release counterpart funds and put pressure on Finance Minister Kamitz to lower inflation and stabilize the economy, so the "Raab-Kamitz Course" was induced by American pressure.[3] The Americans kept using the annual distribution of ERP-counterpart funding after the ending of the Marshall Plan to continue pressuring the Austrian government. The American ambassador "closed the spigot" of ERP counterpart funds in 1958 (not ERP funds, the ERP ended in 1952).[4] Rauchensteiner is correct in arguing that the Americans "were deeply disappointed that a country they had brought back to life, showed insufficient gratitude" (p. 351). Rauchensteiner notes there were 220,000 DPs ("Displaced Persons") "stranded" in Austria in 1955 (p. 288). The occupation powers forced the Austrian government to take care of some 1.5 million DPs after the war.

Bruckmüller's book is a short history of Austria, ending with the Second Republic. Bruckmüller does not use any archival sources in this Austrian textbook history. He covers all the bases of the postwar period, from denazification to economic recovery and the Marshall Plan. He addresses the state treaty and the "reform spirit" of the 1960s, leading to the *Alleinregierungen* of Josef Klaus (ÖVP) and then Kreisky (SPÖ). In his final chapter, he covers the end of the state industries, the end of the old party system, the end of the Cold War, and Austria joining the European Union. Given that Austrian elites consider the country a "cultural superpower," it is fitting that Bruckmüller ends the book with a short summary of Austrian postwar high cultural achievements in literature and the arts (pp. 267–71). Culture gets little attention in Höbelt and Rauchensteiner's books. Bruckmüller also adds reflections on the changing religious affiliations of Austrians, the decline of Catholicism, and the influx of Muslim immigrants from Bosnia and the Neat East (pp. 274–75), as well as Austria's change from "emigration to immigration country" (pp. 271–74).

The massive history of the negotiations and conclusion of the Austrian State Treaty by Gerald Stourzh and Wolfgang Mueller is *the* masterpiece of postwar Austrian historical writing. This is the 6th edition of Stourzh's *Staatsvertragsgeschichte*, regularly updated since its first publication in 1975 when it appeared as the *Kleine Geschichte des Österreichischen Staatsvertrages*. In this edition, Mueller, who teaches Russian history at the University of Vienna, has updated Stourzh's large 4th and 5th edition with new sources from Russian archives after the fall of the Soviet Union in 1991.[5] The result is as complete a history of the occupation decade at the beginning of the Second Republic as we will ever get. It is multiarchival international history at its best, a paragon of engaged historiography.[6]

Diplomaten im Dialog is as remarkable an introduction to highly personal perspectives on recent Austrian diplomacy as you get. This book is a nice compliment to the books on domestic policy reviewed here and informs readers on the foreign policy issues during the Second Republic, on issues like Austrian foreign policy towards the Balkans, or Austria and its integration with the European community. The two top diplomats, Franz Cede and Christian Prosl have interviewed nineteen of their colleagues, plus one another, about their education and career path; each interview concludes with general thoughts on the state of Austrian diplomacy and foreign policy. Cede and Prosl have previously written a small and tightly-argued volume on Austrian foreign policy after World War II.[7] Of the twenty-one top diplomats in the Austrian foreign service interviewed in this volume, seventeen are men, and four are women. They were the generation joining the Foreign Service from the late 1960s to the 1980s (the generation of distinguished diplomats before them, such as Thomas Klestil and Hans Winkler, are frequently mentioned in the book as mentors but do not fit this cohort). What led them to choose their careers as diplomats often was their desire "to go out into the world" (Gabriele Matzner-Holzner, p. 135), or, for those from modest, provincial backgrounds, *Fernweh* (an ache to travel abroad) (Peter Moser, p. 167). Only a few of them knew that they wanted to be diplomats before their high school graduation (Martin Eichtinger, p. 24).

In my review essay cited above, I use Ernst Hanisch's 1999 historiographical review essay to place the books under review into Hanisch's four schools of historical writing in postwar Austria.[8] Hanisch identifies 1) the "German national" school practiced in the years between the world wars; 2) the school of "coalition history" (*Koalitionsgeschichtsschreibung*) practiced from the end of World War II into the 1970s; 3) the school of New Left historiography, the *Gesellschaftsgeschichte* practiced in the 1970s and 1980s: and 4) the fragmentation and atomization of historical writing with the advent of "postmodernism" in the 1990s. Oddly enough, the Höbelt, Rauchensteiner, and Bruckmüller books seem to be a fallback to the paradigm of "coalition history," viewing the Second Republic largely as a success story. Stourzh and Mueller fit into this paradigm too, as the conclusion of the state treaty was unquestionably one of the great triumphs of the Second Republic and the "grand coalition," even though it ended an interminably long military occupation of the country.

Endnotes

1 Günter Bischof, "Austria after 1945—Success Story? Heroic Age? Review of Recent Literature," in *Neutrality in Austria*, ed. Günter Bischof, Anton Pelinka, and Ruth Wodak, Contemporary Austrian Studies 9, New Brunswick, NJ: Transaction 2001, 293–318; see also Bischof, "Zweite Republik," in *Österreichische Zeitgeschichte – Zeitgeschichte in Österreich: Eine Standortbestimmung in Zeiten des Umbruchs*, ed. Marcus Gräser and Dirk Rupnow, Vienna: Böhlau, 2021, 160–77.

2 See his masterpiece on Austria's Cold War security policy, Manfried Rauchensteiner, ed., *Zwischen den Blöcken: NATO, Warschauer Pakt und Österreich*, Schriftenreihe des Forschungsinstitutes für politisch-historische Studien der Dr.-Wilfried-Haslauer-Bibliothek, Salzburg, Vienna: Böhlau, 2010.

3 Hans Seidel, "Austria's Economic Policy and the Marshall Plan," in *The Marshall Plan in Austria*, eds. Günter Bischof, Anton Pelinka, and Dieter Stiefel, Contemporary Austrian Studies 8, New Brunswick, NJ: Transaction, 2000, 247–89 (here 264–65, 279–82); see also Seidel, *Österreichs Wirtschaft und Wirtschaftspolitik nach dem Zweiten Weltkrieg*, Vienna: Manz, 2005, 483–533.

4 Günter Bischof and Hans Petschar, *The Marshall Plan Since 1947: Saving Europe, Rebuilding Austria*, Vienna: Brandstätter, 2017, 248–51.

5 See the lengthy review essays on the English edition "A Cold War Over Austria: The Struggle of the State Treaty, Neutrality and the East-West Occupation, 1945–1955" (trans. by Cynthia Peck), largely identical to this 6th ed. in German, by Charles S. Maier, Günter Bischof, Peter Ruggenthaler, with responses by Gerald Stourzh and Wolfgang Mueller in the FORUM "The Austrian State Treaty and the Cold War: Contending Perspectives," *Journal of Cold War History* vol. 23, no. 4 (Fall 2021): 211–45 (for the publication history of various editions of the "*Staatsvertags*-history", see 211–12, 223–24, 235–36).

6 On "this books reflects the best of international history" (Schwartz), see the "Historiography Roundtable" on the 4th edition with essays by Vojtech Mastny, Thomas A. Schwartz, Klaus Larres, and Anton Pelinka, with a response by Gerald Stourzh in *Neutrality in Austria*, Contemporary Austrian Studies 9, 236–92 (citation 251).

7 Franz Cede and Christian Prosl, *Ambition and Reality: Austria's Foreign Policy since 1945*, Innsbruck: StudienVerlag, 2017.

8 Bischof, "Austria after 1945," 294–96; Ernst Hanisch, "Der forschende Blick: Österreich im 20. Jahrhundert: Interpretationen und Kontroversen," *Carinthia: Zeitschrift für geschichtliche Landeskunde von Kärnten* 189 (1999): 567–83.

BOOK REVIEWS

Tim Corbett, *Die Grabstätten meiner Väter: Die jüdischen Friedhöfe in Wien* (Vienna: Böhlau, 2021).

Evan B. Bukey

Readers of this enormous book should begin by reading its conclusion, or at least those pages that constitute both a summary and introduction to its subject matter. Here Corbett explains his intention to recount the eight-hundred-year history of Viennese Jews from the late Middle Ages to the present, stressing their significance and contribution to the development of city life even when only a handful were permitted to reside in the Habsburg capital. Contrary to prevailing views, the author emphatically contends that the history of both Vienna and its Jewish population have been and remain intimately and inextricably interconnected, even after the Anschluss and Holocaust.

In his lengthy introductory chapter, the first of ten, Corbett explains that 100,000 gravestones from five Jewish cemeteries dating from the 13th century to the present have been used as archival sources, every bit as rich as documentary ones, to supplement existing literature on the Jewish experience in Vienna. Furthermore, because the author is fluent in modern European languages as well as Hebrew and Yiddish, this highly original approach has produced a masterpiece, albeit one that is somewhat repetitious and much too long.

Corbett argues that examination of sepulchral ethnicities enables us to realize that cemeteries and religious monuments since time immemorial have been more important to the living than to the dead. That the wealthy have always erected larger monuments to deceased loved ones from Roman times to the present. In this respect, Jews have been no different from other people, particularly in late 19th century Vienna, where educated and prosperous Jews excelled in constructing elaborate memorials in Jewish cemeteries. These and other grave markers reveal much about family members, except sisters, wives, and daughters, in line with Jewish custom. In late imperial Vienna, Corbett continues, it would be insulting to regard Jews as strangers in a city in which they had been living for centuries. This wildly shared belief can be attributed to the Holocaust, which—until the Waldheim affair—produced collective amnesia both about the size and diversity of Viennese Jewish life and the complicity of non-Jewish residents in the deportation and murder of their fellow citizens.

Corbett's research reveals there were roughly 100,000 Jewish grave markers, including fragmentary ones. These graves can be found in five Jewish cemeteries as well as those of several hundred prominent figures, such as Arthur Schnitzler and Gustav Mahler in secular cemeteries. Combined with published historical works, most notably those by August Ludwig Frankl and Gerson Wolf, as well as others that the author has read in detail, his book constitutes an encyclopedic history of the Jewish presence in Vienna.

Corbett proceeds briefly to recapitulate the history of Viennese Jewry during the early modern period, noting that a handful of Jews, mostly merchants, kept a low profile but were generally left alone. In 1421, however, Albrecht IV undertook a pogrom that murdered or expelled those living in the capital. A century and a half later, enough Jews had returned to organize a religious community. The Habsburgs forbade them from living within the city walls but needed to tax their assets as a source of imperial income. Thereafter, these so-called "liberated" Jews were gradually permitted to dwell in the city though confined to Leopoldstadt. During the Ottoman siege in 1683, they were again expelled, but later returned as "court Jews." In 1782 Joseph II's Patent of Tolerance granted Jews certain privileges, though it compelled them to live in a segregated society. That Jews such as Adolf Fischof played a prominent role in the revolutions of 1848–49 was no coincidence. Finally, in 1867 they were granted full citizenship, enabling thousands of Jewish Austrians from throughout the monarchy to prosper and thrive within Vienna.

Corbett now shifts his focus to the oldest known Jewish cemetery near the Seegasse. He explains that the earliest gravestone is that of a woman who died in 1629. Thereafter, the cemetery became the principal Jewish burial ground, primarily because, at the time, no more than roughly five hundred or so persons of the Jewish faith resided in the imperial capital. In 1782 Joseph II banned Jews from being laid to rest within the city walls but established a common cemetery open to persons of every faith, including Protestants, in which Mozart was interred. Even so, most Jews were buried in the Seegasse or Währing cemeteries until 1879, when the Viennese City Council and the Jewish Religious Community (*Israelitische Kultusgemeinde* [IKG]) agreed to designate the area beyond Gate IV of the modern non-denominational Central Cemetery (*Zentralfriedhof*) in Simmering as the principal Jewish burial ground.

In some of the richest and most informative chapters of his book Corbett contends that the various ceremonial halls, memorials, and tombstones near Gate IV can be seen as a microcosm of the Viennese Jewish population; not least because so many of the deceased had immigrated from far-flung regions of the Austrian monarchy, particularly Galicia and Bukovina. Many had succeeded as physicians, attorneys, bankers, newspaper editors, and other members of the learned professions so as to dominate much of Viennese bourgeois society. Their success, however, stoked the fires of anti-Semitism, most notably under Karl Lueger, so that despite cordial relations with many middle class families and friends, non-Viennese assimilation never took place. Even so, the largely bourgeois members of the IKG worked well with members of the City Council.

Examination of gravestones and other markers reveals that most were inscribed in German rather than a mixture of German and Hebrew, as had been the case before. An exception was made for rabbis. The other markers also reveal the divisions within Jewish society, such as between the Ashkenazi, Sephardim, and younger Zionists. Plots were also reserved for officers of the Habsburg army. Before the Anschluss, relatively few Orthodox Jews were buried at Gate IV; most of them had led destitute lives in Leopoldstadt.

In discussing the era between 1918 and 1938, Corbett points out that because Viennese Jews supported the Austrian monarchy, most notably the middle-class IKG, they found themselves virtually alone confronting anti-Habsburg and anti-Semitic sentiment. Moreover, the influx of 35,000 Galician Jews exacerbated widespread anger and divided the Jewish community into Western and Eastern Jews, with the IKG patronizing the Orthodox "new arrivals." Seeking to overcome these divisions, the IKG in 1933 decided to support Chancellor Dollfuss's prorogation of parliament and establishment of the Christian Corporative regime. Corbett explains that Jewish officials hoped to purge the IKG of its leftist members and ensure the support of the Catholic regime. For some time, this ploy worked, although Orthodox Jews managed to advance their sepulchral agenda, for example, by eliminating fruit trees in cemeteries and removing photographs from gravestones. More significantly, however, the IKG's stance between 1933 and 1938 stoked the fury of Austrian Nazis, who despised both the Dollfuss-Schuschnigg dictatorship and the Jews.

Following the Anschluss, Adolf Eichmann established the Central Agency for Jewish Emigration in Vienna, designed to make the city *Judenfrei* (free of Jews). Himmler's man in the *Ostmark* next authorized the IKG to administer Jewish affairs, giving its officials decision-making authority. Corbett explains the complex, tortuous relationship between Eichmann's office and the IKG in considerable detail. Simultaneously, he provides an interlocking, often repetitious, account of the brutal persecution of

Viennese Jews by Austrian Nazis between the Anschluss and Kristallnacht in November 1938. Relying on official documents and personal accounts, Corbett concludes this part of his study by discussing the expulsion of 130,000 Austrian Jews between 1938 and 1941, and the deportation and murder of 65,000 others until 1945.

For those familiar with the history of the Holocaust in Austria, Corbett's account of these events provides new details but does not significantly alter our knowledge of the persecution of Jews under Nazi rule. That said, the author's sepulchral perspective—the leitmotif of his study—offers shocking new information on what he calls "cultural genocide": the desecration of Jewish cemeteries and prayer houses, as well as the exhumation of human remains, which were shipped to the office of "racial science" at the University of Vienna for detection and analysis of distinctive Jewish morphological features. Furthermore, Jewish burial grounds were regularly vandalized by removing gravestones, which were then used as paving stones or construction materials for buildings or other projects. Ironically, relatively few tombstones were confiscated from Gate IV of the Central Cemetery owing to a 19th-century contract with the Viennese City Council. In Währing, however, the Nazis came close to transforming the cemetery into a park.

Corbett reminds readers that in 1940/41 most Viennese Jews were left in relative peace, usually in public places such as buildings in the Central Cemetery. Burials continued to take place, although frequently without a grave marker. Moreover, because Gate IV was leased by Vienna's municipal government, funeral expenses became increasingly difficult for the financially-strapped IKG to pay. Finally, in March 1942, the Nazis reversed course and banned all burials, except in Gate IV, where the Gestapo assumed the few remaining Jews could stay until deportation to the East. Ironically, the spacious area became a place for rest and relaxation, particularly for youngsters of both sexes. Permitted to hunt pheasants and rabbits, the Jews also grew potatoes, onions, and other vegetables that, in 1942, provided more than enough to eat. However, over time, their numbers diminished so that in 1945 only 5,512 remained in the Austrian capital.

Turning to the postwar period, Corbett offers some of the most fascinating and disturbing chapters in his massive study. The restored Austrian government reaffirmed its recognition of the IKG but also accepted the Moscow Declaration that Austria had been Hitler's first victim. This implied that most Austrians had not been involved in Nazi atrocities, most notably the Holocaust, even though a majority of the population had eagerly supported Hitler's regime and a disproportionate number of Austrian SS officers commanded the death camps. As the filmmaker Ruth Beckermann later pointed out, the main victims of Nazism, Austria's Jews, were left out of the equation.

Under these circumstances, the diminished IKG confronted seemingly intractable problems. In 1945/46, for example, its officials had to deal with Holocaust survivors from Eastern Europe and the Soviet Union, most of whom emigrated to what became Israel. Next, the IKG had to work with several thousand returning professional Jews—engineers, physicians, and attorneys—who had not belonged to the IKG and had no desire to join its ranks. Further, the problem arose whether to disinter Jewish victims buried in various locations and rebury their remains in Gate IV of the Central Cemetery, or leave them to rest in peace. Finally, IKG officials had to confront the problem of Jewish identity. Under Austrian law, the Jewish Religious Community represented all Jews in the Alpine Republic, but the IKG did not represent everyone of Hebrew descent as Jewish.

The most important figure in the postwar IKG was Ernst Feldsberg, an attorney who had survived Theresienstadt, established close relations with Israel, and had become rigidly Orthodox. Prior to the Anschluss, Austrian and German Jews were classified according to faith, not ancestry or ethnicity. According to the Nuremberg Laws, the Nazis defined "Jewishness" in racial biological terms. Ironically, Feldsberg dictated Jewish interment procedures in a way that resembled those of the Nazis, even categorizing the departed as *Volljuden*, *Nichtglaubenjuden*, and even *Rasse* (full Jews, non-religious Jews, and race). He also required visitors to wear yarmulkes and insisted that every gravestone be approved by Vienna's head rabbi. In retrospect, Feldsberg clearly intended to restore traditional Jewish sepulchral customs, but his choice of words and rhetoric provoked storms of protest both within the IKG and the chambers of the city council.

Another problem for the Jewish Religious Community occurred when the Second Republic began portraying Austria as a "cultural nation," albeit with scant mention of fin de siècle Jewish composers, artists, and literary figures. This induced about 10,000 exiles in the United States to request information on the condition of cemeteries in which their families had been buried. A number even visited Vienna in the early 1980s only to be appalled by the lack of upkeep of the graveyards and persistent anti-Semitic views of the Austrian people.

At this point, Corbett passionately reminds readers that Austrians, more than Germans, played a significant role in the persecution and murder of their Jewish fellow citizens. Most of the death camps, for example, were commanded by Austrian SS officers. Further, municipal and federal authorities of the Second Republic stonewalled restitution issues and the restoration of Jewish cemeteries, which admittedly were leased by the state. In 1986 the Waldheim affair compelled Austrians to face up to their Nazi past, though much more gradually than commonly believed. Both municipal and federal authorities equivocated on restitution claims, and Corbett's sepulcher research reveals that Jewish cemeteries were vandalized in recurring waves up to the year 2000. Further, a bitter dispute between Simon Wiesenthal and Feldsberg's disciples within the IKG crippled the Jewish community in confronting the persistence of grassroots anti-Semitic attitudes and behavior.

Even so, the Waldheim affair did constitute a remarkable change in confronting Austria's difficult past, particularly among a younger generation of journalists, scholars, students, and ordinary citizens. As if personally relieved, Corbett describes in detail the efforts of non-Jewish Austrians to renovate Jewish cemeteries and honor Jewish soldiers who had died before 1938, perished in the Holocaust, or fell in the Israeli army. Ceremonies included civil and military officials, and members of the Shalom Society, which restored 1,300 gravestones in the Central Cemetery. In addition, scholars began investigating Jewish history, particularly Austrian involvement in the Holocaust.

In 2001 an addendum to the 1998 Washington Agreement on the restitution of stolen works of art required Vienna to restore and maintain neglected Jewish cemeteries. After intense discussion and debate, the IKG decided to focus on the Währing burial ground, a cemetery that had been severely damaged by Nazi hooligans and Allied bombs. However, because the minuscule IKG lacked sufficient financial resources to undertake the project, its officials requested assistance from the federal government. The government's refusal provoked an angry response by the president of the Jewish Religious Community, who pointed out that the government had ample funds to maintain cemeteries containing the remains of Wehrmacht and SS combatants but preferred to ignore the tombstones of 350,000 Austrian Jews. This nasty dispute, in retrospect, may be regarded as a tempest in a teapot. Nevertheless, the future of the Währing cemetery remains unresolved. As Corbett concludes, the ultimate fate of Jewish cemeteries in Vienna has yet to be decided.

What is one to make of this remarkable book? There can be no doubt that Corbett's sepulchral approach, most notably his meticulous scrutiny of tombstones, contributes enormously to our awareness of the Jewish presence in Vienna from the Middle Ages to 1938—and to some extent beyond. He also reinforces Lisa Silverman's argument that numerous

Jewish writers, composers, musicians, and artists shaped what is nowadays considered a distinctive Austrian culture. Nevertheless, the strength of Corbett's exhaustive study is also its weakness. Aside from being much too long, its focus on Vienna will surely limit its appeal. German-speaking residents or tourists may wish to visit Gate IV of the Central Cemetery but, in seeking information, will most likely purchase a pamphlet or hire a guide. The same could be said of the many descendants of Jewish loved ones living in the United States or Israel, few of whom speak German. This is not to denigrate Corbett's enormous achievement but rather to suggest that it be consulted as an encyclopedia rather than a scholarly monograph.

Heidemarie Uhl, Richard Hufschmied, and Dieter A. Binder, eds., *Gedächtnisort der Republik: Das Österreichische Heldendenkmal im Äußeren Burgtor der Wiener Hofburg; Geschichte – Kontroversen – Perspektiven* (Vienna: Böhlau, 2021).

Georg Hoffmann

The *Heldenplatz*, Austria's central memorial site, often referred to as the '*Hauptplatz von Österreich*' (main square of Austria), is marked to this day by continuing controversies and debates regarding Austria's past. The *Äußere Burgtor*, or Outer Castle Gate, that gives access to the space is a military memorial site divided into a memorial to military heroes erected in 1934, which includes a statue of the fallen soldier, and a commemorative space for the armed Austrian resistance against the Nazi regime, which was opened in 1965. The two memorials inevitably function as opposing poles, making the *Burgtor* a manifestation of Austria's victim myth(s). In addition, the *Burgtor* was and continues to be used by the Austrian Republic and the Austrian Army as a representative site, a backdrop for the *Heldenplatz*, and a site for alternate commemorations of 'heroes' and victims by different protagonists. In 2012 the *Burgtor* and its uses came under sustained criticism, not least due to marches and appropriation attempts by German-nationalistic groups, and fraternities and the discovery of a National-Socialist message placed under the figure of the fallen soldier by its sculptor in 1934. In 2013 the Austrian Department of Defense commissioned a research project, the long-awaited outcome of which was published in 2021 and is now available. The project ran parallel to a process of change and historicization that was first expressed in the official profanation of the Heroes' Monument in 2015.

This 464-page, seemingly monumental publication is to be seen as a scientific basis for classifying and dealing with the *Burgtor*. In this sense, it strives to close a notable gap in dealing with the *Heldenplatz* and to uncover, decode,and analyze the inscribed interpretive contexts and historically formed layers of memory. The chosen academic approach is the term '*Gedächtnisort*', which takes up Pierre Nora's concept of 'places of memory.' It is also anchored in the cultural study of collective memory and the question of identity in the theory of remembrance, as predominantly addressed by Jan and Aleida Assmann or Heidemarie Uhl, in Austria. Regarding remembrance theory, the plural form would have made a better title because the *Burgtor* encompasses not one but several places of memory. These places of memory overlap and define each other, having either altered their significance or retained it beneath the surface. In this respect it is remarkable that, structurally, apart from the Resistance memorial and a memorial to the Austrian Army erected in 2019, there is very little Republican 'remembrance' represented at the *Burgtor*. On the contrary, the site is characterized more by the Republic's handling of the remembrance sites of other eras. Along with its strong focus on remembrance theory and cultural history, the concept of the book, also centers around the study of the site's structural history and a treatment of its administrative history, particularly in the first three chapters.

The book itself is conceived as an anthology. Apart from the three editors, five more authors (Stefan Gugerel, Richard Kurdiowsky, Richard Lein, Peter Pirker und Anna Stuhlpfarrer) contributed to the 19 texts in the book, often providing several contributions. This means that the book is more of a mixed form, rather than a classic anthology. This is particularly apparent in the structure of the chapters. Some of the individual texts are thematically self-contained, rigorously formulated and argued, presenting observations spanning several eras and ending with summarizing analyses. Others are structured in partial chapters, which remain strictly within the relevant time period, and have no conclusion but rather extend over several contributions. This imbalance sometimes results in redundancies with individual subjects covered a number of times.

This publication begins with two forewords, formulated as outlines of the problems, by two of the co-editors: historians and chairpersons of the board of the *Militärhistorische Denkmalkommission* at the Department of Defense, Dieter A. Binder and Heidemarie Uhl. Both describe how the Department of Defense resolved to find a new academic approach to the *Burgtor* and ultimately to incorporate it into a restructuring process for the *Heldenplatz* also by using the *Burgtor* and its surrounding as a place for exhibitions. The forewords are followed by four chapters of varying strength and from different perspectives, which will be outlined here.

The first chapter covers the building of the *Burgtor* as part of the city's fortifications and the entrance to Vienna's *Hofburg* complex up to its adaptation as a military monument during the First World War. Richard Kurdiowsky examines the early phase with the ceremonial reopening of the *Burgtor* in 1824. The connection with the Battle of Leipzig (1813) gave the *Burgtor* the connotation of a triumph arch and enshrined it, without any specific allusion but as a structural whole, as a monument to the victory over Napoleon. As the gate to the Monarchy's seat of power, it promoted a patriotism attached to the Habsburg dynasty. With the construction of the *Ringstraße* and the plan to build a *Kaiserforum*, it largely lost this role. Instead, it became a military functional building, the gateway between the imperial and the civic realms, connecting the inner city and the suburbs of Vienna. The corresponding monumental function was taken over by the equestrian statues of Archduke Carl and Prince Eugene, which were installed on the *Heldenplatz* in 1860 and 1865 respectively. The First World War changed this development for the long term, as Richard Lein emphasizes in his striking article. The wartime aid campaign *Lorbeer für unsere Helden* changed the appearance of the *Burgtor*, covering it with symbols that are still visible but hardly noticed today, and transforming it into a war memorial. This military association would remain the primary feature of the *Burgtor* up to the present day.

However, the most lasting transformation of the *Burgtor* took place between 1933 and 1934 under the authoritarian government of the so-called *Ständestaat* (or to use the actual term: *Regierungsdiktatur*), as described in the second chapter of the book. The chapter's six texts range from the architectural-historical observations of Anna Stuhlpfarrer and several articles focusing on administrative history by Richard Hufschmied, to a thorough and well founded analysis of the symbolism and imagery inscribed into the Heroes' Monument by the *Ständestaat*, written by Dieter-Anton Binder. The authors highlight the dual goal of the remodeling of the *Burgtor* at that time to become a military heroes' memorial to the defunct Austro-Hungarian Army: the *Burgtor* was to historically legitimize the *Ständestaat* through this link with the monarchy and simultaneously mark the image as both Austrian and Catholic. On the other hand, by focusing on the Austro-Hungarian Army and drawing parallels with military traditions as far back as the Thirty Years War (1618–1648), it should allude to Austria's defense against outside enemies in the present as an *Abwehrkampf*. The strong emphasis on the First World War in the form of victim commemoration led to the creation of the *Krypta* as a sacral space, with the central figure of a fallen soldier, and accompanying books of the dead. The latter contained the names of all those soldiers, and occasionally women, who were defined by the *Ständestaat* from a contemporary perspective as 'Austrians,' as well as fatalities; for example, the so-called *Kärntner Abwehrkampf* of 1918/1919. An open Hall of Honor was set up on top of the *Burgtor*, accessible by stairs, with frescoes and imagery that linked 'The Austrian Soldier' with historical military events according to the concepts of the *Ständestaat*. As Dieter-Anton Binder states, it was a manifestation of the hero construct, which spanned the roof of the memorial crypt.

The third chapter of the book, which is much shorter in comparison, focuses on the phase before and after 1938 and deals with the appropriation of the *Heldenplatz* by the National-Socialists and the German Wehrmacht. This part of the book, again, takes the form of observations on architectural and administrative history by Anna Stuhlpfarrer and Richard Hufschmied. The appropriation of the Heroes' Monument to commemorate soldiers and victims related to Germany is illustrated on these two levels. It is notable that even the oblique reference to the Austro-Hungarian Army was not seen as contradictory to the German-nationalist aspect. Against this background, the *Burgtor* can be seen as a materialization of the '*Anschluss*,' as a setting for National-Socialist displays on the *Heldenplatz*. It did not stand for the 'eradication' of all things Austrian but rather for a seamless and functioning integration into National-Socialism and ultimately for the militarization of society and the promotion of ideologized depictions of war. There is much to be said on this subject – a great deal has already been published, whether related to the *Heldenplatz* (Peter Stachl), a treatment of National-Socialist commemoration of the dead (Susanne Behrenbeck), or the inscribing of civilian victims of bombings (Dietmar Süß). However, the texts in this chapter hardly touch on these aspects and publications, being confined from the perspective of architectural and administrative history to an analysis of contemporary media coverage. More depth would have been preferable here – particularly since this National-Socialist appropriation of the *Burgtor* and the commemoration of military heroes and casualties had a lasting impact on the Republic's approach to the site.

The core theme of this publication is to be found in the fourth chapter: how the Second Republic has dealt with the *Burgtor* since 1945 and 1955, as well as the attendant controversies and debates on remembrance up to the present day. The perspective shifts from an outline of contemporary structural adaptations to an examination of the 'battle' over remembrance. In an extensive article, Peter Pirker dissects in his introduction the creation of interest groups and the projection of victimization myths onto the *Burgtor*. At the core of this examination is the integration of Wehrmacht soldiers into the roster of Austrian casualties, and thus their detachment from National-Socialism – a phenomenon that Heidemarie Uhl describes as the second Austrian victim myth. One manifestation of this phenomenon was the expansion of the books of the dead to include fallen 'Austrian' Wehrmacht soldiers. In 1965 a monument to 'Victims in the Struggle for Austria's Freedom' was added to the *Burgtor*. It was no accident that it was separated from the Heroes Monument, as it represented a completely different narrative of Austria's past, the two being unified in the victim role applied to the Austrian nation. Both Peter Pirker and Heidemarie Uhl analyze the attendant battle for remembrance and the subsequent controversies – over the breaking of the *Waldheim* affair in 1988, the continuing thematization of and interpretational debates on the *Heldenplatz* or, for example, the Wehrmacht-exhibition. The examination is focused mainly on the 2010s, when the approach to the *Burgtor* finally changed. The official profanation of the *Krypta* in 2015 triggered a process of historicization and museumization, which would feed into a planned reorganization of the *Heldenplatz* that was never realized. In 2019 an *Ehrenmal* for the Austrian Army of the Second Republic was set up in the Hall of Honour that covers both wings of the *Burgtor*.

The book closes not with a final chapter but with an outlook formulated by Heidemarie Uhl in the fourth chapter. Uhl looks at current developments and parallel processes, ultimately concluding that the future uses of the *Burgtor* and the Heroes' Monument remain open. Today, the *Burgtor* is many things: it still gives access onto the *Heldenplatz* and at the same time it is in part a monument, in part a historical remnant of past times, and in part a venue for exhibitions. It is precisely this consolidation of purposes that allows it to continue to fulfill its role as a place for the discussion of memory and remembrance. For this reason, it would be conceivable, perhaps expedient, to involve the *Heeresgeschichtliche Museum*, which is equally entangled in recent debates on the past, because both 'places of memory,' although different, could profit from a widened and more interlinked approach to memory discourses.

The editors and authors of this book have taken an important step, not only in analyzing Austrian discourses on the past, but also in closing a gap in the examination of the *Heldenplatz*. The various texts serve the purpose of unravelling, problematizing, and contextualizing the enshrined symbols and memory elements; in some cases hidden and with concealed meanings but repeatedly reinterpreted and appropriated by various different groups. In this regard, the book is aimed at a broad readership: those interested in the *Burgtor* and those who use it – the Republic of Austria and in particular the Austrian Department of Defense. It is also an impulse for historical research, which could have stood more depth of study, particularly when looking at the part discussing the Nazi era. It will, in any case, encourage researchers and historians to follow up with further examinations of the subject matter and of Austria's central 'place of memory.'

Oliver Rathkolb, *Schirach: Eine Generation zwischen Goethe und Hitler* (Vienna: Molden, 2020).

Rob Citino

The education of young people is a sacred trust of civilization. Indeed, a wise man once declared that it would be better to be tossed into the ocean with a millstone around your neck than to "scandalize" a child.

If that is true, then the subject of this book, Baldur von Schirach, had better be able to swim. As Reichsjugendführer during the Nazi years, he took the lead in the political indoctrination of millions of young Germans. Standard histories portray Schirach as a kind of empty-headed gym teacher, but he was a figure of considerable importance during the Third Reich. By 1936, when Schirach was only 29, the Hitlerjugend organization (including the Bund deutscher Mädel for girls) had enrolled roughly 6 million members, a stunning example of the mass mobilization of youth. His political career culminated in 1940, when Hitler named him Gauleiter and Reichsstatthalter of Vienna. At one point, Schirach was even in the mix as a plausible candidate to succeed the Führer.

For all these reasons, a serious biography of Schirach is long overdue. Oliver Rathkolb is a distinguished Austrian scholar, and this is an impressive book, deeply researched and elegantly written. Rather than wallow in extraneous detail of the subject's personal life, the author concentrates on deeper questions; such as, the appeal of Nazi ideology to the old Wilhelminian elite (Baldur was the son of a Prussian Guards officer) and the ways that contenders for political influence in the Third Reich could manipulate the levers of power. Finally, the book confronts the key issue: what responsibility does Schirach ultimately share for the crimes of the Nazi state?

As Rathkolb tells it, Schirach owed his rise to three factors. The first was ideological purity bordering fanaticism. Schirach was too young to have fought in World War I, but that didn't stop him from a fervent belief in the alleged "stab in the back," a Jewish plot that brought Germany down in 1918. Being too young for World War I didn't stop him from writing pathetic poems about Germany's heroic wartime struggle ("your father died, so that youth could be free"), or doggerel about the intoxication he felt upon hearing Hitler speak for the first time ("Thousands of you are behind me, and you are me, and I am you"). The latter poem got 17-year old Baldur published in the Nazi press which resulted in a signed portrait from the future Führer.

The second key to his career was his undoubted competence. Schirach had a feel for matters of organization, crowd staging, and popular mobilization. He intuited an essential truth of the modern age: stagecraft and reality are indistinguishable, and the former tends to overshadow the latter. His ability to assemble the (then) astonishing number of 70,000 young people from all over Germany for a "Reich Youth Party Day" in 1931 put him squarely in Hitler's sights, and the size of the crowds only multiplied in later years. Schirach even wrote the official hymn of the Hitler Youth, "Unsre Fahne flattert uns voran," a repulsive lyric calling upon young German boys to die for their Führer.

Neither of these things would have advanced him into the center of power, however, were it not for a third factor: In 1932, Baldur married Henriette Hoffmann, daughter of Hitler's official photographer. Entrée into the Hoffmann family brought him numerous benefits, and it wasn't long before Baldur and father-in-law Heinrich came up with one of the Third Reich's most lucrative schemes: an intimate photo volume of the Führer. *Hitler wie ihn keiner kennt* was a publishing sensation and begot a seemingly endless series of sequels, lining the pockets of Schirach and Hoffmann, not to mention those of Hitler himself. Surrounded by an aura of financial and political success, young Baldur and his beautiful wife, "Henny," were one of Nazi Germany's power couples during the brief peacetime years of the Third Reich.

By the time they arrived in Vienna, however, Schirach's career had already peaked. He'd lost influence over the regime's educational mission, he no longer enjoyed face time with the Führer (essential in the Third Reich's personalist regime), and he compounded his troubles by attempting to transform Vienna into the cultural center of Greater Germany. The new Gauleiter was apparently oblivious to how deeply Hitler resented this polyglot, cosmopolitan city, which he envisioned as nothing more than a provincial outpost of his new empire. From then on, Schirach was a "dead man walking" in the Third Reich's Darwinian corridors of power.

Even under a cloud, he continued to prove his loyalty to the Führer by overseeing the deportation and murder of Vienna's remaining Jews, stealing a huge selection of "Aryanized" art, and working to rid the city of its large and venerable Czech community. His character could be perfectly summed up in his final proclamation, which called upon Vienna's youth to sacrifice itself in "selfless loyalty" to the dying Third Reich; meanwhile, he saved his own skin by fleeing the advancing Red Army. This arch-Nazi then managed to survive the Nuremberg Trials with what one might call a "Speer strategy," which is ostensibly admitting full guilt while including so many personal and intellectual excuses that they obliterate any sense of sincerity.

In the end, Rothkalb argues, Baldur von Schirach bears a heavy burden of historical guilt: for the rise of Hitler, for the murder of Vienna's Jews, and for the senseless slaughter of an entire generation of young Germans whom he groomed for death on the battlefields of Minsk, Normandy, and Berlin.

Peter Becker and Natasha Wheatley, eds., *Remaking Central Europe: The League of Nations and the Former Habsburg Lands* (Oxford: Oxford University Press, 2020).

Susan Pedersen

Possibly because of Britain and France's outsized roles in interwar international relations, but also because of Anglophone historians' outsized role in the historical profession, the recent resurgence of work on the League of Nations has paid more attention to the empires that aggrandized themselves under its auspices (Britain and France) than to those whose dissolution absorbed so much of the League's attention (Austria-Hungary and the Ottoman Empire). However, as this timely volume reminds us, the reconstruction of nation-states and management of transnational crises in Central and Eastern Europe profoundly shaped those states, the League, and the interwar international order more broadly. Born—as most edited volumes are—of conference proceedings and topped and tailed by reflective contributions from two historians who have done much to "internationalize" scholarship on this region (Glenda Sluga and Patricia Clavin), this volume is prefaced by a strongly-argued introduction that tries to marshal contributors behind an ambitious common program. "Our aim has been no less than to introduce a new research agenda," the editors write (3). By adopting a regional focus, they hope to show how, in particular, earlier ideas and practices about "the management of diversity in imperial settings" (4) and the complex agendas of successor states affected interwar regimes of law and governance.

As is usual with edited volumes, contributors only very imperfectly fell in behind these marching orders, instead explaining the significance of their topics and findings in light of scholarly agendas and claims in their respective subfields. This is what one would expect and is entirely fine. Nevertheless, because of the tight topical, temporal, and geographical range of these pieces, and—still more—because of their generally high quality, this volume is indeed much more coherent and more consistently thought-provoking than the average edited collection. Moreover, these contributors are mostly talented early-career researchers, their contributions often precis for books a few years in the offing. Together, then, the essays give us some insight into how deeper attention to this region might shift scholarship in the linked fields of interwar European and international history, the history of international institutions, and to a degree, the history of international law.

Of several revisionist contributions, I would single out four. First, the book significantly adds to our composite portrait of the individuals who shaped the international order in these years. Historians have been too inclined to read the contours of that order off the programmatic speeches and writings of Woodrow Wilson and Jan Christiaan Smuts, even though neither attended a single League Assembly or had anything much to do with the institution's development after its founding. This book offers up a very different cast, one less rhetorically significant perhaps but much more embedded in the day-to-day practices of institutions and states. Some of these individuals, such as the Polish epidemiologist Ludwig Rajchman and the Viennese nutritionist Clemens Pirquet, worked with or within international institutions and foundations and are relatively well-known. Contributions here, however, also draw attention to men who, as national experts or officials, were charged to represent their states or negotiate their interests within new international bodies. The Viennese historian Alfons Dopsch, the Austrian economic expert Richard Riedl, and Vienna's police chief Johannes Schober all had a much more skeptical attitude toward international cooperation, but they knew they had to engage internationally to defend the sovereignty and build the capacity of their successor state. Anything but convinced internationalists, they shaped the international order nonetheless.

This, thus, is the second contribution: the book shows how and how markedly Eastern European precedents and interests shaped emerging international regimes. Poland had long been a focus of the campaign against international sex trafficking, and in the chaotic years following World War I, it was the laboratory for interventions and activism on this question and international health regulation. East European experts used League bodies to build not only transnational regimes but also local state capacities—even, as Sara Silverstein's essay shows, going on to export this model abroad through development assistance, especially to China. Central Europe—or more specifically, Austria—was also the test case for international financial stabilization, and while one might see that intervention as another stage in the long process of subjecting states to the interests of the "gnomes of Zurich" (and London and New York), Nathan Marcus here gives a more generous interpretation. He argues that while the allied and League officials who crafted that rescue package insisted on balanced budgets and austerity, they did resist outside states' predatory efforts to capture revenue streams in ways that would cripple Austrian sovereignty in the long term. The result was a rule-bound international financial order that, while undoubtedly protective of financial interests, was "no longer prone to easy and opportunistic abuse by individual states." Accounts like this rightly resist easy characterizations of the League as "progressive" or "conservative," instead uncovering a much more nuanced process of pragmatic institution-building. David Petruccelli's impressive essay on the 1923 construction of the International Criminal Police Commission, which became Interpol, offers an exemplary case. That collaboration, he shows, was spearheaded by Johannes Schober, the president of the Vienna police, precisely because he doubted Austria's capacity to survive as an independent state and wished to build structures that would help it overcome the serious problems created by the dissolution of imperial bonds. Petruccelli calls Schober's approach "illiberal internationalism" because although it produced measures to combat fraud and trafficking, it was born of a critique, not an embrace, of a liberal legal tradition that took state sovereignty as its foundation.

Other essays likewise show how internationalism could be deployed towards national ends—a third important contribution. In a sense, of course, this is not new: historians and contemporary critics alike marked the extent to which the League codified hierarchies among states and worked to protect West European, and especially British, interests. Here, however, we see both how aware many East European officials were of the interwar order's structural biases, and how diligently they combatted them—often with the aim, however, less of building a more genuinely multilateral system than of enhancing the capacities and power of their own successor state. Insightful contributions from Zoltán Peterecz and Johannes Feichtinger show how specific Hungarian and Austrian collaborations with League bodies were primarily driven by economic desperation and instrumental calculation; Peter Becker provides a limit case by detailing how strongly successor states resisted attempts to get rid of the wartime passport regime and ease border traffic even though there were obvious economic advantages to doing so. As today's right-wing populists know, nationalism can often trump economic interests. Nevertheless, some clever officials and politicians could still see how international engagement might be a road to regional reintegration and fend off poverty-stricken autarky. Madeleine Dungy's sophisticated study of the thought and activism of the Austrian economic official and later diplomat Richard Riedl is most illuminating on this point. Riedl was strongly opposed to the Wilsonian language of self-determination precisely because he saw it as a ruse "to place more than a third of the inhabited world in a condition of permanent economic atomization . . . so that it will be possible for the more organized political and economic bodies of the world to dominate here without using the force of arms" (quoted 223). Riedl worked with Stresemann to promote multilateral economic agreements through the League not because he was an "internationalist" but because he thought such collaboration offered a framework through which Germany and Austria could work towards unification and domination of the East European space. Unsurprisingly, most successor states preferred bilateral treaties that did little for their citizens' well-being but protected their sovereignty.

Central Europe's history weighed heavily in shaping these preferences. Hungarians found it hard to imagine that the Trianon territorial dispensation would stand; ethnic Germans scattered throughout the successor states had even more trouble seeing Poles, Ruthenians, or Ukrainians as fellow citizens. This collection is not primarily concerned with the history of ethnic antagonism and conflict, but it is inescapable nonetheless, and a fourth merit of the collection might be that a focus on transnational activism and institutions allows us to see it in a new light. Antal Berkes' essay on the "Hungarian optants"—briefly, ethnic Hungarian landowners who chose to leave the successor states for Hungary but retained property rights—reminds us of just how wearying, fraught, and protracted the work of adjudicating rival claims to land and loyalty were (in the end, the "optants'" claims were settled as part of reparations negotiations between Hungary and the Little Entente), while two other essays interestingly remind us of alternatives foresworn. National claims, after all, need not—and before 1914 often were not—be settled territorially, and as Börries Kuzmany shows, even after 1919, a few legal scholars looked back to Austro-Marxist thought or Habsburg precedents to imagine arrangements that would safeguard national and cultural autonomy without requiring ethnic unmixing or redrawn borders. Perhaps unsurprisingly, a Czech legal scholar, Rudolf Laun, was the staunchest advocate for such arrangements. However, as Sarah Lemmen shows, Czechoslovakia was also the successor state that sought to capitalize most fully on the global promise of League internationalism—building a large diplomatic corps, "internationalizing" its trade, relying on League guarantees for its security, and even making a colonial claim. Historians often remind us of the high price Czechoslovakia, in particular, paid for its internationalist faith, but this volume refreshingly abjures teleology, allowing us to see the complex landscape of the time as these East European fellow travelers saw it—murky, uncertain, its known pathways mostly obliterated, its new ones poorly signed and leading who-knows-where.

Michael Peneder and Andreas Resch, *Schumpeter's Venture Money* (Oxford: Oxford University Press, 2021).

Janek Wassermann

In this meticulously researched and comprehensive study, Michael Peneder and Andreas Resch explore a relatively neglected aspect of Joseph Schumpeter's economic oeuvre: his "venture theory" of money and economic development. Drawing widely from lesser-known articles and unpublished manuscripts as well as previously unavailable archival and biographical materials, the authors argue that Schumpeter's endogenous monetary theory "deliberately embraced historical evolution and growing speciation of money and finance into increasingly complex social institutions that are malleable to the various needs of entrepreneurial finance." Money, therefore, becomes "the indispensable *alter ego* of entrepreneurial initiative" (5), situated at the very heart of Schumpeter's grander understanding of economic development. With the increasing importance of the nexus of finance and economic growth in the current moment, the authors assert that Schumpeter's monetary theory has greater relevance than ever before. Part economics textbook, part history of economic ideas, part intellectual biography, and part economic history, *Schumpeter's Venture Money* ranges widely and cements Peneder and Resch's status as the foremost contemporary Schumpeter scholars. The product of more than twenty years of work, the book unlocks an invaluable dimension of Schumpeter's thought.

In organizing their ambitious project of contextualizing, reconstructing, analyzing, and applying Schumpeter's monetary theory, the authors divide their monograph into four sections. Although meant to be read together and reinforce one another, these parts are not fully integrated and can be read as standalone essays. Part I presents a fairly conventional monetary and financial history. It begins with an early history of the origins of money as a social institution before looking at the emergence of credit-driven financial and industrial capitalism. It highlights Schumpeter's interest in the role of credit in entrepreneurial activities and economic development. This section tidily summarizes our current understanding of the origins of money, credit, banking, commercial exchange, etc. (chapters 2 and 3) and introduces major milestones in monetary thought and financial innovation (chapters 3 and 4). However, it diverts the monograph away from its main objectives. The exposition on the importance of heterodox thinkers like William Potter,

John Law, and Henry Thornton serves a vital function, yet the rest does not advance the reader's understanding of Schumpeter's own monetary ideas.

If Part I leaves something to be desired, Part II—on Schumpeter's monetary theory of development—is a triumph of historical contextualization and economic analysis. Each chapter breaks considerable new ground not just in the literature on Schumpeter but also in the history of economic thought. Chapter 5 elaborates on Schumpeter's relationship to the marginalist revolution and the Austrian School of Economics. The authors elegantly cover the ideas of Carl Menger, Eugen von Böhm-Bawerk, and Friedrich von Wieser on money, capital, and interest, indicating points of convergence and—more importantly—divergence. This discussion (95–99) is the finest brief treatment of the founding generation's ideas. The incorporation of Knut Wicksell and George Friedrich Knapp into this exciting process of economic ideation provides great insight into Schumpeter's ideas about money as a social institution. The consideration of Schumpeter's place within the Austrian School, vis-à-vis Ludwig von Mises and Friedrich Hayek (106–18) in particular, is also welcome coming from scholars outside the orbit of the contemporary Austrian School.

Chapters 6 and 7 synthesize the insights of the preceding chapters and offer a full account of Schumpeter's theory. They are the centerpiece of the entire monograph and validate the ambitions of this project. Schumpeter's writings on money are scattered across a handful of essays from the 1910s and an unfinished (and posthumously published) manuscript on money. The analysis herein is the first attempt at a comprehensive reconstruction of Schumpeter's ideas. Chapter 6 discusses Schumpeter's rejection of neutral money theories, which maintained that money merely determines nominal values of transactions but does not affect real magnitudes in the economy. Instead of a "veil" over the "real" economy, Schumpeter argued that money was like a "skin," an organ of the economy vital to its existence and functioning. He believed that money's function as a unit of account was essential to the operation of an efficient economy. He prioritized this dimension over others, e.g., money as a medium of exchange or a store of value. Money could therefore serve as an effective means of clearing accounts and as a "claim ticket" for goods. The authors then situate these ideas in broader monetary discussions and the history of economic thought, drawing important connections to Friedrich Bendixen and the early Austrians and distinctions from quantity theorists like Irving Fisher. The authors demonstrate that Schumpeter "lift[ed] the veil of money and rebutt[ed] the postulate of its neutrality, his main assertion was that the endogenous supply of credit renders changes in the price structure an important driver of economic development" (137). Chapter 6 is a tour de force of research and exposition.

In Chapter 7, Peneder and Resch reintegrate Schumpeter's monetary theory into his theory of economic development, highlighting the central role money plays in entrepreneurial creative destruction and the capitalist growth process. Because money was at the nexus of financial innovation and the real economy, it facilitated the "creation and reallocation of purchasing power" (139). Entrepreneurial ventures navigate economic uncertainty and exploit opportunities with the financial assistance of venture investors. Venture capitalists, therefore, get a promoter's profit for their early support of innovation, which results in a brief period of monopoly proceeds. When imitation overtakes innovation, the benefits diffuse outward, prices drop, and real income rises. On its own, this chapter does not offer much more than a summary of Schumpeter's *Theory of Economic Development*, a work that is the subject of extensive literature. However, when combined dialectically with Schumpeter's monetary theory, his major monograph gains far greater clarity and coherence. A digression that examines Schumpeter's theory of entrepreneurship vis-à-vis other Austrians' also offers a welcome illumination of these distinctive approaches.

Like a Schumpeterian business cycle, there is a downturn after the heights of Part II. Part III lacks analytic incisiveness and intellectual innovations, but the archival work on Schumpeter's career as a banker and financier is a major historical accomplishment. The authors reveal themselves to be outstanding historians, adding crucial new details to our understanding of Schumpeter's non-academic career. In painstaking detail, they reconstruct the history of the Biedermann Bank (Chapter 8), of which Schumpeter served as president from 1921 to 1924, and the Braun-Stammfest Industrial Group (Chapter 9), an industrial investor group with which Schumpeter partnered. While neither of these ventures succeeded—for reasons elaborately detailed within these pages—the authors contend these experiences offer meaningful case studies of Schumpeter's monetary vision in practice. This point is debatable, but these studies do enrich our understanding of Schumpeter's biography and the economic and business histories of the First Austrian Republic. The rich archival work at the Austrian State Archives, the Municipal and Provincial Archives of Vienna, and especially the Private Archive of Ulrich Hedtke will undoubtedly influence future Schumpeter scholars and serve as a starting point for all subsequent research. Schumpeter's non-academic period remains somewhat neglected by English-language biographers; the authors show why this omission requires correction. They have done a major service for

Central Europeanists with their comprehensive research on this corner of First Republic history.

The real dénouement of *Schumpeter's Venture Money* is Part IV. Like Part I, the section on Schumpeter's legacy does not fit seamlessly with the central sections. Chapter 11 explores why there has never been anything resembling a "Schumpeter school." Chapter 12 evaluates areas where quasi-Schumpeterian ideas continue to have a foothold in contemporary economic discourse. Chapter 13 concludes with a consideration of where Schumpeterian monetary insights may yield valuable interpretations by examining the rise of venture capitalism, the recurrent instances of financial crises (especially the Great Recession), and the digitalization of money. The first of these chapters acknowledges that the piecemeal nature of Schumpeter's monetary theory and his preference for disequilibrium views prevented a wider adoption of his ideas. His tendency to avoid policy prescriptions also left him in the shadow of Keynes. This chapter and the next read more like economic textbooks as the exposition shifts entirely away from Schumpeter. While the latter chapter attempts to reintegrate Schumpeter's thought into contemporary economic discussions, it does not appear that Schumpeter's ideas deserve so central a position. The introduction of more recent innovations in Schumpeterian economic theory and Agent-Based Models is informative, yet the chapter does not fit well with the preceding sections. The final chapter likewise suffers a lack of coherence. The three subsections have quite different purposes: the first endeavors to show a connection between Schumpeter's thought and early venture capital firms; the second establishes the relevance of Schumpeter's understanding of crises to contemporary economic downturns; the third looks at how Schumpeter's view of money as a unit of social accounts can help to grasp the digitalization of money. While the authors' plea for "biodiversity" in economic thought has a value in and of itself, it is unclear whether that justification will suffice for the book's intended readers (18). "Schumpeterian economists" and historians of economic thought will find this book indispensable, creative, and instructive. As for "non specialists [sic] with a curious mind," it is less certain.

Peneder and Resch have performed an unparalleled service in *Schumpeter's Venture Money*. They have produced a major contribution to the history of economic thought, Austrian history, and the intellectual biography of Joseph Schumpeter. Their work will be a standard reference for scholars for years to come. They have successfully shown that "focusing on the venture aspects . . . one finds a fascinating, visionary, highly original combination of his theory of creative entrepreneurship and neglected heterodox views" (346). In no way do the aforementioned minor objections detract from the brilliance of the book—they merely limit its reach. One hopes that generalist readers will nonetheless dip their toes into the streams of Schumpeter's thought and thereby gain a newfound appreciation of his insights on perpetual change and Heraclitus's mantra, panta rhei ("everything flows," 1).

Evan Burr Bukey, *Juvenile Crime and Dissent in Nazi Vienna, 1938–1945* (New York: Bloomsbury, 2020).

Sarah Fishman

Evan Burr Bukey offers an original, insightful and in-depth look at juvenile crime during the Nazi era in Vienna, the second largest city of the Greater Reich. Starting with the Anschluss, Bukey lays out the existing juvenile justice system and then examines how it changed over time, from the attempts at coordination post Anschluss to the Nazi imposition of special courts and laws during the war through the immediate postwar era. Rather than a simple top down approach however, Bukey enriches the analysis of systemic changes with material from case files that reveal the actual operation of the system from both angles, the courts, laws, judges on the one side and the realities on the ground on the other.

Prior to the Anschluss, Austria's system reflected its Catholic and patriarchal worldview of the delinquent child as disposed to original sin and deserving of punishment.[1] During the brief democratic era after World War I, the 1928 Juvenile Court Law attempted to reorient the system from punishment to rehabilitation. Bukey points out that under the Dollfuss-Schuschnigg dictatorship, Juvenile Courts returned to imposing harsh sentences. Although, in theory, the Anschluss, coordinated the Austrian legal and court systems, Bukey found that existing laws and institutions for juveniles continued to function in Austria, partly a result of shortage of trained personnel. Bukey also points to Nazi jurists' appreciation of Austrian criminal law's "authoritarian legal precepts" (p. 10). Officially dissolved, Austria's Juvenile Courts reconstituted themselves as a branch of the new Higher Regional Court. Aside from Jewish judges fired under Nazi law, Bukey found little change in legal personnel and operations, describing the Austrian system as aligned, not coordinated.

Over time, Nazi leaders layered new laws, new courts, new personnel and new procedures on top of the existing system, creating multiple overlapping legal systems. Bukey's analysis of Nazi War Ordinances on juvenile crime reveals the extent to which they aligned the evaluation of young delinquents with Nazi racial goals. The "Decree Against National Parasites" for juveniles over sixteen rested on the assumption that only some minors merited reincorporation into society. "Parasites and precocious criminals" were to be "excluded altogether from the National Community" (p. 43).

Under the Decree for the Protection of Dangerous Juvenile Criminals, delinquent minors over sixteen deemed dangerous could be sent to adult courts and receive adult sentences. Under the Nazi Decree Against Violent Criminals, both boys and girls over the age of sixteen could be, and were, sentenced to death for actions committed while minors. Bukey examines in detail the shocking cases of minors executed under these provisions during the Nazi era.

In addition to War Ordinances, the Nazis established Special Courts to handle cases of "subversion" involving both adults and juveniles. Per the twenty-seven Special Court cases Bukey found involving minors, subversion included property crimes in addition to overtly political acts. It also included "moral offenses" deemed a threat to the National Community, homosexual acts for boys, sex with foreigners for girls. Special Courts also handled "Jewish-related" offences, young people who concealed their Jewish identity, for example (pp. 108–9). Those cases stopped appearing in the courts after 1942, Bukey notes, because the SS began rounding up and deporting Austrian Jews to the death camps.

Based on careful study of the available documentation, in each chapter Bukey includes details that reveal who the minors were, their background, what they were accused of doing and how the system treated them. Although the University of Vienna "unwittingly" shredded most of the era's case files in 1999, the remaining 437 case files, supplemented with 43 detailed Gestapo arrest records, allow Bukey to give the reader a sense of the range of juvenile misbehavior and of how the juvenile courts responded (p. 5). The cases also reveal much about the reality of life in Vienna as it evolved over those seven years. Minors began stealing items of value on the black market when it began to flourish during the war. Near the end of the war, Bukey's cases included thefts of large quantities of cigarettes which by then substituted for a worthless official currency. In contrast, he did not find the kinds of violent street gangs that developed in cities that experienced much greater wartime destruction. Bukey's detailed recounting of actual cases provides a rich picture of life in Vienna over those tumultuous years, illuminating the lives of people often overlooked, young, poor, working-class. Because the cases are so revealing, my one criticism is that for readers like myself unfamiliar with Vienna, Bukey might have provided more general background information on the city itself, its layout, its urban geography and social divisions.

Bukey's book does delve below the surface of the "popular euphoria" that supposedly followed the Anschluss, examining cases involving minors who resisted Nazi rule (pp. 4, 9). By far the largest group of anti-Nazi youth had been members of the Communist youth movement, but resistance also developed amongst minors from Catholic conservative or monarchist associations. Bukey also scrutinizes a more ambiguous group of juveniles who rejected Nazism without necessarily constituting resistance. Like the "Zazous" in Vichy France and the "Swing Kids" in German cities, a youth counterculture emerged in Vienna: the "Schlurfs."[2] Older adolescents who had no interest in joining the Hitler Youth, the "Schlurfs" preferred to dress in Zoot suits, hang out in bars and cafes, listen to jazz, loiter after dark. The authorities considered their behavior oppositional, but rather than being overtly political, Bukey argues, the Schlurfs just wanted to be left alone.

Bukey found a critical change that took place in the juvenile courts as the war continued. By late 1943, nearly all Austrian men were serving in the Wehrmacht which created labor shortages in essential war industries. Under the Juvenile Court Act of 1944, the system focused on keeping delinquent youth in the labor force. To punish labor indiscipline and absenteeism, juvenile judges imposed harsh penalties, such as solitary confinement with only bread and water. However, to keep delinquent minors in the labor force, judges stipulated that the penalties were to be served only on weekends.

Although the postwar authorities removed the Nazi accretions and established a democratic political system, Bukey's final chapter found more continuity than rupture in juvenile justice. That very retention of local law and identity, he argues, contributed to the success of the postwar transition to democracy. It also led to problems. Bukey found that a number of minors who had been convicted during the Nazi era, even minors punished for anti-Nazi subversion, remained incarcerated after 1945 or struggled for years to get their wartime criminal records expunged. It took Josef Landgraf—sentenced to death for anti-Nazi activities, his sentence commuted so he could serve in a 'punishment' unit of the Wehrmacht—until 1949 to clear his record (p. 103). With the relevant part of the Austrian penal code in place until 1971, Nazi-era convictions for homosexual acts also took decades to expunge (pp.67–70).

Bukey's fascinating study gets at critical questions about juvenile justice, juvenile crime and dissent. It illuminates ideas about childhood and adolescence, highlights breaks and, more often, continuities from pre-Nazi to postwar Vienna. The book thus enriches our understanding not just of juvenile crime and dissent but also of broader issues about the Anschluss, the impact of Nazi racial ideas and the realities of life in wartime Vienna.

Endnotes

1 On the evolution of ideas about delinquent minors in France, see chapter 1, "From Child Criminals to Juvenile Delinquents, 1810-1939," of my book, also cited by Bukey, *The Battle for Children: World War II, Youth Crime and Juvenile Justice in Twentieth-Century France* (Cambridge: Harvard University Press, 2002): 11–44.

2 On "Zazaous" in France, see Jean-Claude Loiseau, *Les Zazous* (Paris: Grasset, 1990); On the "Swing Kids" in Nazi Germany, see Michael H. Kater, *Different Drummers: Jazz in the Culture of Nazi Germany* (New York: Oxford University Press, 2003); In the US, Kathy Peiss, *Zoot Suit: The Enigmatic Career of an Extreme Style* (Philadelphia: University of Pennsylvania Press, 2014).

List of Authors

Bernhard Alexander Achhorner is a PhD candidate in the Department of Musical Science at the University of Innsbruck

Günter Bischof is the Marshall Plan Chair of History and the Director of Center Austria: The Austrian Marshall Plan Center for European Studies, University of New Orleans.

Evan B. Bukey is Professor Emeritus of History at the University of Arkansas.

Vanessa Maria Carlone is a PhD-student in the Department of Musical Science at the University of Innsbruck

Rob Citino is the Samuel Zemurray Stone Senior Historian at the National World War II Museum in New Orleans

Jason Dawsey is Research Historian in the Institute for the Study of War and Democracy at The National World War II Museum.

Sarah Fishman is Moores Professor of History at the University of Houston.

Winfried Garscha is retired senior historian at the Documentation Centre of Austrian Resistance, Vienna, and co-director of the Austrian Research Agency for Post-War Justice.

Georg Hoffmann is a historian at the Austrian Department of Defense.

Christian Karner is Professor of Sociology in the School of Social and Political Sciences at the University of Lincoln, UK.

Marc Landry is Assistant Professor of History and the Associate Director of Center Austria: The Austrian Marshall Plan Center for European Studies, University of New Orleans.

Christoph Leschanz is currently working on an Austrian Academy of Science-funded project about the "Austrian Literary Field" in the post-war period at the Department of Comparative Literature at the University of Vienna.

Joseph W. Moser is Associate Professor of German at West Chester University of Pennsylvania

Sarah Oberbichler is a postdoctoral researcher and works at the Institute of Contemporary History at the University of Innsbruck

Susan Pedersen is Gouverneur Morris Professor of British History at Columbia University.

Eva Pfanzelter is Associate Professor in the Department of Contemporary History at the University of Innsbruck

Gerald J. Steinacher is the James A. Rawley Professor of History at the University of Nebraska-Lincoln.

Alexandra Sterling-Hellenbrand is Professor of German and Global Studies at Appalachian State University in Boone, North Carolina.

Janek Wasserman is Associate Professor of Modern Central European and German History at the University of Alabama.

Judith Welz is a PhD-student in the Department of Contemporary History at the University of Innsbruck.

Contemporary Austrian Studies

Günter Bischof, Anton Pelinka/Fritz Plasser/Ferdinand Karlhofer, Editors

Volume 1 (1992)
Austria in the New Europe

Volume 2 (1993)
The Kreisky Era in Austria
Oliver Rathkolb, Guest Editor

Volume 3 (1994)
Austria in the Nineteen Fifties
Rolf Steininger, Guest Editor

Volume 4 (1995)
Austro-Corporatism: Past—Present—Future

Volume 5 (1996)
Austrian Historical Memory & National Identity

Volume 6 (1997)
Women in Austria
Erika Thurner, Guest Editor

Volume 7 (1998)
The Vranitzky Era in Austria
Ferdinand Karlhofer, Guest Editor

Volume 8 (1999)
The Marshall Plan in Austria
Dieter Stiefel, Guest Editor

Volume 9 (2000)
Neutrality in Austria
Ruth Wodak, Guest Editor

Volume 10 (2001)
Austria and the EU
Michael Gehler, Guest Editor

Volume 11 (2002)
The Dollfuss/Schuschnigg Era in Austria: A Reassessment
Alexander Lassner, Guest Editor

Volume 12 (2003)
The Americanization/Westernization of Austria

Volume 13 (2004)
Religion in Austria
Hermann Denz, Guest Editor

Volume 14 (2005)
Austrian Foreign Policy in Historical Perspective
Michael Gehler, Guest Editor

Volume 15 (2006)
Sexuality in Austria
Dagmar Herzog, Guest Editor

Volume 16 (2007)
The Changing Austrian Voter

Volume 17 (2008)
New Perspectives on Austrians and World War II
Barbara Stelzl-Marx, Guest Editor

Volume 18 (2009)
The Schüssel Era in Austria

Volume 19 (2010)
From Empire to Republic: Post-World War I Austria

Volume 20 (2011)
Global Austria: Austria's Place in Europe and the World
Alexander Smith, Guest Editor

Volume 21 (2012)
Austrian Lives
Eva Maltschnig, Guest Editor

Volume 22 (2013)
Austria's International Position after the End of the Cold War

Volume 23 (2014)
1914: Austria-Hungary, the Origins, and the First Year of World War 1
Samuel R. Williamson, Jr., Guest Editor

Volume 24 (2015)
Austrian Federalism in Comparative Perspective

Volume 25 (2016)
Austrian Studies Today

Volume 26 (2017)
Migration in Austria
Dirk Rupnow, Guest Editor

Volume 27 (2018)
Austrian Environmental History
Patrick Kupper, Guest Editor

Volume 28 (2019)
Democracy in Austria
David M. Wineroither, Guest Editor

Volume 29 (2020)
Myths in Austrian History
Christian Karner, Guest Editor

Volume 30 (2021)
Visual Histories of Austria
Martin Kofler, Hans Petschar, Guest Editors